Pink Heart ©
By Shannon O'Shea

Pink Heart

"Pink Heart" is an anthology of my life as Shannon O'Shea, her insights and memoirs as a transgender woman. It includes my unique vision of the transgender condition, as well as how it has affected me, and those others like me walking the same paths.

It is my hope that my personal experiences will present the reader with a clear picture of the risks, rewards, and challenges that my trans-sisters and I might expect during and after transition to our new feminine gender.

All rights reserved
ISBN: 978-1-955736-10-7

This book, or parts thereof, including all photos cannot be reproduced in any form without the permission of the author.

Library of Congress Control Number 2009910820

Copyright © 2009

Dedication:

A great and wise philosopher once said in a cartoon, "**Don't worry about life ... none of us are going to get out alive anyway**!" By the way, have you ever noticed in cartoons that some of the male characters often become a "cross-dresser" and dons themselves up to appear like a pretty snazzy-looking femme?

Before I thank those to whom I shall dedicate this book, I hope that somehow in this book, I asked and answered the right questions.

This introspective, autobiographical work is therefore dedicated to all my "**trans-sisters**" and to those of you out there who seek, find, and perfect the gender of the person you wish to be. This is to **Diane,** for finding her life and then going on before us to reserve our place in paradise. To **Nicole,** for becoming my best friend, my life partner, for her companionship, her undying love, and for always believing in me.

To my brother**, Vern,** for his unconditional love, being my friend, and for supporting and encouraging me when others I loved ... turned away and ostracized me from their lives. To my good friend, **Andy,** a staunch Republican with whom I often wrangle about politics. To my **children**, my **ex-wives,** and hoping that one day they'll all understand why I became Shannon. Thanking **God,** my Creator for the gift of life, and to my Lord and Savior, **Jesus Christ** for sustaining me through it, for the forgiveness of sins, and the hope and promise of resurrection and a life of eternal peace. To **Dr. Rita Cotterly** for guiding me through the process of discovering my true self. To all my **Trans-sisters** and **Trans-brothers** ... I send to you my prayers, my hopes for your happiness, and that you too have or will find true peace and acceptance of who you are.

Pink Heart

Definitions of Abbreviations

TS -TG = <u>Trans-woman</u> = Someone who was born male but wishes to assume the gender opposite from their anatomical birth sex.

MTF = <u>Male to Female</u> = A trans-woman that is born anatomically male, but seeks to transition and live life as a female. Someone FTM a female seeking to transition as a male.

GRS = <u>Gender Reassignment Surgery</u> = Surgical modification of the external genitals to conform to the TS's preferred gender.

Pre-Op = Often referred to as a **<u>Preemie</u>** or someone that is a **<u>Pre-Operative</u>** trans-woman, perhaps living full-time in their chosen gender, but has not undergone GRS surgery.

Post-Op = <u>Post-Operative</u> - Someone that has had GRS alter their genital sex to conform to their preferred gender.

RLT = <u>Real Life Test</u> - A Trans-woman living full-time (24 – 7) in their chosen gender role for one year before being eligible for GRS.

TG = Transgender = All-encompassing term for those who are gender variant, but some may or may not seek GRS surgery.

GLBT = <u>Gay, Lesbian, Bisexual, Transgender</u> = Associating or describing this grouping of individuals as being socially connected … as in a political or minority group.

X1, X2 = Shannon's <u>Two Previous Ex-Wives</u> = No disrespect meant here. This is merely an attempt to designate anonymously each of my former mates without the intent of being condescending.

Shannon – Smiling at You

FACTS YOU SHOULD KNOW:

1. I always wanted to have dark brown eyes, so I often wore **brown color contacts** for cosmetic effects. It gave me a variable appearance rather than just showing up with **dark green eyes**. It was like using any accessory, such as earrings or other jewelry. As I aged, my vision worsened and I had to wear glasses, so I didn't wear the contacts as much after ten years as Shannon.
2. I "love" having long hair and styling it as I please. I experimented with various colors and styles. Another outlet of expression is "**wigs**." I've bought and worn many styles of wigs, which will be evident in the photos I post herein. My hair, eventually turned to a platinum, then white color, a fact I truly like. I wear my hair with bangs and that has become my look. I love variety, which you'll see in my photos of differing hair flairs and dimensions.
3. Until 2003, I did not own a digital camera. Most of the photos posted within this book will be from either a black and white Polaroid, a Kodak camera, or Nikon. I did pose for several studio type photos and posted a few of those herein. Most photos were taken by friends when I was at home, outdoors, shopping, in restaurants, at concerts, or out and about in Dallas/Fort Worth.
4. My gender counselor does not like me posting photos displaying bosoms with cleavage. In my first manuscript, I posted but a couple such photos. However, that display was a part of my life's story, so I include that now in this newer version. There are a few such photos posted herein, and I hope they do not offend you. After breast augmentation, I sometime wore and was photographed in low-cut blouses (not nudes) and displayed my feminine assets. As I became, older, that trend faded in me and I am more conservative now.

PINK HEART
By: Shannon O'Shea

INTRODUCTORY

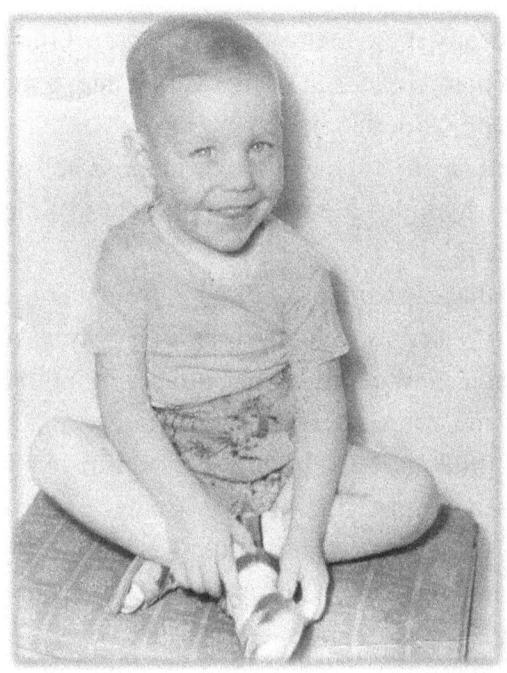

What Child is This?

Consider a moment the photo above of an infant child. What is it you see? Is your perception from the observation that this is a boy child? Every "normal" physical indication leads one towards the assumption that the photo is that of a male child. The photo depicts a baby with sparse hair, wearing button-down suspender pants, and appears to have on male shoes. Isn't it obvious then to assume that even without visual evidence of this child's genitalia, that what you are looking at is a boy?

What is your reaction if I inform you that you are incorrect in the presumption that the child is a boy? I proclaim to you that the child in the photo above is a little girl. Huh? How can I make that statement? How do

Pink Heart

you now view the photo? Perhaps you have a degree of cynicism, declaring my statement to be misleading. Does my declaration change your perception of the child? Do you acknowledge in your mind that this charming little person, with attractive eyes and an endearing smile, may indeed be a girl child? No, it probably does not.

She has long lashes, as do many female children. Granted, she has sparse cranial hair, as do many infants at such a young age. She is quite a cute girl and seems very happy, doesn't she?

But if the child is a girl, then why is she in those boy clothes? It's a posed studio portrait, so why didn't her parents place her in a nice frilly pink dress with bows in her hair?

The answer to that question is: Although from all outward appearances, even though being raised as a young boy with normal male anatomy, the child above that you view <u>is</u> inside her infant's mind a <u>little girl</u>. Despite how she is raised and what others think of him/her, that is how she'll soon come to see and think of herself. She'll grow up <u>longing</u> to be the girl perceived in the second paragraph above. Being female is the gender that more truly identifies her soul and the one in which from age four she will always seem more comfortable. Can any one of you actually "see" the little girl inside that little boy? I doubt it, but I assure you she's there.

Over time, as that little boy grows and the little girl inside him becomes more curious and disappointed by the fact that she can't live as a girl, life becomes more and more confusing and frustrating. Not wishing to cause her adopted parents any heartbreak or worry, the little girl remains concealed and quietly exists behind those mysterious, green eyes, just inside that little boy's mind and body. She waits, hopes, dreams, and prays for a solution to escaping the nightmare that continues to grow ... as <u>she</u> does.

This girl child constantly undergoes intense self-scrutiny, as her heart is filled with a great sense of loss, vulnerability, and low self-esteem. At age four, this child learns to overcome her inner urges and to display a happy, contentment before those she loves (parents, siblings, family) and with whom she comes into contact (playmates, teachers, coaches, public).

Is it so surprising that this little girl resents being born with male genitals? Is it any wonder that as she grows, she chooses not to humiliate herself by confessing her innermost desires? Instead of displaying her true feminine characteristics, she lives through childhood and into adolescence and represses those things that might give others the suspicion and impression that she is not normal. She allows others only to see the person and traits that they expect from her male self.

Imagine the conflict, frustration, and fear she feels. As a result of her uncertain future and growing incongruity with her birth sex, she chooses instead, as do most others of those like her, to mask that which is to her a basic of instinct and desire ... to be a girl and to be feminine. As with all children, and teens she wants to be liked and to have an easy and pain-free life. Within this context, she like all humans seeks to avoid conflict, which results in compromise and resisting overwhelming urges.

She later learns that when any one of us attempts to make some change in our lives, we can be certain that somebody is not going to like it. She discovers while still a child and young adolescent that if she chooses to make a gender change, she might face harassment, criticism, ostracism, or perhaps even personal attack for being different.

Like all of us, she has aspirations to be normal, but in her heart knows she never will be. During young adulthood, her fears of disapproval are often so great that she finds any change efforts may never start let alone become complete. So that's how it is for this child that becomes a young adult, for even though she longs to be a real girl, she foresees only doom and gloom if she carries through and confesses to anyone her true feelings.

As a child, she knows nothing of the sexual aspects confronting post-pubertal human females. All she discerns is that nothing about being a boy feels right to her during childhood or on into adolescence and adulthood.

As the years pass and ten becomes twenty, the little girl inside does not like the direction and consequences of her self-denial, yet she learns to cope with her fate. Nevertheless, at no time does she give up hope of one day becoming real and being a woman.

From her time in school and gathering feedback from the mainstream society in which she exists, she comes to learn that those like her are often labeled as outcasts, queers, pedophiles, perverts, deviants, or someone with a sick mind and low morals. She learns that those like her are labeled as being <u>transsexual and transgender</u> and that those truly committed to the task can and do find relief from their inner conflict by seeking help via counseling, psychotherapy, hormone therapy, and ultimately sex reassignment surgery.

Even with such options available, the reality of such a thing happening to her seems remote. Nature's final cruel trick upon her is to balloon her height till she is almost six feet tall. Her feet seem larger than most females and there is scarcely anything about her male physical presence that appears feminine. Her nose is crooked and thick from being broken three times in sports before she graduates high school. With anguish and a heavy heart, she comes to accept (for the time being) her self-imposed imprisonment within her male body.

Such a fate seems inescapable at this point in life. Her trans existence fosters fear of the unknown and the inner conception she has about her sexuality and gender identity. For numerous reasons and using various excuses, she just cannot muster the courage it takes to dismantle the life created by her male self, albeit one in which her true self exists out of view of everyone ... save herself.

It should come as no shock that this girl bonds herself to a genetic female and receives a woman's hand in marriage (the first of two such marriages). Doing so is but one more example of what she does to conform to being born into a male body. In effect, it is <u>his</u> pre-transition attempt to be the person others expect of <u>him/her.</u>

Although the reasons for entering marriage have many variables, the primary one is that the two people involved love one another and are indisputably concerned about the welfare of their marriage partner. They enjoy the union and although she's a gender variant person, she does not disclose the depth of that fact to either of her two mates. She does not doubt that doing so would end any hope of acquiring and keeping a spouse.

Having no demonstrable congenital deformity or defect, she is quite capable of consummating the marriage, as is evidenced by her eventually becoming the parent and sire to three children from two matrimonial relationships. Being married seems a good option at the time and she hopes love lessens the impulses inside that make her want to step out into the open and reveal her femme self to the public, her spouse, kids, parents, friends, and family. She cannot find the courage within her to disappoint those she loves most, or to make the tough choices. Life becomes like treading water, as she seeks to simply stay afloat.

Most wedding vows include a part about seeing each other through tough times: "For better or worse, in sickness and in health ... till death do you part." Although great sentiments, in reality, such vows belong more in a fairytale and imaginary existence, for they are sorely tested when one of the members of that marriage reveals "herself" to be transgender. What happens when the presumed <u>male</u> in this union confesses the aspiration to become female and then decides to seek help, and then does so? What happens then to the little girl above when she decides to transition and undergo a gender/sex reassignment? Making this bittersweet, yet the excruciating choice confronts her and all trans-women in time.

That such a choice is belated until the calendar clicks over forty years from her birth makes the deferred accomplishment seem even harder. The question on everyone's mind that knew HIM...is why? Why now after all these years does this person choose to leave <u>his</u> life behind to chase after a "mystery girl" dream that began when he/she was but an infant that somehow became aware of the desire at the age of four years?

Dealing with non-familial relationships after such a revelation is difficult at best. Now she also has to deal with revealing her intent to her spouse, children, siblings, and other relatives and loved ones. How does she do that? By now, her parents are all deceased, so that is one less obstacle to confront. She later realizes that her reluctance to "come out" and confess her urges to be female was due primarily to not wishing to allow her beloved parents to know her desires. Instead, she became a "lady in waiting" until God called them all home.

Up until then, she's lived the way others expected her to live. No longer able to suppress her obsessive feminine side, at this time, after choosing to go forward and bring out the inner little girl still inside, she finds many challenges and barriers over which she must leap. The masculine career she carved out under the guise of manhood all of the sudden becomes like a crash head-on into a brick wall. She learns far too early on in her transition what it means for a woman to deal with the corporate glass ceiling and the inequality of female wages compared to her male equivalent.

She faces her lifetime separation anxiety from her birth mother, father, and siblings; an agonizing, dangerous service in her nation's military, and suffers severe intra-psychic conflict, frustration, and trauma from a rape by a gay male before the age of ten.

After two trying divorces, she faced bankruptcy, lost her home, car, job, and almost everything of monetary and material value. Most of those that were "his" friends avoided her. They did not condemn her, but simply separated themselves and ostracized her from their lives. To her, it's as if they were pretending that she doesn't exist.

It's a gross oversimplification and misconception to express in this discourse that her family is losing their brother, sister, cousin, friend, or father. Instead, they are simply seeing more now of who she is than they have seen before. Their relative and friend is finally opening up to them, being herself, and hopes they begin to understand who she is and what she kept hidden from everyone. She does not love any of her relatives or friends less. Given the chance, she will be able to more clearly express her love and peace with herself, the world, and her family knows that she's opening up. Unfortunately, very few of her family or old friends allow her the chance at an audience with her new femme self. To them, she becomes an aberration, a sad entity that they cannot embrace or condone. This saddens her and makes her have regrets, although once she begins the journey ... she knows there is no turning back. It both frightens and excites her.

Except for her oldest brother, her other siblings divorce themselves from her as well by letting her know she will never be accepted as their <u>sister</u>. For a while, she forages through her new life, groping for sustenance, sanity, new friends, and a way to survive in this new femme-world with incredible obstacles to overcome. Her self-respect is challenged, but she is a stubborn person and refuses to quit or give in. Though earlier on in life, she contemplated the choice of suicide, that is no longer an option. Such a reaction would only serve to bolster the "I told you so" people that criticized her most. No, it takes far more courage to live and face those things within her psyche that declares she is a woman in a man's body.

After it happens and choices are made, despite the challenges and high costs, the genie is out of the bottle and it is not going to go back inside, no matter what the expense.

Her previous life was a perpetual lie. It was a painful life where every passing day and year left her with sorrow rather than joy. Even being a husband, father, son, or brother did not quench her thirst for peace or contentment. The overwhelming need to become female was always there inside her …like a mystery girl … that obsessed her, causing her to cross dress when alone and then become a male again by morning's reality. Up till now, she ignored and exhibited self-denial about the essence of her being. Life before transition was no life at all.

Why did all this happen to the little child above? Today's scientific and medical community confirms and biological rules declare that in a resting state, every fetus is female. If during pregnancy, nature withholds androgens in improper amounts during fetal life, despite genital sex, behavior and anatomy typically do not coincide. Thus, the mind of such a child as the one above, and others like her later display those inner female tendencies and confirm they are transgender and likely being feminized before birth by some action or consequence inside the womb. As a result, such instincts and feminine desires are inborn and become part of nature's program inside the child's brain before birth occurs. This obsession with being feminine comes from a legitimate physiological, genetic, plus biological reason and becomes a part of the process, similar to those which cause the child to have red hair, green eyes, or light-colored skin.

Maybe you can accept she is transgender and that a child like the one above deserves the chance to live the life for which she longs. Sadly, far too many folks deny her the respect that she and others like her warrant. Still others "do" come to accept her and life … as Shannon becomes a reality.

In attempting to relate to the world in which she lives, family, friends, and others in the general populous that encounter her and others that are transgender should learn to come to terms with the veracity of the situation. If they do, those folks will discover that transgender folks need assurances, not criticisms; they need your blessings, not your curses; offer them your hand, not your backside. The trans-woman yearns for compassion and craves social acceptance. Is it too much to ask from today's open society that they permit transgender people to walk upright into the wind with their face into the sun? Why must those that are different hide who they truly are and live as if they are sub-human rejects who have no honor, pride nor are deserving of respect?

In the state of confusion, I mean Texas, this child born with male genitals is considered to legally be a "he" despite surgical intervention and confirmation by medical or psychological diagnosis stating otherwise.

Consequently, any marriage she engages in before transitioning from a male to female ... remains legal and binding, even after sex reassignment surgery's extreme physical modification. Such a marriage can only end if it is by a voluntary legal divorce agreement.

As perhaps you've guessed by now, that child in the photo ... is **ME!**

Eat, Drink, Relax ... Sit, Read, and Learn

There's some evidence that an MTF trans-woman's brain resembles a female one, but other than that there's little use in looking for a reason of what causes one to be transgender under a microscope. You won't find any answers under there.

Early HRT Photo with My Youngest Daughter
* * *

"But all you have to do is knock on any door and say, "If you let me in, I'll live the way you want me to live, and I'll think the way you want me to think," and all the blinds will go up and all the windows will open and you'll never be lonely ever again."

This passage is a direct quote from defense attorney Henry Drummond, in the movie "Inherit the Wind." He goes on to imply, that if one chooses another path, *the only sound* that person might hear is the sound of his or her *footsteps*.

Though he hadn't intended them to be, that character's words present us with a profound example of what it is like to be *transgender*. As long as we, that diminutive minority of humans that *are* transgender, <u>deny</u> our true selves, remain imprisoned within our body, and go along with the way others want us to live and think ... then the world will open up to us.

However, if we as human beings have the audacity to <u>follow our hearts</u> and seek our gender path to self-understanding and inner peace, we may discover the only sounds we hear are those of our *footsteps* as we search for friends or family ... and find only ourselves making this journey *alone*.

Pink Heart

In the following text, I attempt to explain about the HOW and WHY others and I are transgender. In essence it's similar to being on trial in life's courtroom. We are on the witness stand presenting our testimony before the court of public opinion.

As stated earlier, you never get to know someone until you see things from their point of view. For those who hear only the echoes of your footsteps, I bid you come. For others who are curious, you may seek a better understanding and perhaps seek to learn more about what drives someone to seek a change of gender.

Life is not the candle or the wick, but rather it is the burning. Kissed by the flames of femininity, each of us that is a male to female transgender human has inside us a bonfire that often burns so intensely and uncontrollably that only <u>SHE</u> truly understands what it is like living with such a raging, ceaseless inferno from within.

Is it then ... an obsession? Indeed, it is and one that no matter what ... will never go away, regardless of how much the individual attempts to hide or suppress it. Its power is engrained in the very soul and the only relief comes when the individual accepts that feminine side and chooses to do something about it. Ding so, may be complicated and be the cause of much tribulation for the transgender woman and for those in a relationship with the "woman" within.

COMMENTARY

Why is there so much suffering in this world? How many times have you asked yourself that question? Recently, the world's population has had to contend with a viral pandemic known as Covid 19. How many thousands have contracted that virus and how many worldwide have died from it? Who among you ever thought we humans would have to wear masks when in public to prevent us from contracting a deadly virus? Who thought a pandemic would cause us to sequester in lockdowns at home, or that we'd not be able to dine out at our favorite restaurants, attend stadiums with maximum capacities to watch our favorite sports teams, or do dozens of our *normal* daily or weekly routines without risking getting the virus or passing it along to an elderly loved one?

How many people have lost their lives in natural disasters or accidents this past year? How many American mothers' tears have caused hearts to rust due to the untimely deaths of their sons or daughters killed in the war in Afghanistan or other conflicts? How many died this past year or week of AIDS, cancer, heart attacks, diabetes, Alzheimer's, or some other debilitating disease? Why in 2001 did a group of terrorists' kidnap jet airliners and use them as attack missiles to bring down the World Trade Towers, damage the Pentagon, and cause chaos, death, and destruction within our homeland? How many parents agonize over a young child that suffers from cancer and seek help from the Saint Jude's Cancer Hospital for children?

How many horrible incidents within our nation occur where some people are persecuted or killed because of the misfortune of merely having black skin? Why are some that enter this land of the free seeking asylum and escape from oppression? They see a better opportunity to achieve an improved life for themselves and their children. Many enter illegally and are often turned away, sequestered, separated from loved ones, and generally unsure how to enter our nation legally to become citizens.

Who can say why these types of things happen in our world? I certainly don't believe it's the result of a vengeful, wrathful God. As children of a *loving God*, I can only conclude that death and suffering are merely a part of our human existence. It always has been and always shall be. I would speak to the lack of concern and how some folks turn their eyes from the suffering of their brethren.

To what degree and what manner of tolerance and compassion should we exhibit toward our fellow humans? At times, I believe all of us are guilty of heartless laissez-faire reactions to the plights of others. Sadly, that too is human nature. Still, I would declare that inside most of us there is a conscience that often causes us to do marvelous, generous things and display great compassion for others in need.

In my lifetime, I've seen horrific things happen to others in my own family and the immediate world. I've attended the bedside of my parents' last hours on this earth before they slipped away into the hereafter. I've attended far too many funerals of relatives or friends and attempted to comfort those close to them whose loss I also felt.

The implication here is to admit that there are <u>far worse</u> things in life that have happened and are happening in our world and to its people than that which is the subject of this book. This melancholy reflecting upon the precariousness of life and the misfortune of some, like myself, that must deal with being transgender pales in comparison to those who have suffered far more traumatic things in their lives. Although being transgender/transsexual is not a frivolous misfortune, neither is it comparable to some dreadful calamity that annihilates or extinguishes life itself. In a sense, those who travel down this path must hold private funerals for the person they "used to be," as they set off on an amazing, challenging journey to become that which they have always dreamed of.

However, there is a small percentage of transgender humans that suffer from severe depression and a feeling of hopelessness that turn to suicide as an alternative means of escaping their unhappy reality.

Manifestly, the multitude of humanity is spared from having to endure life as a transgender/transsexual, and for that, they should be thankful. Being transgender, I cannot hypothesize what the collective response to the sufferings of those that are transgender might be among those who will read this book. reading this should weep for those others or me that are transgender, nor do we want or seek your pity. We would, however, seek your tolerance, a degree of understanding, and a measure of consideration.

Instead, save your tears for those angels of honor who defend our nation and first responders who rush in to save lives in flooded-out areas after a storm, or brave collapsing, burning buildings to rescue survivors inside. Bestow your tributes upon those skilled nurses, surgeons, and heroes who save countless lives each year and those who peer through microscopes to discover vaccines, and cures for disease. Pay homage to those who travel to where disaster strikes in our world to lend a helping hand, pass out food, clothing, offer a smile or just embrace a child and deliver a message of hope.

What's a transgender woman? I would tell you to walk over to your fax machine and send a copy to whomever you please. What you would be doing is about the equivalent of what is a male to a female transgender person. There is no such thing as a true biological "sex change" so, the best a transsexual can hope for is to become as close a facsimile of a woman as possible. SHE has fashioned genitalia that appears to be female and partakes of enough estrogenic hormone therapy that her secondary sex and blood levels slant toward the feminine. Each of us that are transgender depends on the best medical science can offer us to achieve such a status. For those who believe themselves to be transgender: The cave they fear entering contains the treasure they seek. (Quote from Joseph Campbell)

I am now a retired and have enjoyed my past twenty-five years living as a female. The photos of me herein are mostly of a time when I was aged in my forties. To my delight, progesterone and estrogen gave my body a boost of youthfulness and I looked like I was in my thirties instead.

In today's world, as is evidenced by the many videos on YouTube, transgender women and men are leaping into their transition and gender change journey far earlier in life than most in my generation and others did. There is more tolerance and more information about the condition and an eagerness on the part of well-informed young adults to make their change and transition as early as possible in life. I admire their courage and conviction. Many trans-women are quite beautiful and one would never know that they were born as males. I was amazed at how feminine and lovely I became as Shannon.

Chapter 1:
You Call This Progress?

    I was raised at the advent of the atomic and jet age. In the span of my lifetime, I have seen countless scientific, medical and technological marvels come into being. The inventive, creative imaginings of mankind have driven human beings to achieve and bring about a myriad of remarkable innovations into our realm. I have seen the world develop from the vacuum tube to the transistor, and then be thrust into a cyber world that is ruled by integrated circuits, megabytes, microchips, and information gathering so quickly that it comes to us at the speed of a mouse click. Others and I who were born during this period have in our decades of life witnessed a medical, technological, and industrial surge like no other in human history. Mankind has even walked on the surface of the moon, not just once, but several times.

    The innovations and advances achieved over the years have been staggering and altered our way of life and how we view our world today. No doubt the discoveries of this past half-century have saved countless lives and created for all of us a more convenient world. Still, in our exuberance over the incredible advances and devices for making our lives easier, have we manifested change as progress? If indeed this were advancement, I would declare that it has come to us at a piercing price.

    In these modern times, humankind developed the ways and means to examine the minutest elements of life itself here on earth. It extended its vision to the dark outer reaches of the universe to study the beginnings of new stars, solar systems, discovering exoplanets, and the existence of other worlds like our own. Researchers discovered numerous ways to slow or defeat many forms of cancer and made huge advances in treating heart disease and other human diseases. Technology has made our world smaller and nations became part of the global community that finds itself more interdependent than ever on other countries to supply its citizens' needs. Progress indeed harnessed the energies of the atom and abundant strides have been made to improve our world and make it a better place in which to live. Was it worth it? What were the true costs of this progress?

Reports tell us that the rainforests of our planet are being destroyed at alarming rates and that when they are gone, so too shall be many species of life and possibly the hope of finding cures for many diseases that plague humankind. Thanks to inflation, if you've had to take out a loan to fill your truck or automobile's gas tank of late, you know too that world oil reserves are dwindling and that the gluttony for fossil fuels caused many of the world's underground seas of oil to become barren.

There are still places on our earth where extreme poverty exists and children die each day of starvation, where diseases run rampant, and where waging war and killing is an everyday occurrence. Industrial progress advanced global warming and the depletion of the earth's protective ozone layer. Don't believe that? Come to Texas in July or August and endure the dry heat with extended weeks of temperatures topping the century mark.

Look around us at the rising sea levels and falling levels of our lakes and reservoirs. The wild fires in California, Oregon, Washington, and other western states are due to severe drought. In our crowded urban cities, we must check our nightly weather reports for ozone alerts and air quality to find out if outdoor activities the following day will be safe.

In our own country, social progress advanced the causes of many minorities, including improved civil rights for Black Americans, Hispanics, Orientals, and others within our borders -- which daily are still being invaded and crossed by those entering our nation via illegal means. Black Lives Matter has called into account instances of police cruelty and violence dealing with the arrests or containment of black men or women.

Unfortunately, there are still enough addicts in our society to support the drug cartels of Asia, Mexico, and South America. The violent crime rate is rising, as does the ever-growing population, which tops out to over three-hundred million humans in our nation.

The economic gap between the poor and rich is increasing and large conglomerates, such as megalithic social media platforms on the Internet practice censorship and are gobbling up the smaller enterprises of America causing near-monopolies. Higher prices for food, clothing, fuel and energy continue, and meager stimulus packages by Congress during the pandemic do little to avert the economic crisis caused by Covid-19 shutdowns.

Pink Heart

California urban areas of Los Angeles and San Francisco bulge with the filth and disease from the increasing homeless populations and encampments on beaches and city streets.

Inflation is rampant, plus health costs are staggering and the poor are left to depend on government-assisted programs and welfare when major economic and health issues arise.

Despite all our scientific, social, medical, and technological advances and our own nation's affluence, for many in our world and society, there's still a <u>lack</u> of true progress or <u>meaning</u> in their personal lives.

The churches of our land are overwhelmed with those seeking answers and guidance from God, atonement for sins, and responses to the same questions our ancestors asked hundreds, even thousands of years earlier. Sadly, church attendance is decreasing, as fewer citizens make it a priority in their spiritual lives. Foreclosures on mortgages are only topped by the seeming foreclosures on moralities and the death of the American family as it once existed. A higher standard of living does not necessarily bring about fulfillment, happiness, or a better appreciation or understanding of life.

Disenchantment with the fast-paced society in which we live has many of us longing for the slower, simpler, less complex lives of our childhood and those of our ancestors. We wax nostalgic, looking backward in time at the wake of vanished days and a lifestyle that is indeed "Gone With The Wind".

For certain, our higher-octane world is much less safe today than it was when I was born. It has become a powder keg of crime and violence whereby communism, terrorists, and religious zealots threaten the very core of our freedom. Has the mindset of our world progressed? Has the human desire for power or domination truly diminished all that much amongst world leaders over the past seventy years? Have those nations, world politicians, and leaders that were greedy or corrupt become less so? Have the weapons of war been laid down and has peace now come to every land? Has the threat of nuclear annihilation waned any? Unfortunately for all of us, the answer to those questions -- is no! Ask the Ukrainian people.

Lost in this entire ostentatious leap into the Internet world and the allurement of this advent of such incredible progress -- is this FACT: We live in a wondrous time in history and now have amazing tools and machines to assist us with improved living. However, we seem to understand the basic complexities of physics, mathematics, electronics, and engineering <u>better</u> than we do <u>the labyrinth of possibilities</u> and the function of our <u>hearts and minds</u>.

Modern science and psychiatry introduced us to anti-psychotic drugs such as Prozac, and other such drugs designed to temper mental instabilities. Our children have been dosed with Ritalin to better focus their attention on learning. The clergy, therapist, counselor, psychologist, and psychiatrist have all become more in demand as people seek help with answers to everyday problems that they face in this fast-forward world. With all the wonders of this contemporary age, it is this fascinating superb instrument of reason, **THE HUMAN MIND**, which remains the world's greatest mystery.

Other than life itself and an eternal soul, the mind is the most precious gift that God has given us. In our struggle to survive, most of us want there to be meaning and purpose to our lives and so we seek peace, fulfillment, and to discover WHO WE ARE and what is inside our hearts. We all seek proof that we are more than just some random sequence exuding from a genetic spin of the roulette wheel of life.

The progress humankind has made over the past six decades, I present you with another question: Have we humans become more tolerant, compassionate, and considerate of others? In some ways, perhaps we have, but we still have a great way to go. Some people apprise me that human tolerance these days is more <u>indifference</u>, choosing not to become involved or mixed up in the lives of others. Thus, for some, they do not do unto others -- they simply avoid them and let others fend for themselves.

As it applies to this book, I would cite a good example of such an apathetic, callous attitude being the lack of tolerance and understanding that some people have for those that are gay, lesbian, bisexual, or TRANSGENDER. Some people understand the complexities of $E=MC^2$ and might even totally grasp how Quasars are formed. Others might know the composition of a DNA helix or that a certain computer hard drive has a hundred gigabytes of memory storage – and yet they cannot conceive something so simple as to why one male might find it preferable to have another male as a mate and partner. I wager that even the smartest of contestants on Jeopardy would probably fail to know much about why or how a person becomes transgender or what the procedures are to "switch genders and the challenges involved in that endeavor.

Many people are lost in comprehending why or how a human-born male could possess an impulse and desire to become female. Depending on their religious, ethnic, or social background and the way they were brought up, such a concept might be as foreign to them as a first-grader trying to understand advanced calculus or physics.

How much real progress have we made when our world and nation are divided about hot issues such as: Which political party holds the most promise for the future? How do we prevent wars? Which religion is the most divine and offers the true path to God and enlightenment? As a Christian, my answer to them is obvious. Still, try convincing a Jew, Muslim, or Hindu that Jesus is the Messiah and their personal Savior.

Which methods of governing are best for all? How do we prevent terrorism? How do we best control the burdensome population growth and stem illegal immigration? How do we best protect our freedoms? How do we solve world hunger? How do we address controlling crime and deciding proper punishment? Should abortion be outlawed? How do we protect the sanctification of marriage and why shouldn't gays and lesbians have the right to do so?

Probably somewhere near the <u>bottom</u> of that list of questions and human concerns one might ask the following: <u>What is transgender that is known as a gender identity crisis</u>? Can it be cured or prevented? Is it a disease or sickness of the mind? How many are affected by this condition known as GID (gender identity disorder)? Are lengthy therapy and gender-reassignment surgery really necessary, or is there a better way to cure or solve the issue about those who claim to be transgender/transsexual?

Since this human condition is so rare among the populous, it is not perceived as a priority concern ... except to those few minorities of humans directly affected by it. Admittedly, there are many more issues of importance for humankind than being transgender. Still, if YOU are that one in a hundred thousand or one in a million who is or believes him/herself to be transsexual, THEN it becomes an important issue. For those then, our bodies are likely to become our autobiographies.

My favorite hobby is writing lyrics and melodies for my music. To date, I've written many songs. I've had some of them made into professional demos, but haven't tried marketing them yet.

Being transgender is not an illusion nor is it unimportant. Ask those left in the wake of carnage by some loved one or friend who is transsexual. To those wives, husbands, children, friends, or others that endure the trying times of having to deal with a transgender person going through transition, I assure you it is not a trivial ordeal or condition.

In keeping with the theme about the progress of humankind, I herein address what progress has been made concerning this transgender condition. For that reason, as much as any, I wrote this manifest.

Chapter 2:
It's Not Easy -- Being PINK!

For most of my childhood and adult life, I felt much like Peter Pan chasing around after his lost shadow. The difference being, the shadow I sought was not that of some boyish imp cast upon a bedroom wall, but rather a covert, elusive, womanly silhouette embedded within the shadow of my mind's eye. This feminine phantom lingered therein and patiently waited to be set free -- to <u>cast her own shadow</u> upon the wall of life and in the sunlight.

However, for me –Never-Never-Land did not produce the same promise or implication of hope that it offered for Peter Pan. To me, the idea of being a **boy** that never grows up is tantamount to existing and enduring in the worst type of purgatory. To my old friends and family, it probably seems I've become more akin to the winged fairy Tinker Bell than the impish Peter Pan. Would that I was as cute as she.

No, my Never-Land represents something entirely dissimilar. In that place, it seems I am more like <u>Pinocchio</u> – for there – my chromosomes are forever denied the privilege of becoming a <u>real girl</u>. From all the hidden truths, excuses, and lies I told as my boy self -- my NOSE grew ten feet long and a family of egrets nested therein.

It saddens me that have a Y chromosome and will never possess the proper double X chromosomes that would, in my adulthood result in menses and provide me with a biological ability to have vaginal moisture, intense orgasms, become pregnant, bear a child, or become a mother. Never will I know the joys of what it is like to breastfeed an infant produced through the fertilization of an egg in my womb-less body.

Although my voice is somewhat feminine, never again will I experience the felicity of having the cute soprano voice I once had before the onset of male puberty. Never will I possess the smaller, 5'6" shorter type skeletal frame which many adult females inherit. Adjusting my estrogen levels provides me with and permits me to have proper feminine curves in all the right places, but my skeletal frame won't shrink to allow me to shop for petite womanly-sized clothing and shoes.

Thankfully, I have been able to experience what it's like to possess a natural feminine appearance facially. My dream was to have a young man look upon me, gaze into my eyes, dream of the future, and desire to have me for his mated wife. Some, no doubt has and ... there was this one guy, but that's another story. Never will I be blessed with having been born into the gender with which I feel most comfortable and NORMAL. Never-Land? Yes, I've been there -- and as far as I am concerned, Peter can keep it.

This then is the story of ... ME

Gender Counseling Group – '99

Oh, by the way, my name is **Shannon O'Shea**. It wasn't always so, for you see although I am a female (a trans-woman), I was born with improper genitals. Does that statement confuse you? Keep reading and you'll come to understand what I mean.

Once upon a time, my name was **Gordon**. He was a nice enough fellow; he just wasn't the actual, factual -- me. Then who am I? I am tall, have somewhat shaggy platinum blond-hair and a trans-woman (turning white-headed with age) with fair skin and emerald green eyes made even greener by the envy I have for those of you fortunate enough to have been born female in the first place. I'm connected by a dear friendship and love to another transgender lady whose name is **Nicole.**

Pink Heart

Nicole – My Beloved Best Friend

Are we homosexual lesbians? Negative! But that's beside the point. We jokingly refer to ourselves as being <u>Transbians</u>. All I know is she loves me and I love her. We are best friends and have a home and have lived together for twenty years. In that sense, she is my <u>mate</u> and someone with whom I feel privileged to share my life. We are an emerging writing team and have authored several fiction novels, manuscripts, and screenplays.

I've two ex-wives, sired three children, parented one step-daughter, and have five grandkids. As I stated before, both my adopted parents and biological parents have passed onto into the hereafter. I've two brothers and one sister (that died last year of Alzheimer's). Professionally, I have been in construction, sales, and management for most of my adult life. I've got a business degree from Baylor University and was born and raised in Waco, Texas. I studied Psychology in online classes for several years. There shall be more on my childhood and personal life later in this text.

Despite being transgender, I profess myself to be a decent person. For the first seven years of my journey as Shannon, I did exhibit low-cut styles and femme "boudoir behavior" habits, but I was not immoral. I wore less than conservative dresses and tops that were somewhat exhibitionistic. Partly because the summers are "hot" in Texas, but I admit it was also because I enjoyed my newly acquired bosom, sexy figure, and all my femme assets. I was not nude, but certainly provocative, mostly in private, but also when at parties, dancing, and such. Still, I believe I was a decent spouse, parent, and never strayed far from my core moral beliefs, but admit to some failings in each of those categories.

I have enchantment and a passion for writing stories, songs, and poetry. I smile more now and I am confident and comfortable with whom I am. I enjoy sports, music, poetry, art and design, live theatre, reading, the Internet, and most all things feminine.

I view the world with a glint of wonder and awe, longing for an occasional snowy, rainy, or lazy day and loving to swim, play golf, go fishing, watch spectator sports, and attend a concert or a play. Like all women, I take great pleasure from shopping, going on a picnic, camping outdoors in an RV, getting dressed up, going out to dinner and a movie, dancing, playing in the paint (make-up), getting my hair done, being pampered at a salon or just crashing at home with Nicole.

I delight in people with a keen sense of humor, a positive attitude, confident yet humble, generous, moral, and honest, believe in the Almighty, and are open, committed, loving, and friendly.

I dislike braggarts, apathy to others, dishonesty, extreme profanity, immorality, violence, addiction to drugs or alcohol, agnostics, stinginess, and impatience. That's enough with the "I am, I like, and I enjoy." Let's move on.

As I begin my tale, let me quote a comedic lady named Rita Mae Brown, whom I've not yet had the pleasure to meet. Once, while onstage, she stated the following:

"The statistics on <u>sanity</u> are that <u>one</u> out of every <u>four</u> Americans is suffering from some form of mental illness. Think of your three best friends. If they're okay ... it's probably you!"

I wonder where Ms. Brown got her information. Whatever! I shouldn't worry, for my three best friends are as nutty as fruitcakes, so I imagine the odds are that you, the reader is just fine. Nevertheless, if I still seem crazy

Pink Heart

to you, ignore your instincts, for I proclaim that I am just as lucid and rational as you -- lest you doubt that from the beginning. (She says with her tongue planted firmly in her cheek)

In a trans-woman's life, she will likely build a <u>dam</u> to hold back the bitter waters of <u>lies and deceit</u>, which she hides from those she loves. Not that she wants to, but it's her only way to live the life <u>expected</u> of him/her. I envy those youngsters of today who confess their gender dysphoria and come clean with parents, family, friends, and medical professionals. By starting the journey when young, fewer loved ones will be lost or upset in the transition process.

There will come a time when a trans-woman has to "suck it up," come clean, and to paraphrase Larry the Cable Guy, "Get <u>her</u> done."

Shall we continue then? Hey, wipe that smile off your face or someone watching you read this might begin to suspect that you're about to enjoy perusing a story about a trans-person, and then they really will think you loony.

While I'm at it, there's another old saying "It is better to keep your mouth shut and seem a fool than to open it a remove all doubt." Oh well, I suppose it's too late to try and get that horseback into the barn.

In that case, you readers will certainly be seeing my mouth wide open and what brains I have spilled out all over the ensuing pages. Any doubts about my sanity, sensibilities, or seeming a fool to you will become entirely evident long before you reach the end of this story. Whatever conclusions to which you arrive, I trust that you will be entertained, enlightened, informed, and possibly a tad more tolerant, understanding, less apprehensive, and familiar with a portion of the human race that many of you may never have before encountered -- or perhaps were even aware exists.

First Year of My Fulltime Journey
✱ ✱ ✱

If you are truly seeking to learn more about trans-women, then I welcome you. It's my sincere hope that in some way the personal insights into my own life's story, as told herein will inform you and touch you in a manner as to make you more aware of <u>what a trans-woman is and isn't</u>.

The information I've gathered herein comes from many years of reading about and researching the subject, plus more importantly from my <u>first-hand, personal experience</u>. After you've read this material, you can draw your subjective conclusions about how accurate you think I portray this condition and whether or not you agree with my opinions.

Perhaps afterward, you'll be more prepared to react or deal with someone who is transgender. If your post-reaction is favorable, then it might

Pink Heart

lead you to become more open-minded, accepting, receptive, and less suspicious about those gender variant people whose lives are different than your own.

Though the phenomenon of being <u>Gender Dysphoric</u> happens to those of <u>both sexes</u>, in this book I <u>primarily address</u> those who are going from being **male** to becoming **female.** It is not my intent to slight those individuals going in the opposite direction from my own, it's just that my main interest and experience has been in dealing with those who are male to female (**MTF**) transgender/transsexuals (**TS**).

I would like to add that I have personally met and been befriended by several females to male (**FTM**) transgender/transsexuals. These <u>men</u> are marvelous human beings and I feel privileged to have gotten to know them. One had his surgery over twenty years ago and he's married to a dear and great lady. They make a very convincing, cute couple and most people have never had a clue that the male in that union didn't start in life that way. The other FTM I know is dating a woman and he's an active and talented member of a church orchestra. Both these people are quality individuals and pass as men extremely well. Being transgender, I have a great appreciation of what they've accomplished and for the successful transition that each has had. I admire and respect them both and my heart goes out to them and to all that are FTM and seek to live the life they choose.

Those of us, who fall into the category of being transgender, are not a sub-human species. Most of us are not perverted, nor are we a contagious blight ready to swarm over the earth and contaminate it. For the most part, we are stable, intelligent, caring, and responsible citizens who obey the law, pay our taxes and contribute in productive ways to our society. Many of us are parents, and maybe even your best friend. Some of us might be your husband, your brother, your neighbor, co-worker, or even worse -- your boss!

Each individual with this condition has various unique and complex reasons for having obtained this desire to be female. I will touch on some of those reasons, but it is a fruitless effort to attempt to explain them all -- even if I knew them all, which I don't.

To some of you, this condition might seem like an aberration, an abomination, or bizarre behavior at best. I don't deny that being transgender deviates behavior from the norm, but I assure you most that are transgender are reasonable, sober of mind, and the majority have had to meet head-on a quandary that has had a lifelong vice-grip on their psyche and soul.

OR Although a genetic female just is, an MTF trans-woman must become a female ... by whatever means available to her ... via medical science, chemistry, and surgery.

What's Ahead?

As for what issues I shall address herein, first I will establish my genesis and **her story** and the rather odd childhood circumstances that lead to my guardianship, and the effects that situation had upon my psyche and my mental development. Along the way, there shall be commentary and explanations about certain aspects of being transgender. Then I will present a **question-and-answer** format that will be used to convey certain of my thoughts about issues that affect other trans-ladies and myself. During that section, the surveyed opinions of several prominent sex/gender reassignment (**GRS**) surgeons will be stated, as they comment about the effectiveness of these types of surgeries upon those that seek them.

I shall, throughout this entire book self-analyze and self-evaluate my transgender nature, at times exhibit self-deprecation, my failures, disappointments, aspirations, and successes that I've attained in my having lived upon this planet.

Pink Heart

The world as we know it changed in 2020 when the pandemic came to our American shores and everyone had to shelter in place at home. At the writing of this story, I have both my vaccine and booster shots. I pray God helps me and those I love to avoid this deadly plague. God be with all the families of those poor souls who have died from returning to normal.this terrible affliction. Here in 2022, we seem to have turned the corner, and thanks to the vaccines, life as we knew it is slowly but hopefully

This book is a chronicle of my having lived my life in a male's **blue** world -- but all the while possessing a woman's **pink heart**! So pull up a chair, sit down, get comfy, and if you need them, locate your reading glasses and follow along as I expound on that last statement. As Ricky Ricardo told his zany red-headed wife, "Lucy: "You got some 'splaining' to do!"

When the trans-woman has her "aha" moment: the intense build-up of pressures … the dam breaks, and the truth floods There's forth with such a force that it's like taking a wrecking ball to her former, fraudulent self.

Now, leave any bias or preconceived notions behind and keep your mind open as we commence this marvelous, fascinating, compelling odyssey.

Chapter 3:
The Invisible Me

As stated before, I am Shannon and this is my story -- and one I expect is similar to the other thousands of male-to-female (**MTF**) trans-women like me. No, it is not the story of that false male image that I presented to the world and who everyone expected me to be. Rather, it is the story of the **true me**, the transparent me (yes, I was a trans-parent) -- the invisible, feminine me, which was kept hidden beneath that dark cloak of masculinity all those years among those with whom I came into contact.

This is the story of me that loved and was loved. As I mentioned, after my transition from Gordon into Shannon, I became separated and fell out of favor with almost everyone that had up till that time been important in my life. Why did that happen?

Like the zebra that grew up asking if he was WHITE with BLACK stripes or BLACK with WHITE stripes, I grew up and wanted to know – Am I a WOMAN in a MAN'S **body,** or am I a MAN with a WOMAN'S **mind**?

As John Money and Patricia Tucker pointed out: "When you see a (TS/transgender), it's no use asking is she still a man or was he a woman all those years? The question is meaningless."

The answer I'd give is that I desired to be one thing -- as a whole a female as I could be. My older brother, Mack would tell you that, zebra-wise, he sees me as definitely being WHITE ... but with PINK stripes.

I love that concept and I see it as being pretty accurate. Then am I some new flamboyant breed of Flamingo or did my kind simply evolve from a branch that fell off nature and God's tree of life? Perhaps, but it wasn't an act of natural selection that helped form the person I am today.

Like all humans, I contemplate and wonder why I'm alive, where I came from, and where I am going. Being raised a Christian -- I doubt that my heritage sprang forth from the sea or just because I once enjoyed climbing in trees that my ancestry evolved from apes. But why, among all humans do I feel like God should have made me into a GIRL ... instead of a BOY? Or did HE and all I had to do was to recognize it and work to earn the right to obtain and maintain that gender?

There is no denying my anatomical biological birth sex, for I was born with male genitalia (Yuck!), but there is also no doubt or denying that mentally I've always felt like a female. That is a fact that has caused my loved ones, others, and me much confusion, sorrow, and heartbreak in our lives.

Every MTF transsexual/transgender I know, including myself, has envy and covets that which every genetic Ciswomen has been born; that being <u>a female in body, mind, and spirit</u>. It's the physical asset that we trans-women are not born or blessed with at the time of our birth.

Many that are transgender can never fully attain the equivalent physical assets, social acceptance, status, or beauty as those that are fortunate enough to be born <u>naturally genetic females</u>. To an MTF transgender, those being born female have been presented with a great, extraordinary gift and blessing -- that <u>none</u> of them should ever take for granted.

I cannot recall at any moment in my life when I was completely happy being a male. Sure, there have been joyful, loving times in my male life -- plenty of them in fact, but my being a male caused me far more anguish than it did elation.

After my youth had been spent, for some reason it just wasn't in my cards to meekly accept my fate, or to leave my destiny to genetics and forever deny the intense longing that I had within me to become female. So, I made the tough life-changing decision to leave behind the life Gordon fashioned and became a trans-woman and as close a facsimile as medical science can in today's world accomplish.

Some women and men that I have met or known who consider themselves to be <u>normal</u> and who have never questioned their sex or gender have spurned me. Some looked down their moralistic, heterosexual noses at me because of my desire to be female.

I would remind these folks, especially those who were born female or who tout their perceptions of morality to me that they did nothing to earn their beauty and grace, or their right to have a vagina with the ability to have orgasms or bear children. Neither did they earn their heterosexuality or their morality. They were, as I pointed out earlier, the fortunate ones whom God graced with the gift of being born female.

The same God that gave me this innate desire to be female gave these women their natural physical gifts and their so-called normal status. One being transgender does not make that person immoral, nor does it mean that person is homosexual, for those two considerations and conditions are completely different and separate.

I have lived a dual life in two genders and that part of me that is Shannon is woven deep into my psyche as well as my physicality, much as normalcy/commonality is to those that have it. If you are comfortable within your skin, with who you are, and what sex you are -- <u>consider it a great blessing</u>.

However, I would urge you who are so fortunate to please not <u>judge or condemn</u> those of us who questioned our gender and felt compelled to change it. The transgender condition cannot be reduced to some simple choice, a character flaw, a bad habit, some mental defect, or an addiction that can be cured by attending a seminar with a twelve-step program for recovery. It's a condition that cannot be identified by drawing blood or found by peering through a microscope at cells or tissue.

Before transitioning into our preferred gender, most of us that are transgender have lived like squirrels feverishly turning in our revolving cages, seeking to escape the existence and environment in which we felt entrapped.

We often build our prisons, much like the invisible fences and the electronic collar that a dog wears to prevent him from straying beyond his master's boundary. Below the surface of our varied personalities, our real, true self lies immobilized in a palisade of detached emotions resigned to offer up an infinite number of excuses as to why we can't become the <u>she</u> that we desire to be.

Many MTF trans-people are married, and like myself have children or even grandchildren. Though many more are open these days to society and transition in their 20's or teens, some still feel self-defeated, for they can't find it within themselves to come clean and confess their femme desires to parents, friends, or employers. Instead, they withstand the inadequacies and unhappiness that the deception creates in their lives. The creation of the trans-woman's femme personality may require years of <u>living through</u> the causes of the excuses and waiting for the right time and proper place to act upon her innermost desires.

For example, an MTF transgender may choose to wait until his parents have passed away, as I did. He ... might wait until his children graduate high school or college, get married, or perhaps wait until after a divorce or some other incident happens that will allow and present the transgender with the opportunity to seek a change of gender. For others, a sense of desperation creates an urgency that cannot be denied, no matter what their circumstances. I admire those that come out early in life and decide to transition. Parents these days seem more accepting and educated about their child's gender dysphoria, and are more willing to become involved in supporting that child's desire to become congruent with how they feel toward becoming female instead of remaining unhappily in a body that does not fit with how they feel and cope with life.

For some MTF trans-women, there is still the issue of self-deception and self-denial. The male side of him refuses to believe he can't defeat those feminine desires that threaten to alter or perhaps destroy the life and existence that he created for himself. Hiding from one's self so as not to face the troubled soul and the female within only serves to delay the inevitable. One cannot create a living FACADE and expect it to last forever. Sooner or later, the bubble bursts and that person endures the exercise of having to face up to the truth.

We MTF trans-women often build for ourselves barriers that serve as mere artificial platforms made up of agendas that detract us from seeking the truth. Eventually, the fragile foundations for those platforms (marriage, over-achieving machismo, hiding behind a mustache, or parenthood) crumble, and our life and the lives of those we love most become scattered amongst the ruins in a total shamble. Usually, when this happens to an MTF trans-woman, he/she feels as though she's become like an actor, impersonator, performer, or role-player. He / She lives and breathes, but is he/she truly alive?

For some trans-women, life becomes like a sad melodrama of pretense, whereby he/she finds support from a wardrobe of masks that out of necessity he/she uses to adapt and accommodate those who <u>expect</u> him to be the man they know and love. He / She conforms, but he does not transform -- and therein lays the problem, for as a male, he/she feels like he's caught in a hypocritical charade. In such a circumstance, life takes on a stifled aspect for the MTF trans-woman, as the pretentious mechanisms of conformity and attempts at normalcy only lead him/her down unhappy paths. The Roy Orbison song, "Mystery Girl" tends to make me envision that the "she" in the song is a transwoman prior to transition. The male part of her imagines the female part of him to be like another entity, a mysterious female that beckons him each night to dress and become her. As the song states, "she tears against my bleeding heart … I want to run; she's pulling me apart. Falling angel cries, and I just melt away. She's a mystery to me." Then morning comes and "her heaven" returns to the hell of living as a male. I doubt the song was thought of in that manner, but listen to it on youtube.com. The address is below and follow along the lyrics to see why to me it relates to being transgender The URL is below:

https://www.youtube.com/watch?v=CfCYSW3Xl6E

His male life becomes a <u>distraction</u> as if he/she is corrupt and shortchanging himself out of his / her future or any chance at true happiness. At the same time, it feels like he/she is cheating his spouse, kids, friends, or employer by not giving them the full attention or love they deserve. Often, an MTF transgender that buries himself in such falsehood winds up becoming emotionally bankrupt His / Her life turns out to be mundane and pretentious. I can attest to this fact, as I write this from personal experience.

For some of us that are adult MTF trans-women, we took on the role of husband, father, friend, boss, or being bossed and model our male image by what others and we think we should be. However, in this daily round of living, at some point in time most of us that are MTF trans-women modify our behavior. If not via permanent changes, at least through temporary fixes that satiate our overwhelming desires to be feminine.

Some of us do this via cross-dressing, experimenting with make-up, allowing our cranial hair to grow and styling it in feminine ways, or perhaps immersing ourselves with perfume and wearing jewelry. We may acquire acrylic nails, shave our legs, chest, and underarms, lavish ourselves in sexy lingerie, or for some perhaps experiment with hormones and electrolysis. For the true trans-woman, they will not be happy until their GENDER IDENTITY is made right and all these temporary fixes become permanent. How is that accomplished?

It's not as simple as some people think. Ask a non-trans-person about how a male becomes female and they are likely to tell you, "They have a sex-change operation!" The truth is, as I pointed out earlier, the surgery to alter the genitals from male to female does not change a person's chromosome sex. It does fashion for an MTF a natural-appearing labia and vagina. Still, this operation is but one step among many in the process of the transition.

To some people, perhaps the acts above might seem like a fetish, but they are not really. It's only a part of the charted course to become feminine. All those things and more are how trans-women seek to use and attain when passing from one gender to another -- into the gender role they prefer. In this odd journey through life, many trans-women feel themselves to be fractured souls, separated into disjointed entities with dissimilar parts and an incoherent voice with fragmented identities.

For pre-transition trans-women, life can be sort of like stumbling through the darkness, seeking self-comprehension, all the while tossed around in choppy seas during a storm -- never being quite able to obtain an accurate compass heading for the destination she hopes to obtain.

Even a person that is transgender and achieves professional and financial success, fame, or rises to the top of the athletic, social or cultural ladder, will experience less than complete satisfaction with whom and what they are if they deny their true self and gender (Bruce/Caitlyn Jenner). This is something I speak of to others when I try to explain self-harmony, peace within, or synchrony with one's gender. The synchronization connection between mind and body with inner identity is not something a non-trans-person can always recognize or understand.

Most non-trans-persons may understand the physiological aspects of cross-living and identity, but most fail to comprehend the complex neuropsychological effects the mind plays in determining the role of who we are and what we think we should be.

Gordon – Soldier   Grdon – age 31 –'88

Gordon at Age 5   **A PeeWee Leaguer**

Pink Heart

Before Shannon There Was Gordon

Assuming that the condition of Gender Dysphoria / Gender Identity Crisis affects about 1 in every 50,000 to 100,000 humans, with an estimated U.S. population of 350 million that would put the numbers of transsexuals in our country at about 7,000 That is .00002 % of the total population.

Mental disorders are common in the United States and internationally. An estimated 22.1 percent of Americans ages eighteen and older—about 1 in 5 adults—suffer from a diagnosable mental disorder in a given year. Four of the ten leading causes of disability in the U.S. and other countries are mental disorders ... major depression, bipolar disorder, schizophrenia, and obsessive-compulsive disorder. Many suffer from more than one mental disorder at a given time.

Does this mean that someone can be transgender and also be bipolar, obsessive-compulsive, bulimic, and anorexic, suffer major depression, post-traumatic syndrome, and possibly even have schizophrenia? Yes, it does.

Chapter 4:
The Other Side

The following is an interpreted excerpt from a newspaper article written in the "Fort Worth Star-Telegram" about a member of my gender counselor's support group. She was a gender specialist, now retired, and counseled at the Sexuality Education Center there in Fort Worth.

※ ※ ※

Her office is quiet and softly lit by the table lamp next to the sofa. The counselor takes a deep breath and squirms in her upholstered armchair, as she listens carefully to the tribulations of the troubled young man sitting across from her. As founder and director of a Sexuality Education Center in Ft. Worth, Texas, she has counseled many others like this young man that has come to her requesting private sessions to discuss his feelings of gender confusion and ambiguity.

This young man is attempting to sort out his inner feelings about whether or not he should attempt to alter his gender and live full-time as a woman. He confesses to the counselor his secret desires to do so but tempers his enthusiasm by expressing self-doubts as to whether he can pull it off by presenting himself as a female. He tells her he worries about what others might think of him, what his friends and family might think, or that perhaps his employer might react negatively.

The counselor leans forward in her chair, uncrosses her legs, and then looks her client directly in the eye. She points her index finger toward the office entry door and sternly remarks, "How much longer are you going to let what goes on out there" -- she returns her pointed finger toward her client's chest -- "control what's going on inside your own heart? Build your dreams, or someone else will expect you to build theirs."

Did You Hear the One About?

A river separates two blondes. One yells across at the other, "Hey, how did you get to the other side"? The second blonde yells back, "Huh? You ninny! You are on the other side".

Pink Heart

Finding My True Self

The point is that life, as we know it depends on our PERCEPTIONS of where we are in it. For many, like that client of the counselor's and those two blondes, it is simply a matter of seeking to get to the "other side," yet not knowing exactly how to achieve that feat. The truth in this world depends on our perspective of not only knowing where we are but also <u>who we are</u> and <u>what we are.</u>

Some things most humans just take for granted. A black person knows they are black. An Indian ordinarily knows he's an Indian. Sounds a bit obvious, doesn't it?

In most cases, the physical, cultural, and mental properties that exist within each of us are indeed apparent. It is interesting, however, to note that not all human beings are a hundred percent definitive about the gender to which they believe they belong. Many of you that read the above paragraph about the two blondes probably took for granted that I was referring to two blonde women -- when in fact I did not mention their gender. Most of you probably just presumed the joke was about two blond females. Aren't some men also blonde?

That is how <u>perception</u> and <u>perspective</u> can influence and direct our lives. Most of you reading this also take for granted the sex that you were born with. The genital anatomy that declared you male or female <u>was</u> and <u>is</u> that <u>gender and sex</u> that you believe you were meant to be. It is simple and self-evident. Thus, most people never question the sex or gender to which nature selected for them.

I would wager that few of you have ever encountered any doubt as to what is your sex or gender. From early childhood, you just knew and accepted that if you have a penis, you are a boy, or if you have a vagina, you are a girl – period -- even before you've had one! Pun intended.

Chances are, that on the day you were born, other than being given the gift of life, two other important functions occurred. They are:

1) You were assigned a <u>NAME</u>   2) You were assigned a <u>SEX</u>

In both cases, which assignment you were given was determined by visual examination of your genitals for evidence into which sex you would be categorized. Your father, the sire, and your mother the procreator, along with all your ancestors passed on their genes to you via the genetic imprint of what you became, both physically and mentally. Keep in mind the differences between what is SEX and what is GENDER.

Sex is the biological aspect of being either male or female. Gender is the SOCIAL and CULTURAL characteristics associated with biological sex. Therefore, besides the two above assignments made, whether your parents realized it or not -- they also assigned your gender at the time of your birth. It happens almost instantly. In the nursery, a little boy is wrapped in a blue blanket and a little girl is cuddled into a pink one. From those early beginnings, our gender role is that which tells us how we're to act ... as either a MALE or FEMALE.

<u>Nature</u> does not always follow rigid genetic codes. Nature proves far too often to adhere to something more akin to being <u>guidelines</u> rather than <u>ironclad</u> certainties.

What happens if you do have feelings of doubt about your gender or there is something inside you that makes that perspective and perception seem awry and <u>out of synch</u>? What if you grew up with sexual confusion and mental ambiguity as to which sex and gender you should be despite the genital evidence that declares you one sex or the other? What would you do then?

I referred to the fact earlier about a trans-woman not being able to accept his / her gender fate or leave their future to what has ascribed them at birth. As trans-women, <u>do we all control our gender destiny,</u> or is it some unchangeable biological definition that is set by nature and is unalterable? No, it is not.

As trans-women, should we follow our heart and soul to where it leads us, or must we instead be steered by biology, society, and tradition to travel roads where our anatomy and others would have us to go? No, we do not.

Must those who endure gender uncertainty live according to the gender expectations and perceptions that social culture and their outward biological body decrees? No, we do not!

Must those, who for some inexplicable reason <u>question their gender</u> live in a world where they are always seeking to get to the other side, but are never quite able to arrive there? We encounter so many questions. Who then has all the answers? Do you? Do I?

The answer to that is that probably nobody does, which is why this is such a frustrating condition. The indications of why it exists and how to define it aren't always obvious or easily attainable to the counseling gender specialist, psychologist, or psychiatrist.

Where does one go to find answers to such hard-hitting questions about such a basic human assumption … as to which sex and gender you are <u>or believe you are</u>?

Does the counselor know what's best for her client? Do you? What would happen if someone you knew told you that he or she felt uncomfortable with their gender? What if they said they wanted to explore the possibility of crossing that gender line, forging the gender waters, going over to the other side, and living out their lives in a gender role that is the opposite of their birth sex?

How would you react to such a revelation? Would it offend you or your basic, fundamental societal, and religious beliefs? What if that client of the counselor was your <u>husband, brother, father, son, a dear friend, or a co-worker?</u> Would you attempt to exhibit compassion, understanding, and sympathy toward this individual, or would you instead be confused, filled with anger, apathy or suspicion? Would you embrace this person and make an attempt at understanding, or would you shun them and ostracize them from your presence? How much diversity would you be willing to accept in your world?

Assuming

Assume for a moment that you are my counselor's client. What if it were you that had been withholding your true feelings all these many years from your loved ones, friends, relatives, or employers? What if it were YOU that kept this secret sheltered deep within you and lived in silent agony, resented your own body, and rejected your own sexual and gender identity?

All the while you felt yourself to be a falsehood and living a pseudo existence. Out of fear of humiliation, ridicule, and even harassment, up until now, you have told no one. Rather, you chose to abstain, as best you could from divulging this thing inside you that haunted you for as long as you can remember. Now, for some reason, you look across life's abyss at the other side and yearn to go there. Even you aren't entirely sure why that is. This challenge to seek a pathway to the other side seems to present before you a great canyon, a crevasse with a seemingly impossible expanse. How can you ever make it across? By what means can you ever hope to reach your aspiring destination?

What is it that compels you and draws you to attempt to leap over that mighty river and divide that separates you from your goal and dream? What are those things that drive you to seek the truth about yourself and to leave behind those you love, the deceptions, and all those other fears that have prevented you from seeking to do what is in your own heart? What is it that forces you onward, toward total self-annihilation of that person you were born with, yet incessantly beckons to you from the other side to seek the new self that you hope and pray to become?

The only way for me to answer all those questions is to present you with my perspective and opinions. Therefore, be patient as I delve into the depths of my feminine psyche to explain what it was like being physically born a male, yet all the while feeling myself to be female.

Why would I, at near the end of middle age, sacrifice that life and all that I'd achieved to opt for the chance to stand upon the opposite shores of truth? To do this meant attempting to become as much a female as is scientifically and medically possible. Still, think I'm rational and sane? "Maybe not, Clarice, but quid pro." You let me tell you why, and then I'll share a nice Chianti and some Fava beans with you."

Pink Heart

It has been at times a bizarre, yet often life-affirming, invigorating odyssey. It is a journey that has been fraught with much pain and sacrifice, but one also laden with joy and relief. Like that young man in the counselor's office and so many others who have traveled this path, I have had to face my own worst fears and deal with self-doubts. In the passage, I have been deprived of friends, employment, and much respect. As a result, I am separated from most of the loved ones that were once so dear and close to me. Still, having lived all those years in the dark, the promise of the illumination by the light of femininity spurred me onward.

I would declare that mine is a compelling story, but one not unlike the thousands of others of my transgender sisters or brothers that have crossed the same valleys or forged the same rivers to arrive upon the other side of their own true and sacred shore. What perhaps is different is my spin on the condition, my narrative interpretations, and my perspective that will allow you, the reader to form your perceptions about trans-people from what I reveal herein. I seek to relate to crossing over to a place that I formerly had only dreamed about and one that few other humans ever seek to go ... into the inner sanctum of the human mind, heart, and soul of someone transgender.

Step inside the pages of my <u>Pink Heart</u>. Walk around in my skin and shoes. You might not be all that comfortable in them, but after you read this book, you will at least have had the opportunity to become a bit more aware of what it's like for other trans-women and me.

Chapter 5:
A Hometown Visit

About five years ago, I was on vacation and had to make a return trip to my hometown of Waco Texas to conduct some business. I hadn't been through some of the old neighborhoods in over ten years. On that bright, sunny January day I made my way down north 18th street, onto Trice Avenue, passing by the small wooden house I grew up in. I then drove towards Lake Waco and veered off toward Cameron Park. In passing down streets that were once very recognizable and businesses that as a kid I used to frequent, I noticed the following:

1. What was once the Children's Hospital was now a boarded-up vacant building with a chain-link fence was around it. The Providence Hospital that was once next door to it was no longer there.
2. Where my old West Junior High building had been there was now only a vacant lot. Even my high school building was closed up and had been consolidated to God only knows where.
3. What used to be George's drive-in (by today's vernacular, a convenience store) was hardly recognizable and it was now a beer joint. George's store was a place I used to visit once a day. I'd collect and redeem soda pop bottles and the elderly and dear Mr. and Mrs. George would pay me two cents per bottle for my efforts. A candy bar was a nickel in those days and a coke came in an eight-ounce bottle.
4. The Jones Café where I'd visit every morning after I threw my paper route was now some sort of janitorial supply house. Dear Mr. & Mrs. Jones used to serve me up a piece of their famous chocolate pie for a quarter and a nickel for a Coca Cola.
5. Brickman's Salvage & Wholesale that used to sell discount furniture and appliances was boarded up and looked to be a lifeless old shell.
6. Where once stood a corner Rexall Drug Store had now been converted into a Goodwill store.

7. The Cameron Park playgrounds in which I used to run, laugh and play ... a place with the old hillside slides, the crisp, crystal clear, natural springs that poured from a fountain to pool after pool ... all were extinct or virtually unrecognizable.

8.
The Point Being: Things Change

The indications being that what I wrote in the preface rings true; THINGS CHANGE. Time does indeed change everything, including buildings, businesses, parks, hospitals ... and PEOPLE. Except for the Lord Almighty, nothing in this world or life remains static. No matter how much we wax nostalgic about our past, it has to be bid farewell and things move on as well a life -- to the next stage and the next level. The old things give in to cultural progress and new technologies. Older generations must step aside and yield to those who will live on after them. Their memories, legacies, and heritage can be passed on, but they are relegated to our history books and the past. The bygone era we so loved about our youth and days of innocence is thereby filed away into the minds and memories of those who experienced them. The life we confront in the now of today must conform to the society, the time, and the space we occupy in present ... the one each of us lives in with every breath we take and each beat of our heart.

Time can bring about startling changes to people. Some get an education; receive degrees, pedigrees, and some who we once thought were smart turn out to be those that do some of the dumbest things. Some grow taller in time, and then still others in time seem to shrink, shrivel, or stoop. Everyone we know has gotten older, some go bald, and others grow beards, let their hair go long and wild, or else now wear it shorter. Some have hair that turned gray; others now dye their hair darker, or even bleach it and go blond. Some who were well are now sick and some that always seemed ill are now well. Some who were skinny are now fat and some that were overweight are now fit and trim. Some who were single are now married and some that were married are now divorced and single again. Some who we thought were straight are now gay or lesbian, and then some we figured for being gay or lesbian are married and have four kids. Some who were poor are now wealthy and successful and some that were wealthy have lost it all and are now poor.

The position is that few, if any of us, remain the same throughout our lives, either physically, socially, economically, or otherwise. Many factors, such as fate, our genetics, and other issues within us somehow influence us to change. For certain, I would categorize the changes made in my life be extreme, but from my perspective, I evolved into what and who I am because in time I came to realize that for me life is a much better fit as a female.

Perceived to be Believed

Remember what I wrote about perception? Having been in sales since I was nineteen years old, I have learned one thing about people and the world. What we perceive, we tend to believe. In other words, to most people perception -- is reality. What people perceive, then that to them is the truth.

How someone perceives another person is to that someone the reality of what the other person is. In my life, before my living as a woman, I was perceived to have been a male, a friend, a husband, a father, a brother, and a son. For the better part of half a century, I did nothing to dispel that perception or detract from it. Yet, these perceptions were ones belonging to others, and ones that they had of me, not those that I had of myself.

In a way, the image and identity that I presented to the world were like an illusion -- a slick sleight-of-hand magic trick for they saw what I allowed them to see. They believed what they saw, which to them was their reality. Confusing? I suppose, but there is but one truth, despite this slight of words and misperceptions.

Smoke and mirrors? The true reality is that I was not at all what I appeared to be to others. I was never completely a male, but rather more of a non-male. I was never quite the husband, father, brother, son, or friend that others perceived me to be. What was I then? Was I female? Not quite yet, but I was not entirely male either. So where did I fit in the spectrum of gender and sexual identity? My biological and anatomical sex was undeniably male, but to me, what was between my legs was not the true determining factor for my gender identity. Besides, what I have under my skirt should be of no concern to anyone but me or an intimate partner.

I was compelled at a young age with the desire to be a girl. To this day, I have no definitive proof of why I felt that way, I just did! In future paragraphs, I shall give you all my theories as to why I believe I am, and perhaps many others, are this way. As odd as it may sound, I have known since I was three years of age that I was meant to be a girl. Why then did I wait and in middle-age feel so compelled to finally do something about my obsession and the innermost dreams and desires that haunted my every waking hour? I had endured that long in life, why not just ride out the storm and let this obsession remain hidden from others? I'll try to explain that later on in this narrative.

Defining what gender I am is simple, but defining other parameters about myself is not such an easy task. Most clinicians would easily confirm that I am a Secondary type trans-woman (having lived my childhood and mid-adult years with male privilege as a guy).

In all my years of dealing with those that are transgender, I have never known someone that can be described as a Primary transgender. By that, I mean someone that has never created a male personality. Although they exist, such people are rare, for this is a person who from their earliest childhood moments has never accepted their male genitalia or their gender role. Their every trait is feminine and they make the subjective choice from the outset to assume the role of a female. That's not an easy thing to do when one is a child or pre-adolescent. Despite the physical evidence presented by their natal sex, they are always effeminate and thus consider themselves to be female. Although this is rare, by the Internet (You-tube) and information gathered from network television shows on the subject, some pre-adolescent children have been open about feeling like they were born into the wrong body and gender.

This results in a person that grows up wanting to or does wear femme clothing and dresses, whereby some parents wanting the best for their child, learn about the condition and through counseling to the child and educating themselves, some parents agree to raise the child as a female. For the child, this is akin to coming out of the egg kicking a screaming to be given the right to live as the girl they believe themselves to be.

They receive puberty blockers that not only delay puberty but steer it in the direction of them developing the secondary-sex characteristics of a female when puberty does occur. In such cases, the effects of progesterone and estrogens upon their pre-pubescent body are startling. Most develop into lovely young women, just as they'd hoped and planned.

That stated, let me now imply that <u>every</u> trans-person that I've ever known feels <u>the same way</u> as those above. The only difference I've noticed between a Primary and Secondary trans-person is usually circumstance, environment, and the passage of time. The depth of the obsession is usually the same, only their social situations and commitment are different.

All of us that are transgender have those early gender indicators in our lives that we should not be boys, but for reasons not always under our control, we do not act upon our feminine impulses. Consequently, we wind up forming our artificial male personalities and creating a life that from the outset feels wrong. I envy any primary trans-child, for they are the far more fortunate ones in this journey. The social and personal entanglements for them are much less than those of us that try to carve out lives based upon falsehoods and our parent's outlook for our future.

A Work in Progress

Despite my physical changes after all these years, I shall forever see myself as a work in progress. That's more mental now than physical, for I've taken the physical as far as possible. Expressing my femme self, exploring and presenting to my friends, family, and the public my feminine identity provides me my biggest joys in life. I consider my femme self to be a work of art whereby the artist lopped off something other than an ear. All I can say is, "Viva la estrogen and vaginoplasty."

Having been twice married, each time to a genetic female, I shall discuss some of the pitfalls of such unions when one spouse is transgender. I reveal some of the external stresses I received from having lived as a male and from having had spousal and familial responsibilities. I'll explain what it's like coping with the incongruity over my biological sex and gender. I'll discuss the timing and motivations that finally lead me to my decision to act upon the option of transition to become a female.

Casting aside male clothing, the MTF trans-woman sheds the male identity like a snake sheds its old skin. Likewise, I assumed the full-time feminine role of my gender of choice and now live my life as a woman.

As with any true trans-woman, the <u>transition process</u> includes several procedures that I will address more in detail as this story develops. Those others and I in this select group of individuals have found that Gender Reassignment Surgery (**GRS**) proves to be a very satisfactory final solution to solving the genital unconformity and mental distress related to having been born into the wrong sex and gender. Surgical modification is both restorative and healing. It is the goal of almost every true trans-person, but it is evident that it is <u>not the sole means</u> of transition into the gender role or identity of a female. Although most receiving this type of surgical transformation do have positive post-operative lives, some do not experience the hoped-for results. I will touch upon some of these perceived factors, as I see them, later on in this book.

To display my sense of humor, I inserted numerous "**true, but funny**" vignettes of my life. I call these breaks from the serious, moments…**Huh?** Here's one below:

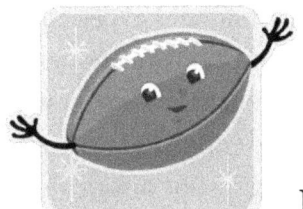

Huh # 1: Jose, Can You See?

Do you know the way to San Jose? In November of 1980, my adopted dad and I attended a Baylor football game. It was a day game and unseasonably hot for that time of year. Baylor was on a roll that year and had won nine straight games. The Baylor coach rested his starters for most of the game, but after the first half Baylor trailed by a couple of touchdowns. Later, they went on to lose that game, the only blemish that year on their regular-season schedule.

At halftime, dad went down to the concession stands to stretch his legs and get us something to drink. While in line, he saw a man wearing a San Jose State baseball cap. He smiled, and asked the guy, "Y'all are playing a great game. Where is this San Josey State? (Heavily emphasizing the **Joe-Zee**)

The man, sweating profusely smiled back, got his coke, turned to my dad, and replied, "it's pronounced San Ho-Zay State, and we're from San Jose." My dad looked confused. The man clarified his statement, "You see, it's a Spanish name, so for that reason in California we pronounce J's … like an H.

Dad just shrugged, got his two cokes, and then turned to leave. The man, still sweating asked him, "Is it always so hot this time of year?" My dad grinned, and replied, "This is mild, but it gets hot here in Hune and Huly." It seems that my dad was a **cunning linguist**.

Chapter 6:
Frankly My Dear ... I Am What I Am!

In a classic book, it claimed, "It was the best of times; it was the worst of times." As a child growing up in Texas, like other children I experienced many joyous, rapturous times and have hundreds of precious memories of both my birth parents and adopted parents. I relish the moments spent with my siblings and playmates. Irrespective of that, my childhood was also traumatic and confusing. Often, I found myself feeling lost or disoriented.

Why was that? What caused the conflict between living a total utopian existence versus one laden with psychological disturbance, great unhappiness, as well as intense self-doubt? It came about from several circumstances, with the most overriding reasons springing forth from two questions:

1. "<u>Why did my birth parents give me away</u>?
2. "<u>Why was I a boy when I felt I should've been a girl</u>?"

Although many speculate and debate on what causes the dissonance of gender identity within a young child, I can only relate to you that it is not a pleasant thing to endure ... at any age. My problem was exacerbated by several developments after birth, not the least of which was that my birth father decided to offer me to be raised by another married couple with no children of their own. There was little doubt in my mind that my gender confusion at such an early stage in life and having the <u>longing</u> to become a girl stemmed both from this circumstance, as well as being born with the anomaly in my brain that I was a girl.

Despite no physical deformities or outward defects, regardless of my having possessed a penis rather than a vagina, I was certain nature made a terrible error with me. Yet, like all trans-children, how could I express my true nature and desires to the two adoptive parents who raised and loved me as if I were their child? The answer is, I couldn't...show or tell them. Nor at that time did I have anyone else that I could've spoken to about this dilemma. It's difficult for people to comprehend what they haven't experienced. Thus, as is the case with most trans-children, I kept my questions and the <u>longing</u> a secret and buried it deep within my heart and mind ... uncertain of what to do about it or what life might have in store for me.

* * *

When I was born in 1957, Dwight Eisenhower, the Army General who directed the U.S. troops in Europe during World War II and accepted the unconditional surrender of the German Army was now entrenched as the thirty-fourth President of these United States.

In my hometown of Waco, Texas, six years later, I was a child with carrot-colored hair, emerald eyes, and a rosy red nose already blistered from playing in the intense Texas sun. I was aglow with eager anticipation that comes from the beginning of education and the first-grade school year and the end of a summer full of exciting adventures.

My adopted parents were planning a vacation to Missouri that summer where even as a young child I'd get to witness a great major league baseball game with all-stars like Stan "The Man," Musial, and "Jolting Joe," DiMaggio play "Old Timers Day baseball. I don't recall any of it except what I saw in photos.

By age nine, my talent for the game was apparent even amongst playground and sandlot peers. That summer was to be my first experience in organized peewee baseball. It would be the inauguration of a lifelong love affair that I would have with sports and our country's beloved <u>National Pastime</u>. Besides the love of the game, I found it to be a distraction from other confounding problems that would arise throughout my young life.

That ninth summer, I was also to be introduced to some real treats that remained locked in my memory for all of the time. One such delight was a visit to downtown Waco and Mrs. Keaton's bakeshop, next to the lavish old Waco Movie Theatre. My birth mom had a Saturday off from nursing and arranged to take me to see her favorite movie, "<u>Gone With The Wind</u>." She'd first seen it when it came out in 1939, and now it was showing again in Waco. She wanted me to experience the classic tale of the Civil War and the Old South. I'm not sure why none of my other siblings were there, but whatever the reason that was to be a very special day. That majestic motion

Pink Heart

picture was also to be the first movie I'd seen in <u>glorious color</u>. Up until that time, all the cinemas I'd seen were in <u>black</u> and <u>white</u>, like those in a <u>Tarzan</u> jungle movie, or perhaps, in a shoot-em-up western.

What my pre-pubescent eyes would behold that fine day upon the silver screen would become emblazoned forever in my mind! With my mother beside me, in that dark theatre, I experienced my first conscious reaction to a situation that would haunt me the rest of my days. As this melodramatic movie about the Post-Civil War South unfolded before me, I recall having feelings that both delighted me and yet bewildered me as well.

Captain Rhet Butler, was to me the epitome of what a <u>man</u> should be. Up on there on that big screen, he was larger than life and so perfect for his part. He was tall, dark, handsome, and gallantly portrayed a southern gentleman, albeit one with a rough exterior. Rhet even appeared at times to be a scoundrel, yet he genuinely loved Scarlet and his child with all his heart. To me, he had many redeeming characteristics. Secretly, I wished my father adored me as much as Captain Butler did with his precious daughter, <u>Bonnie Blue,</u> but then, <u>she</u> was a girl and I -- <u>I … was not!</u> At least, I wasn't outwardly.

I came to like Clark Gable as an actor, then and always. He, John Wayne, James Stewart, and Kevin Kostner became my favorite male actors of all time. Besides their talent, I think the reason I found them each so fascinating was that they were everything I wasn't. I admired the strong, but sensitive macho images they each portrayed. I knew I'd never be like either them -- or for that matter any other macho male.

The female star of the movie was divine and perfectly cast in the role of, <u>Scarlet O'Hara</u>. The impact of her celestial image there upon that mammoth movie screen was to become a defining moment for me. I watched her magnificent performance in complete awe, even a reverence. Her silky raven-colored hair, those gorgeously seductive eyes, her somewhat innocent, yet cynical smile and irresistible laugh, her every movement with that diminutive female body drew me in and captivated me. I was consumed with a desire beyond definition, or of my comprehension.

I do not believe my desire for her was a carnal one. Then again -- maybe in an odd way it was. Like the giddy young southern beaus who surrounded her on-screen, I too swooned as Scarlet swished and swayed her way so gracefully at parties, dances, and social events in all manner of astonishingly frilly, feminine dresses. She was the consummate southern belle. To me, she was the loveliest cinematic creature I'd ever seen. I listened intently to her Dixie darling and pixie voice as she'd shout, "Fiddle-Dee-Dee," and throw her tantrums … as <u>Mammy</u> tried to lace her corseted waist back to eighteen inches.

    I witnessed the way men fawned over her and how she used the power of her youthful feminine wiles to beguile them into carrying out her will. She had few scruples, was conniving, and married men for profit that she didn't love. She coveted another woman's husband and then took Rhet for granted, the one man that loved her more than anyone. Still, like those giddy men in the story, I looked past all of those flaws in her because I was so enthralled and enchanted by her magnetism and beauty. I was entirely smitten, for Scarlet O'Hara also captivated me. My prepubescent response though, was not as one might imagine.

    The temptations and imaginings that Scarlet O'Hara created within me did not formulate the desire for me to <u>have her</u> in any sexual manner. Back then I was but a child and void of any real sexual urgings. No, instead I found the emotions that stirred within me were those of envy and even … resentment. I didn't want to <u>HAVE</u> Scarlet. I wanted to <u>BE</u> Scarlet. That I could not be like her that day caused me great sadness and bitterness. I had been born into the world as an unwanted **boy**.

    In that melodramatic darkness, I sat there within an arm's reach of the woman who bore me and brought me into this world. Yet, when we each left that theatre, I knew she would not take me home with her when the movie was over. Hers was a home where I was excluded and where my ill-tempered, indifferent father, two brothers, and my sister waited for her to love and embrace them. No, I was to go and be dropped off at my adopted parent's house, which was to be the loving home in which I was raised. Yet, \regret followed me all my days as a child and I never felt whole or completely loved, even though my adopted parents displayed and gave to me all the love any child could ever hope to have.

Pink Heart

Yes, I envied Scarlet, as I was certain in my heart that if <u>I</u> were as beautiful and feminine as **she**, then <u>no one on Earth would defy or deny me anything I wished</u>. And wish I did, for years and years after that. However, that was one wish that in my childhood and young adulthood did not come true … was delayed, but eventually, Shannon won out.

I felt that nature dealt me some poor cards and that it was an oversight by God that I had been born a boy. The uncomfortable feeling of not being a girl made me despondent. I reasoned that if I were a beautiful young girl, then I would not have been resigned to a life apart from the woman sitting next to me there in the dark, or from my two brothers and sister whom she had awaiting her at <u>their home</u>.

The feminine pattern and idea were even further reinforced and would forever alter the self-perception, I had of myself. That oddly exhilarating self-realization of the extraordinary notion that I desired to be FEMALE will possess and obsess me the remainder of my days. My life has been as much an emotional drama as it was for lovely Scarlet in "Gone With The Wind." For years, I wondered if anyone truly did "give a damn."

Chapter 7:
Gen-a-sis

In the book of Exodus, the Bible states that Moses was born the son of a daughter of Levi. The Pharaoh commanded that every son born be cast into the river. Fearing for her son's life, his mother placed the infant Moses in a basket made of bulrushes and then daubed it with pitch and tar. She laid the baby Moses in the basket and set it adrift amongst the reeds along the riverbank of the Nile. As the Bible records, Moses was found by the compassionate daughter of the Pharaoh of Egypt and was raised as her son.

I do not claim to be <u>SHE</u>, who shall deliver my Trans- people out of oppression and bondage, nor have I seen any burning bushes, but I will tell you that Moses and I do have one thing in common. I also became a child that was cast afloat, only to be plucked from the choppy waters of life's river. I too was raised by a woman that was not my birth mother; rather I was gathered in by a woman and her husband that were kind, compassionate, loving, and would offer me their all in an attempt to bring me up as if I was their child.

Unlike Moses, I knew very early in life my true ancestry and those that were my birth parents. Follow along as I now relate to you my <u>Exodus</u> and how I came to be led out from the enslaved subjugation of that male existence into which I was born.

The mental commandments given to me, though perhaps not divine as what Moses received, were indeed just as self-demanding and unrelenting as those to which **God** Almighty Himself wrote for Moses into those stone tablets there upon Mount Sinai. For you see, inside <u>I too was on fire</u>, yet unlike Moses' divinely celestial burning bush ... I <u>WAS</u> being consumed. All of me that was and shall always be Shannon became my <u>holy ground</u> to be sought from within. It was she that became embossed into my heart and carved deeply into the rock of my soul. As Moses asked, so too do I beseech you God with the question, "Who am I, Lord"? As God answered back to Moses, I would also say to those who herein read these words, "Tell them, I am -- who I am"! Thus, **God's** answer to Moses became -- **my own!**

Pink Heart

Into the Breach

I came kicking and screaming into this world around 8 a.m. on a December morn in a central Texas town that people would later come to sadly refer to as, "Branch Dravidian" territory. As I stated earlier, I was born and raised in Waco, Texas. Besides being the home of Baylor University, thanks to Chip and Joanna Gaines, Waco has become "Magnolia City, with tourists flocking there to see the HGTV Network's stars of "The Fixer Upper" television show. Thousands visit the old grain silo area that I used to see and smell from the ancient and no longer present, "Katy Ballpark" where the Waco Pirates played minor league ball.

On that fine morning in December, I became the fourth and final child of parents that did not need nor particularly wish for any more children.

My father's name was Mack. He was a descendant of Irish heritage and a carpenter by trade. When I was born and for as long as I knew him, he was bald and rugged looking. Still, he was a man who fancied himself to be attractive to most all women. No doubt he was to certain types of "morally bankrupt" women.

He wasn't an evil man but paid very little heed to his bird in the bush wife, my mother, or of the physical and spiritual needs of his family. No, he was not a bad person per se, but neither was he the type of loving man who doted on his family. According to most of my siblings, he was sexually impulsive and a skirt-chasing, lousy parent and probably an even lousier husband to my mother. Though he showed little remorse at that time, to his credit later in his life he would come to express many regrets for his earlier indiscretions, for his sins against God … and mostly those against his family. I believe that my father died with a humble heart sincerely repenting of his sins, possessing a sincere and earnest love and fear of God, and expressing his personal beliefs that Jesus was his Savior. I do not wish him any malice and I pray for his soul and eternal peace.

Oddly enough, he was a likable old rogue, already forty-seven when I was born. As I grew older, I found him to be an interesting man who realized the foolishness of infidelity and his mistakes far too late in his life. He did attempt to make amends with those in his family that he could, but some would accept no apologies and ostracized him from their world. I know what that feels like. To many of my relatives, that seems to have become a habit in our family.

He was a very talented carpenter and always worked diligently and hard for his money. His vices were women, profanity, gambling, booze, dominoes, and country dancing. He had little formal education, yet was schooled in the ways of life and even brilliant in many ways. In our adult conversations, he always had remarkable tales to tell and could spin a yarn about as well as anyone I've ever met. He seemed proud that even though I had a college degree, I still chose to follow in his trade and become a carpenter, builder, and contractor of homes. I found early on that my endurance for the heat and physical stress of doing carpenter work could not match his.

After I graduated from Baylor and became disillusioned by the politics of corporate structure, I became a general contractor and let my sub-contractors do all the demanding physical work. I was ingrained and trained from my studies at Baylor to work smarter, not harder. I should have combined more of the two attributes and maybe I'd been much more of a success. However, the fact that the President directing the Fed Chairman back then raised interest rates to over 20% that put me and about every custom builder during that period in the late '70s and early 80s out of business. After that, few, if any, of those who wanted new homes could afford to build and finance them.

One of the most amazing feats my father did was when I first started as a builder. I contracted him to frame my first new home. He did the entire carpenter framing work by himself; in mid-July and August, when in Texas it was over 100 degrees for about two months straight. Every morning he'd come to the job site, put on his nail apron, and get to work. He did a great job and the house is still standing today and looks as good as ever. He was seventy-four years young at the time, and his efforts would have worked ten men half his age under the table. Secretly, I had to wonder if he didn't go home every night during that period, soak his feet in ice, and then just collapse in pain. From wherever his stamina came, he never complained and I never forgot or appreciated his accomplishment.

Pink Heart

Something inside me, perhaps inherited from him, has always driven me to be creative, whether it's building, writing a poem, a song, novel, screenplay, or this memoir. For certain, I undoubtedly understood his fascination with building and fashioning housing structures, for that inclination and desire also became my own. To this day, even as a woman, I have the acumen for construction and building. For the past twenty-nine years, if I was not contracting new homes, then I was involved in the selling or manufacturing of some sort of building materials. Nicole tells me that I seem happiest when I have a "fixer up" project going on around our home. She's right, for I do love to remodel and do repairs around the house.
My birth mother was a five-foot-two-inch short, sweet, jolly, good-natured, good-hearted Christian woman of German heritage. So, you can see I'm from a German / Irish lineage. Perhaps that explains it! ;o) I shall never forget her joyously, infectious laugh and a distinctive German accent.

She showered <u>most</u> of her kids with affectionate love. Shy and without much self-esteem or confidence, she made every attempt to avoid a verbal or physical conflict with my birth father. From my perspective, I think she feared him as much as she loved him. She would simply fabricate any story she could to protect her children from him scolding, whipping, or beating them with an old razor strap that he kept to discipline his brood. She knew all too well that he cheated on her with other women, but yet she stayed with him because of her commitment to her children. In her mind, I believe, because she felt she had nowhere else to go.

She and my <u>sister</u> shared a very special mother-daughter bond that I came to envy and covet. She manifested my sister with affections that neither the other boys nor I received. Throughout my sister's adult life, my mother was never far away. Though I don't think she ever fully realized the extent of her favoritism, it was obvious to all the rest of us kids that my sister was very special to her. This exposed evident fact did not escape me … even as a young child.

Mother worked hard all her childhood on a farm in nearby Riesel, Texas, and then as a married adult, she toiled in a garment manufacturing facility in Waco for minimal, meager wages. A few years after my birth, she would become a vocational hospital nurse. A great irony to me was that this woman who was not there to change my diapers, would in her caregiving career come to change a multitude of bedpans and care for and nurse thousands of patients back to health in numerous hospitals in Waco and throughout California. Looking at my situation now through adult eyes, from my perspective this fact was indeed puzzling, but not her fault.

My opinion now is that she was a grand and noble woman and one I loved, admired and that I believe earned her angel's wings long ago.

My mother did not fare well after my birth. I came along at the end of a complicated pregnancy that culminated with me being a Cesarean-born child. During the difficult ordeal, she hemorrhaged, got sepsis and remained in the hospital for weeks after my birth. My Father worked and certainly he had neither the desire nor inclination for caring for a newborn infant. Besides, he had three other rug rats at home for which to care. Therefore, he consented to let a close lodge brother and friend keep me temporarily until my mother could get back on her feet. However, though I believe it was his original intent for this arrangement to be temporary, this childless couple that agreed to look after me would wind up doing so -- <u>permanently!</u>

Was that the plan all along, or was it simply something that just happened? The only people who knew the answer to that question never told me the accurate or complete story. Thus, for whatever reason, I became the adoptive child of **RED,** my Father's lodge brother, and his wife HATTIE. They lived only three miles from where my parents lived, a fact that would later prove incredibly frustrating and confusing to me.

If the story had ended there, and I'd not come to know who my birth parents were, or that I had three siblings, perhaps my life's story would be different today. Still, I <u>did</u> get to know them all, and for that reason, even at a very young age, I faced some very profound dilemmas. As a result, I suffered many self-esteem issues and questioned my self-worth in the world. My young innocent mind often pondered, "What's wrong with me? Why was I the one that was given away?"

This inner conflict and concern greatly contributed to a growing incongruent attitude toward my sense of self -- and especially that of my <u>gender identity</u>. At some point, I reasoned that if I'd been born a <u>girl</u>, then my parents, and especially my mother, would have wanted me, kept me, and I too would've become a favorite child of hers. It was a fool's folly, I know, but it is how I felt at that time.

Though in my heart I knew I was loved and adored by Hattie and Red, I felt slighted that my birth parents had cast me aside, as if I were some unfit offspring that didn't belong in their litter. I confined the anguish and disappointments, burying the grief I had deep inside me. I groped my way through early childhood and adolescence seeking answers to questions that <u>no child</u> should ever have to ask.

My adoptive parents were like my guardian angels. No youngster could have ever asked for more dedicated or loving parents. I cannot embellish them with enough tributes or admiration. Hattie was a very wonderful and unique woman. She was very likable, but when some problem concerned me, she could be tenacious and like a pit bull or a protective lioness. Anyone who made trouble for me incurred her wrath and though I'd have preferred she didn't, she fought many battles for me.

She went to her grave unaware of the secret I kept hidden from both her and Red. If either had known I was transgender, I feel certain they would have sorrowed over that, perhaps blaming themselves, but they'd likely have adjusted to the idea and become a staunch proponent to me -- as Shannon. That's how much they loved me.

Still, because I too loved them -- so much, I could never find the courage within my heart to make them, or my biological parents suffer through such a revelation. As a result of that inability to reveal my true desires, I resisted the yearning to become Shannon and let the years of my adolescence and young adulthood slip away. In retrospect, if I had it to do over, I do believe I would have spoken up sooner, preferably before my first puberty. My goodness, but life would have certainly been interesting had I done that.

I mentioned earlier about those who are Primary Trans-persons. It's interesting to note, that if an MTF trans-woman were to begin a female hormonal regimen before the onset of puberty, that individual would likely exhibit little to no male physical <u>secondary-sex characteristics</u>. The estrogens would feminize the pre-pubescent male's body in a way that would mimic that of a female in every way other than establishing menses or the presence of a vagina.

The male testicles would be chemically castrated and would not develop, the voice would remain high-pitched, estrogens would close off the ends of bone growth, so the person would not be as tall, male beard growth would not occur, and body hair would develop in a feminine pattern. The estrogens would initiate breast growth, put weight on the hips and buttocks, soften the skin and keep the hair soft and shiny.

In short, the body would be re-programmed to develop feminine secondary sex characteristics, not male. Most of the prettier trans-sisters I've known began their journeys early on in life to take advantage of their youth. I wish that I had been so brave and fortunate.

Hattie was obsessive toward insulating me from many of the ugly things in the world and once even went head-to-head with a school bully twice her size to help protect me from his teasing and cruel pranks. Neither she nor Red was oblivious to the pains of rejection and confusion they witnessed pouring forth from my sad eyes. They saw in me the hunger that I had for the affections of my birth mother and father ... and for that of my siblings.

Though I loved Hattie with all my heart, I don't think she ever felt completely at ease the entire time I was growing up. In the back of her mind, there seemed to always be this sense that she was an imitation mom and that my real mother and father were going to come to snatch me back someday... and that she'd lose me forever. So far as I know, neither of my birth parents ever gave Hattie any real reason for concern in that regard. Still, I know she thought of it often, for we discussed it more than once. I would always assure her that although I was curious about what my life would've been like within my birth family, I would never leave her or Red. Thus, Red and I became her sole focus in life and she doted on both of us like the mother hen she became.

Let me state equivocally that God never breathed life into a gentler, loving soul than that of my dear, sweet mom, <u>Hattie</u>!

During my early years, Hattie worked hard at being a mom, a housewife, and selling shoes in a local department store. While she worked, she had a kindly old Negro woman that I very much came to love, keep me during the day. My young heart had no bias even back then, and even as a child, I came to recognize discrimination and injustices. I grew to have a great deal of

Pink Heart

respect and admiration for the oppression and plight of <u>colored folk</u>, especially there in Waco, that southern city and Mecca of Texas and Americana.

Back then, Black Americans were forced to drink from separate water fountains, ride at the back of a public bus, and educate their children in segregated schools for black-only students. They were compelled to work for wages far below that of privileged white folks, and most lived in poverty in a segregated poor area of town. Though I was a lower-class <u>white boy</u>, I never came close to having to face the prejudices that came to those whose skin color and race were different than my own. Even the Asians and Hispanics of that day suffered the indignities of discrimination. I took no particular pride in being born into the white Anglo world; it was simply my fate, just as it was my being born with <u>male genitals</u>!

Though my adopted parents earned a meager living, I never knew or felt deprived of anything. All my basic needs were met and I was mostly a contented child. From all outer appearances, I must have seemed to be <u>ordinary</u>; at least that's the semblance of what I bestowed to others. However, my psyche was like an iceberg, and more than three-fourths of my true nature was there below the surface. Deep inside me were hidden a myriad of emotions and anxieties of which even those closest to me were not aware. The secrets I longed for were buried deep below my epidermal exterior and remained concealed behind my eyes. Even those who thought they knew me best, including my spouses, kids, closest friends, or family members, in reality … <u>they did not</u>!

Red was a very decent, humble, and honest man who worked as a meter reader and in collections for the local Texas Power & Light Company. He and I became very close and he was the one man on whom I knew I could always depend. He had little formal education, but like my birth father, he too was very shrewd and schooled in the ways of life. I often sought his sage advice and he always taught me to <u>do the right thing</u> when dealing with people in life or business. Always doing the right things in both my personal and professional life later became a challenge that I found to be difficult and almost unattainable. Red's simple lifestyle was predicated on an 8 a.m. to 5 p.m. job that he worked loyally and diligently at for 36 years. His home had an ideal 50's type atmosphere, with only the essentials in simplistic furniture and appliances. Extravagance and luxury were words that didn't exist in his vocabulary or budget.

Growing up, I never knew what it was like to have a window air conditioner much less central heat and air. Even our automobiles were devoid of any luxuries, as Red stated, "They were hard on the battery, engine, and fuel efficiency." Yes, he was a frugal man, but not stingy in any way. Societal arts and culture to him seemed something for rich folks, so we were truly simple folk with few wants or needs. A major regret was that neither Hattie nor Red thought it necessary for me to learn music or to play an instrument. Thus, as a novice songwriter today, I am musically illiterate. I can speak the language; I just can't write it. Therefore, my musical creations are the combined result of my lyrical talents, plus my abilities to get my ideas and melodies across to more talented demo musicians who formalize my songs into an instrumental and a vocal rendition of what I create.

Red's family was close-knit and numerous (ten siblings). He and Hattie together had over thirteen siblings, so as a result, I had dozens of adopted cousins and so many aunts and uncles that every weekend it seemed we were off visiting another of the clan. My home with him and Hattie was somewhat like living with a combination of Ozzie and Harriet.

Hattie, who worked in retail and was required to dress appropriately, had a complete wardrobe of wonderfully feminine dresses, numerous pairs of high heels, and some very frilly outfits ... that my pre-pubescent body would later find to be a delight to wear ... while in a guarded covert mode. Red and Hattie were wonderful people with whom to share my childhood and growth years. I was so blessed to have them as my caregivers.

The two of them were very much in love. They attempted to see to my every need, took me to church, and started my feet on the proper path to righteousness. As I looked up from my cradle, it was their faces I saw; their arms that embraced me, they that clothed me, fed me, gave me a home ... and made me feel **loved**. From my point of view, Hattie and Red were wonderful parents, and I ... was ... their only **son!**

Chapter 8:
Becoming One Voice

 Living as a male restrained my psyche, causing me a distorted gaze upon a disorientated world … one in which fear made me afraid and silenced my voice. After I became absent from maleness, I developed a clearer vision with which to look at the world into that which I was born.

 I know that the torrid experiences of a trans-woman are foreign to most Americans to whom education concerning those that are transgender is nearly non-existent. Those people accept the gender of their birth and take for granted the freedom of their heritage. The <u>quest for justice and truth</u> should touch the hearts of every trans person all over our world today. I feel that the caring, involved transgender community of America has a moral obligation to remind the nation of their plight; their right to a pursuit of happiness, and to make right the injustices dealt them by discriminatory laws. When the world hears the voice of a repressed trans-person in America, remember that <u>it is but one</u> voice, yet it cries out as if a chorus of truth for <u>liberty</u> and understanding everywhere!

Male ___ Female ___ Other ___

 The world then has indeed changed and life itself is filled more each day with a vast array of C O L O R! There is a correlation between descriptions of color and how those hues and contrasts might be applied to those of us whose lives are so colorfully influenced and decorated by being transgender. Oh Great! Let me expound on that before your mind conjures up images of Ru Paul or some ditsy blond transsexual you saw on the Jerry Springer show. My point in all this is the world and gender, as well as all in it or around it, can no longer be conceived in mere black and white. That same reasoning applies to the binary idea of linking everyone into but two genders. The advances in science, engineering, computer electronics, medicine, and construction bear evidence that there exist many more ways of doing and improving things of material matter or biological origin than having but two choices to do so.

Thinking outside the box is a modern contemporary way of describing integrated, progressive thinking and acceptance of things outside the norm, or in the usual way of accomplishing something.

The same can be said of having to make choices concerning humankind itself. As stated, we still live in a binary society that most often believes all humans are either male or female. Yet, many people have realized that in today's world we cannot simply slide every human being neatly into one category or the other. The choices today are more imprecise than ever, and if nothing else ... they are certainly more colorful.

For certain, the choices are no longer as simple as many would like them to be. There still are those who would declare that God made but two sexes, male and female. The so-called normal folks often try to embrace and clench onto those two principles and ignore those who are different than them. They might even try to shake those differences into compliance and relinquishment of their compulsions to be different. Most cannot seem to fathom that we transgender folks desire not their guidance nor their attempts to save us from discovering our true self. Their crabbing and grabbing at us is as ineffective as trying to take hold of water with a bare hand.

Allow me to interject one point of view that came out after Nicole and I attended a support group meeting in Ft. Worth. In that meeting, our facilitator let us all view a Kate Bornstein video. The topic of the video concerned Kate's view of gender and the conclusion she came to as to her choice of gender and how she feels about her transgender situation. She stated that, after much deliberation, she found she didn't fit totally into the gender choice of being male or female but instead fit into another box, she would check as being -- Other. Whoa! Talk about ruffling an old girl's feathers! Mine were molting and standing on edge.

Afterward, we were all asked to comment on this matter and how we each felt about the video and its implications. Upon further review, although I suppose I can understand Kate's personal opinions and personal feelings, I do not agree with them as they apply to my own. Although the world is no longer black and white and how some folk perceives what their gender might be. Still, I believe that if one is a true MTF trans-woman, neither do they wish to be known as an Other. Like me, they do not aspire to be an

<u>MTO</u>. There is no way a male wishing to become female wants to become such a thing as a <u>Male to Other</u>. This is especially true of the MTF that is post-op, and someone living 24 / 7 as a woman.

I Don't Feel or Look Like "Ann-Other"

    The MTF trans-woman simply sees herself as a female … period, even if she's never had one. She's just another woman. She attempts to live, work, and socially interact as a woman and most would likely be disappointed and possibly offended if someone didn't consider her to be that. If a genetic cis-woman knows or comes into contact with a true trans-woman and <u>doesn't accept the trans-woman as a female</u> and someone of the same sex as she, then that genetic female is for sure going to frustrate and offend the trans-woman by her non-acceptance. The defenses will go up and arguably the trans-woman will anger and support herself as being as feminine as the cis-woman.

    It has been my experience that at times, some genetic females might act indifferent and snobbish to the MTF trans-woman. However, most I find are accepting. Of course, there are exceptions to everything, so some might see a trans-woman as being unworthy of checking the box marked FEMALE.

    That then would be exhibiting an air of sexual arrogance and is a hurtful bigoted bias directed toward the trans-woman. The more passable the MTF trans-woman is the more likely she is of being accepted as a true female. Painting the trans-woman black or white is sometimes difficult to do, even if the MTF trans-woman passes well and would prefer to be accepted only as a female.

That being stated, what of those trans-women who are already **out** at work and are open to others about being transgender? Are there those that consider themselves to be an-other? There is, for I know some trans-women who simply don't care what anyone else thinks. Some transgender sisters may not aspire to alter their genitals and may be satisfied with their status as others. Some that are post-op even have this attitude, which I find puzzling. However, if it works for them -- so let it be. The bottom line is that the ultimate category or label of choice should be the solitary selection of the trans-woman and should not one bestowed upon them by those with whom they come into contact. Nevertheless, such a scenario usually only exists in a perfect world.

Quite often, when a binary-minded person comes into contact with a true trans-woman that has been through their transition, that person is not likely to even be aware that the **female** before them is different or wasn't born into the sex and gender that person is portraying. As I stated, if the male to female trans-woman is truly maintaining and presenting herself in a passing mode, then whomever she comes into contact with will likely fit her into the category from which she appears to belong -- that of a female.

Though the choices are more than black and white, this does not, in reality, mean that one shall be given more than the two choices if one seeks to become genuine and live without conflict, ridicule, humiliation, or suspicion. The less conspicuous and more easily an MTF trans-woman can blend, the better off that person will be at interacting within society. As stated earlier in this text, I do think today's civilization is more sophisticated and tolerant than when I was a youth, but the sad fact is the world in general still judges a book is by its cover. Society has got a long way to go before it completely accepts the existence and rights of those that are transgender, gays, lesbians, or those with some other form of psychological or gender variance.

Pink Heart

New Puritans and Femancipation

When many of our founding forefathers and relatives were persecuted by injustice in Europe, they sought to make a new life for themselves in this new land. They were called <u>Pilgrims</u> and <u>Puritans</u>. As we all know, in Salem Massachusetts, Puritanical zealots accused several women of being witches and being possessed by Satan.

In the name of God, those pious clergymen tried and condemned many of the town's women of witchcraft. Mercilessly, they convicted these women to be hung, drowned, or burned at the stake. The irony of that situation is that most of those pious folks took flight from their own old countries and came to a new land because they sought relief from the oppressions and indignities that they received from domineering monarch lead governments.

Although slavery was not new to America, the advent of its prevalence came into focus in the Old South during the 1800s when plantation owners sought, by use of slavery, to maintain
their farms and estates. As a result of this, black natives from the far away continent of Africa were stalked, trapped, and brought back in chains to the south by <u>slave-runners</u> to fill the quotas of plantation overseers who ran the farming operations for the owners.

Those <u>Blacks</u> were degraded to the point of being no more than mere chattels, like draft horses for their masters who became the flesh dealers and purveyors of racial crimes, some comparable to that of the Nazi Holocaust. Though some would eventually earn privileges, they could never aspire to anything other than being owned and told what to do.

Thus, in this <u>one nation…under God</u>, supposedly conceived in <u>liberty and justice for all</u>, these black humans, these slaves … were denied that. In the Old South, a government claiming states' rights and the legitimacy to "own" slaves seceded and broke away from the Union. This action instigated the most horrific war this nation has ever endured.

Most assuredly, this moral outrage was as dark a period in human history as mankind has ever faced. What those affluent land and slave owners did induce toxins into the race relations in this country for as long as the United States shall exist. Those stolen souls directly affected by the sting of slavery have long since passed from this Earth; however, their descendants bear the mental and social scars of those who were denied their freedom.

Our nation's history is riddled with racial cruelty and injustices. Consider those Japanese Americans during World War II who were forced from their homes, had to give up their possessions under suspicion, and were assigned to internment camps for the duration of the war. Consider the Chinese who labored and died building the transcontinental railroads connecting the east and west coasts of the U.S. Even today U.S. businessmen use illegal Hispanic immigrants to farm the fields or man their factories, all in the name of commerce, at wages far below the poverty levels of most American citizens.

It begs us all to ask, where does one look today in America to find it's tired, it's poor, and its huddled masses yearning to be set free? Are there not enough broken, dysfunctional families, economic inequities, and lingering racial unrest in our country that we Americans can simply stick our heads in the sand and pretend all our problems are solved? Despite what our political leaders would declare, we are a diverse and, in many ways, a disunited populace. The tumultuous Afghan and Iraq war is evidence of that fact, as are the numerous opinions on what we need to do to solve the health care crisis, Covid 19, the burgeoning budget deficit, poverty, inflation, homelessness, or even defining marriage.

Like those slaves and other oppressed people, we trans-women of today are similarly denied many of our rights and freedoms. <u>Transgender</u> folks in many ways are social <u>outcasts</u> similar to the <u>colored folks</u> of a bygone era. Like the blacks were back in the Old South, as I've noted, we are a very slim minority of the populace. Our window in time is now opening, but it won't remain that way forever. Thereby, I contend that trans-women must become more involved with their destinies or remain satisfied that we too will always be confined and <u>driven</u> by someone other than ourselves.

Some religious denominations and legislators formulate new ideas or laws that define and characterize their description and means of deeming what our true gender and sex are ... to then enslave us with opinion and

Pink Heart

legalities that become <u>our chains</u> of injustice and misunderstanding. What sort of justice is it that declares we must bear the indignity that empowers religious denominations or judges and courts to declare that we trans-women are nothing more than effeminate, mutilated, and <u>castrated males</u>?

As trans-women must we continuously guard or defend ourselves against such ignorance, discrimination, bias, inequities, and injustice that is reigned down upon us? Why suddenly are so many others afraid we'll disrupt their social order, or bring down religious or family values? Must we trans-women choose to remain silent ... to go quietly about our lives and remain <u>seated at the back of the bus;</u> letting others compel and take us to where <u>they want us to go</u>? Or, should we become like those proud, defiant Black brothers and sisters, those Native American Indian Warriors, those persecuted Jews during World War II, those Japanese Americans made prisoners in their own land, those American Women who were subjugated, abused, and denied equality? I declare that we trans-women can become the <u>New Pilgrims</u> of today's America. I would declare that if we choose <u>to do nothing</u> ... <u>then nothing</u> is exactly what will be done.

It is very important to let the others among the general public, the leaders and lawmakers of our country know <u>what we stand for</u>, but it's equally as important to make known to them that we <u>won't stand for</u>. Is the Post-Civil War equivalent of <u>transgender reparation</u> to offer us up "40 acres and a mule," or comparatively speaking to <u>let us exist</u>, but only on their terms, by their definition, and their ground rules? However, what happens if we as a group of human U.S. citizens, <u>who just happen to be transgender</u>, take a stand and battle for our freedoms? Might we not revolutionize the thinking of those that would oppress and deny us the basic human dignity of choosing our way of life and that sex and gender in which we choose to live? Otherwise, those Puritans of today might just renew their <u>witch-hunt</u> and decide to accuse trans-people, or even gays and lesbians of being possessed with evil, immoral, satanic intent. Some already are accused of exactly that. The Baptist faith proclaims all trans-people are sinners and should repent from their desires to change genders and conform to what they believe is right in the eyes of God. That's why I'm a Methodist.

Don't think those kinds of folks are still around? Visit the Cathedral of Hope church in Dallas some Sunday and watch how some fanatical, Puritanical zealots of today picket the streets as parishioners exit the church. Listen to how these hecklers "<u>damn</u>" all those that attend this non-denominational church. It's a Christian church that welcomes all people, where gays and lesbians in Dallas are safe and can congregate to worship God and their Lord and Savior, Jesus Christ. Over loudspeakers, the hecklers warn of how wrong those attending there all are; that they are being lied to and that the hecklers themselves are the ones who know God's will for those men and women attending that church.

The hecklers boldly invade and intrude into the worship services and seek to cause mayhem wherever they are able. So far as I know, none of the congregation there have been hanged or burned at the stake, but they are constantly threatened. The church's clergy have even had to resort to using the city's police force before, during, and after worship services as a means to keep these "holier than thou" zealots at bay and protect the church members from their verbal onslaught. Folks, I am here to tell you, violence against those who are gay, lesbian, or transgender folks does occur every day in America. There have been several trans-women slaughtered by those whose motives for such murders were because the victim was transgender.

I'm very aware of the desire and the need for any trans-person to remain out of the eye of the storm. I also believe that wish to remain clandestine generates much of our problem. Because all of us who are transgender cherish our privacy and anonymity, we tend not to be as vocal as perhaps we should be. Thus, our voices most often remain mute and have not yet become that <u>resounding bell in the ears of lady liberty</u> or among those who need to hear the clanging.

Legal decisions in minor court cases all around the country have had a profound negative impact and effect not only on those to whom they were decreed, but the resulting spillover has trickled down to affect the legal rights and lives of every trans-person in the land. There shall be no public outcry, no demand from the masses that these inequities be resolved. For the most part, probably 98% of the general population has no idea that such legal action has even taken place. Nope, the only voices those legislators or

Pink Heart

judges might hear ... are our own. Unless we instigate the changes, I have serious doubts that they shall ever occur.

An unjust law cannot be administered impartially. It can only obliterate and punish those who lie beneath its oppression. Summarily, it will in turn destroy the freedoms of its supporters as well as those that oppose it. To me, such laws as the ones I speak of above, especially the Littleton case in Texas and other laws directed toward those that are transgender is <u>immoral, and unjust law</u> and should be repealed.

Fortunately, there are those among our community of trans-people and those concerned caregivers and citizens that do lobby for positive change and to revolutionize thinking amongst the public and those lawmakers. There are some voices of those in government, in the medical and psychological professions that do speak out on our behalf and do make valuable attempts to seek and effect positive change.

Tolerance seems to be like a virus and it is catching on more and more. Attempts are being made to legislate commonsense, compassionate laws that would make violence directed toward trans-people a "hate crime" and such acts would carry severe penalties for those perpetrating such acts of violence. The problem, as I see it, is how serious of consideration do lawmakers give to such a brief minority of their constituency. For most, I think they merely allow the transgender segment of the nation to let off steam, and then the lawmakers comply with those individuals that have stated the transgender point of view. They declare that they will "take it under advisement" ... only to have the requests fall into the cracks, by the wayside, or be voted down by the less tolerable or conservative councilperson, representative, or senator. Even former President Trump disbanded a decision to allow trans people to serve in our nation's military. The current President re-instated that transgender policy and once again allow those who wish to serve in our military may do so, no matter they're being transgender. Effecting change shall require such good intentions; good fortune, and a whole lot more of shaking the tree of justice.

In Dallas and Ft. Worth, as in other cities of the country, city councils are adopting laws that make it illegal to discriminate when hiring or in the dismissal of a trans-person, calling it a criminal misdemeanor if the employer does do so. Though encouraging in their intent, in practicality I question the ability of civil governments to enforce such laws. For certain, it did not help my employment situation when it came time for me to first transition on the job. More on this will be covered later on in this text.

There were those from my local support group, including our gender therapist who trekked down to Austin every year and made their voices heard in the halls of justice in our own state Capitol. Some still work the Internet and lobby in Washington for Gay, Lesbian, Bisexual, and Transgender Rights. I pray that in the future years, our nation will follow the lead of several pioneering progressive states and nations seeking to become more lenient and less intrusive into the lives of those of us who are bi, gay, lesbian, or transgender. In a movement that I call, <u>Trans-Femancipation</u> we MTF trans-women must join hands to break these bonds that refrain us from enjoying the life, liberty, and pursuit of happiness that we too are promised by the U.S. Constitution.

Our nation, despite all its frailties and flaws, is still our beloved homeland. Though imperfect, all of us still alive are riders/passengers upon this same good ship Earth. Among nations, ours is still the most just and the one that holds the most hope and promise for the future of freedom and humanity. All Americans, whether they are transgender, bi, gay, lesbian, or otherwise should be honored and proud to be a citizen of the United States. Despite my annoyance with some leaders and injustice, I still always consider myself to be a patriot and loyal American.

I certainly am not one to try and reinvent the wheel, I simply want to replace some outdated parts, squeeze a little oil on some antiquated old bearings and make the wheels of justice roll a little smoother for all of us who are transgender.

I am annoyed with certain political and judicial decisions, but I hope that trans people will be given the understanding, dignity, and rights that we deserve. Our great nation must recognize that there exists a sort of Transgender Apartheid and real separation of human rights that does not allow <u>all of its citizens</u> those equal rights its constitution promises. Though we have problems here in the U.S.A., I still have faith in the system and that right and truth will prevail.

Chapter 9:
The Gatekeepers

This rare condition known as being transgender is technically <u>Gender Dysphoria,</u> or <u>GID</u> (Gender Identity Crisis) is a <u>behavioral phenomenon</u>. Thus, it is neuroendocrinological. That's a big word meaning that the condition is as much <u>psychosexual</u> and <u>psychosocial</u> as it is one driven by the tangible desire to alter one's genitals as well as gender.

Among those trans-women I have known, the few that had GRS have <u>any</u> post-op regrets. Other than perhaps some that might rethink who they would let perform their surgeries, for the most part, all seemed pleased with the fact they had the surgery. In panel discussions during group sessions, all related their individual experiences and none issued any remorse for their actions, even though for some the whole process was devastating financially. Some lost touch with loved ones, old friends, or had issues with their employers. <u>All</u> noted they now felt more congruent in their new chosen gender and more complete as human beings … and felt like women. Why is that? I'll discuss the issue of effectiveness for GRS later in the text.

I would attribute that success as much as anything to proper screening procedures that are done by<u> gender counselors, psychologists, and psychiatrists</u>. A <u>one-on-one </u>formalized<u> session</u> is completed whereby the individual undergoes intense counseling <u>and/or</u> psychotherapy. During the sessions, experienced and learned counselors will encourage the trans-woman client to include themselves in the participation of local support group meetings dealing with those who possess similar conditions as their own. By attending such meetings, he or she can communicate to others with related desires, challenges, or obstacles in the process of seeking answers to why they are the way they are.

Usually, within this assemblage, the conceivable trans-woman might form constructive, <u>therapeutic alliances</u> with her peers.

During this period of psychological evaluation, an observant gender specialist might further assess and evaluate the client/patient's attitude about her gender situation. In the group sessions, a <u>cordial, less structured atmosphere</u> is established whereby a proficient counselor/therapist may assess whether or not the conceivable MTF trans-woman can relate to others as a female. During these casual group sessions, a wise counselor may pick up on several keys to a trans-woman's attitude and expectations. Within a group setting, it's been my experience to witness others open up more and express the problems, concerns, challenges, and reality of what they anticipate as well as what they desire. In such a setting, a counselor can more readily comprehend that person's overall mental health and either affirm or refute the readiness and desire of the TS to have surgical intervention through GRS.

In other words, this time spent in a group, assists the counselor, as well as the trans-women in forming subjective opinions about persons that she/he may have about a client or ones that might become clients later. It broadens the picture and allows for better input into the psyche of those present. However, as some trans-women are rather introverted, a counselor should be cautious about jumping to conclusions without good evidence that a person isn't responding because of shyness, rather than due to lack of commitment.

As you might imagine, there are strict guidelines that a gender specialist/psychologist/psychiatrist must use to ascertain treatment options for some deemed to have a gender identity disorder. The guidelines that have been established by the psychological and medical community incorporate the <u>Benjamin Standards of Care</u>, named for the renowned pioneering sex reassignment surgeon, Dr, Harry Benjamin, for anyone seeking gender reassignment surgery. Thus, most gender counselors abide by those guidelines when they work with someone that is transgender. Do trans-women accept and agree with all the guidelines outlined in these standards of care? I would estimate that most of us see the value of having a blueprint in place, but once again, I would remind counselors, readers, and those physicians that administer to the transgender that in this world it is <u>not</u> one size fits all.

Since each trans-woman individual situation is unique, I do not believe that every person should be required to strictly adhere to the same regulations. However, the exceptions or exemptions to following the guidelines outlined in the Benjamin Standards are rare. Should a candidate for GRS wish to speed up the process due to some logical or pertinent reason, then the more than required two signatures of a gender counselor or psychologist should be closely scrutinized. A third counselor or fourth may be a wise suggestion to further eliminate legal ramifications after the trans-woman has had the surgery performed. After that happens, it is too late.

The counselor attempts to establish that their client's motives for requesting counsel leading to hormonal therapy are well-founded and will be of benefit. If in the opinion of the counselor their client is <u>perceived</u> to be rational and deserving of assistance administered by a medical physician, then that counselor will usually then write a letter or contact the attending physician and arrange for or recommend their client for hormonal therapy. To the person that is a trans-woman, this is a <u>major step</u> in the process and the gender specialist must have an accurate accounting of the individual's psychotherapeutic and personal history. To me, this was the most important first step of my transition.

The trans-woman must possess a clear understanding of her situation and be able to make smart, coherent decisions concerning her gender transition. It is paramount that each MTF transsexual knows what her <u>self-perceptions</u> are of what they hope to achieve from estrogen/androgen hormone therapy or surgery. A few trans-women I've known enter hormonal therapy with unrealistic expectations, expecting that alone to remake them into a passable female.

Upon corroboration that the client/patient is transgender, of a healthy mind, and has undergone profound analysis and inquiry from their primary gender specialist (the <u>gatekeeper</u>), that gatekeeper will be asked by the trans-woman to sign off on that person receiving estrogenic hormonal treatments. For trans-women, that is a major accomplishment in the transition process. However, I would note that the ultimate decision to prescribe or not prescribe hormones is always up to the <u>medical physician</u>. In due course, the doctor's choice for prescribing a female or male hormonal regimen depends as much on the <u>physical</u> health and medical history of the patient as well as their perceptions and assessments of the recommending therapist and their assessment of the patient's mental and emotional stability.

Typically, any trans-woman's first visit to an endocrinologist, gynecologist, or some medical physician who can prescribe hormones is one filled with anxiety, anticipation, angst, or in other words ... a bad case of the jitter*s*. When a post-op transwoman's feet are in stirrups ... and I'm not speaking of being on a horse, there is a major degree of anxiety. This nervous anticipation and fear of being rejected often drives up that person's blood pressure and can lead a doctor to possibly misread the individual's health condition. My initial visit to my gynecologist was just such an incident.

Notwithstanding, I was fortunate that the kind-hearted doctor wisely knew that letting his transgender patient calm down beforehand would make the entire process less stressful. His psychological understanding of apprehension was greatly appreciated, as was his compassion and the signed scripts for the hormones I would need to begin my journey into womanhood.

The trans-woman must freely choose to assume their new gender identity and live, work, and exist on a full-time basis for <u>one year</u> in the female gender of her choice. Once the gatekeeper is convinced of the trans-woman's intent to complete that process, the gender specialist will then be asked to provide a <u>written referral letter</u> for their client/patient recommending she be permitted to have her GRS.

The next step in the procedure usually entails meeting with a second clinical behavioral scientist (psychologist/psychiatrist). During that interview, this second gatekeeper will then evaluate the primary gender specialist's records and either affirm or deny the evaluation and whether or not to endorse the client's / patient's request for GRS. The basic goal is simple. Usually, this second evaluation is far less lengthy and is more of an assessment of the diagnosis, rather than the cause of why the person feels they want the surgery. The primary aim is to avoid signing off on any male-to-female trans-woman the second gender specialist doubts is sincere about becoming female or having the surgery. The practitioners also seek to avoid future legal litigation and to provide improved diagnostic and selection criteria for pre-surgical preparation.

In due course, for others and me, the outcome is dependent on our <u>motives</u> for desiring the GRS surgery, our expectations, and ultimately the quality of the surgical procedure that is performed. I have known some that have had a botched GRS surgery or at the very least was done poorly. Those trans-women suffered some physical malformation, had inadequate vaginal depth or sensation, and some later developed a vaginal fistula, infections, excessive bleeding, nerve damage, no vaginal or labial arousal by stimulation, or extreme soreness and discomfort. The likelihood of those women being content and happy as a post-op is going to be lessened and marginal at best. I might add, however, that aftercare is essential to any post-op and it becomes the responsibility of the patient to follow strict procedures for hygiene, dilation, and prevention of infection if GRS is to be a total success. Many of those I referred to above <u>did not follow</u> the procedural guidelines for dilation or aftercare and thus wound up with problems that could have been prevented.

GRS for the MTF trans-woman creates the external appearance of female genitals and a skin-lined (penile skin turned inside out) vaginal canal. The surgery must also allow for normal urinary function and hopefully, the trans-woman will be capable of experiencing some degree of sexual clitoral sensation. The resulting depth of the vaginal canal is dependent on several factors, including the amount of donor skin, the source of which is the penile and scrotal tissue of the patient herself. If there is adequate usable tissue, then the use of a skin graft can be avoided and the trans-woman should have an adequate vaginal depth to become capable of future sexual intercourse, should that become her desire.

In some cases, from those who have thought of themselves as transgender, I have witnessed <u>resentment</u> when they find they have to endure counseling or therapy sessions with a mental health professional or appropriately trained gender specialist. They either thought it to be unnecessary, too expensive or merely too burdensome. To me, such an attitude is folly and the person who denies they need help is likely the one who needs it the most. Sometimes, fear is another reason for avoiding treatment or therapy. To some, spending time and money on psychological services implies that one can't solve their problem. For some male-to-female trans-folks I've known, they perceived this to be a weakness and flaw in their character. I would tell you that is sheer nonsense. It isn't being weak to admit you need help, rather it indicates that this is a journey only you can decide to take, but not a journey you can make alone. It requires the help and assistance of many professionals and as many friends as you can acquire.

By speaking to and confessing their innermost thoughts to an authoritative party, one that is trained in dealing with sexuality and gender identity issues, the transgender person will be compelled to face their uncertainties and tackle their problems. They must quit making excuses and avoiding the real issues confronting them. To me, the gender specialist or therapist has a very real and positive impact and brings to light the choices confronting a trans-woman and what that person can do about the <u>medical mandate</u> that requires them to go through such therapy before being approved for hormonal therapy or surgery.

The phrase, "No Man (or Woman) is an Island" is very appropriate when one considers the choices confronting a trans-woman. As stated above, this is a journey that is reached by <u>solitary commitment but not made by solitary means</u> of confinement. One that is male cannot fully attain the status of becoming a female without first having made the trek through psychological and physical assessment by medical and gender specialists. GRS is not a DIY (do it yourself) project that is completed at home on the weekend.

A gender counselor takes on many roles, not the least of which is to guide and direct the person seeking to transition. The counselor must clear away the vague ideas of folklore, falsehoods, and misinformation associated with what it takes to transition. Far too many people I've known have envisioned a grandiose journey whereby they would contain the high costs of transition by retaining their existing lifestyles ... only doing it as a female. The result for most of these people was that they were not able to remain static in either their social lifestyle or in containing the costs. For many, they were met with disdain or opposition from their employer. A spouse that started out being supportive wound up eventually choosing to separate from the blossoming woman ... that before was her husband. Kids and other family members found themselves turned off to the emerging woman that was replacing their father. Those people's grandiose vision of this journey turned into a grandiose nightmare.

In short, the counselor must often assist the trans-woman through an emotional minefield that occurs during almost every trans-woman's transition. The trans-woman is somewhat like an onion, and it becomes the task of a skilled counselor to peel away the outer stratum and expose the inner layers of the heart and desire of the person that presents herself to the counselor. If must be determined the trans-woman's intent is going 24 –7 as a woman, the trans-woman is sincere and has realistic expectations about her transition. The pseudo male facade she put forth for all those years will eventually fall away ... piece by piece to reveal her true inner-self that was submerged and repressed all those years. That's how it was for me and so it is for most that make this journey.

The counselor may also find that not everyone she counsels should be given an endorsement to begin hormones and for certain should not be considered a candidate for GRS. It is not so much separating the wheat from the chaff, as it is identifying the truth and sincerity from the lies of the demented. Unfortunately, some that present themselves as being trans-women are far from it.

They play-act, making it appear as if they are transgender, when in fact their intent may be sexually perverse and their goal merely to deceive others ... as well as themselves. Such people do exist, as I have met some that are like this that have tried to "dupe" a counselor, a support group, or physician into letting them begin hormones or having some ill-advised surgery.

Astute observers in a group will usually weed out these transvestite phonies or weirdoes and steer clear of them. These types of individuals are afflicted with other mental problems, such as psychosis and neurosis that require advanced psychotherapy. Some such individuals seek out trans-women, or attend group meetings and speak of transition, telling of all the things they are "going" to do and in the end, never accomplish any of it. Why is that? It's because they were never serious about it in the first place. Instead, they live vicariously in a fantasy world created by them ... for them. Such folks use gatherings or Internet chat rooms as outlets.

Shopping with a Friend **Supermarket Shopping**

Windy Day ... Shopping **Sofa-r... So Good**

Pink Heart

A true trans-woman will be tested each time she steps out the door to attempt passing as a female in public. Before doing that, work on the image you present, and I advise first having been on an estrogen regimen for several months or years before committing to make the full-time switch to your new gender.

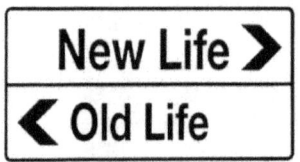

Once the choice is made and **"she"** commits, plan on leaving that old nest and male life behind ... and possibly with it a loss of economic and social status achieved by your male self. Reinventing one's gender identity takes courage and a willingness to accept the physical and economic challenges presented by the switch from male to female.

* * *

The trans-woman is going to need the best medical care she can afford to find when making the "change." GRS is not cheap to acquire financially, nor psychologically. Do your due diligence and decide who will best serve your needs for everything from hormones, to facial feminization surgery, electrolysis, breast augmentation, and GRS. Failing to plan, as they say ... is planning to fail. Get right with your physical conditioning, save for the expenses of your surgeries and other procedures, build your femme wardrobe, and be smart about what you plan to do to be self-supportive during and after your transition.

Chapter 10:

Managing the Realities

Managing one's transition is of paramount importance if one is to experience success at becoming the gender opposite to which he or she is born. I once thought it might be easier for me to become a Negro, Hispanic, or even a Gorilla ... than to become a woman. Gad! Can you imagine the electrolysis bill for that kind of hair removal? Anyway, I was wrong! Though the task has not been simple or easy it has nonetheless proven to be ... attainable.

If a person is to succeed at going from being a male to female, then one has got to obtain and have a complete understanding of the realities of such a challenging undertaking. One must become educated and well-versed in all aspects of gender change and what such an endeavor may entail. Above all, I want to reiterate to anyone reading this who might consider herself to be a trans-woman to realize that deciding to change one's gender identity is not for the timid. There may be apprehension, but there can be no lack of total commitment if one is to succeed at reinventing his or her complete gender identity. The personal costs of transition are often extreme and can be devastating, as was the case in my own life. Notwithstanding, rewards do come to those who persevere, set their sights on succeeding, and do not fear pain or accept failure as an option.

Even if a trans-woman is no bathing beauty, their gender presentation should always be 100% female, thus each should be perceived to already be a female by those who know her at work or in public. Personally speaking, the emotional anxiety, discomfort, and mental conflicts I once had lessened when I began living and working as a female. Thus, the outcome for my transition from male to female was acceptable and I am happy with my journey's transition and the results thereof. Success at passing will present any trans-woman with greater emotional stability, improve her relationships with others and especially with her friends or the mate of her choice. This exploration onto gender shores opposite that of their birth will be enlightening to her physically, socially, and spiritually.

Pink Heart

I heard one trans-sister describe being transgender like someone walking a tight rope. For the trans-woman to survive, she must maintain a <u>balance</u> between her personal and professional relationships. Realizing that what she is doing will impact the various people in her life; the trans-woman must pose her wants to then balance short-term desires with long-term goals and needs.

Living in Texas where tornadoes occur every spring, and with the rash of hurricanes our nation has had lately, I and other transgender folks often feel like it is <u>we</u> who are in the <u>eye of the storm</u> where the turbulent whirlwinds push and pull us in several directions simultaneously. When we find ourselves leaning too far forward into the wind to keep our balance, the wind all of a sudden may reverse its direction, and cause us to lurch forward … as stumbling … we sometimes fall face-first onto the ground. When we finally do pick ourselves up again, gathering our legs beneath us and regaining our balance and equilibrium, the gale-force winds rapidly change directions again. Accordingly, the trans-woman will spend a great deal of time and effort, just trying to keep <u>balance</u> in her life.

Hard choices must be made and the fulcrum will tilt if one chooses to follow the path that will lead to going full-time as a woman. When that happens, and the trans-woman is blown in the direction of seeking her peace, more often than not those whose she loves and cherishes most will have to forfeit theirs. Have you noticed … this is a common denominator in many a trans-woman's transition?

For me, it was a question of could I disrupt the lives of my entire family or was it possible to simply ride out the storm and finish up my days on this planet as a guy. I knew I didn't want to divorce either of my wives, but neither was it fair to them to hold on to a marriage that became an illusion at best. I didn't want my kids, and especially my youngest daughter shunned and ridiculed by schoolmates and kids in the neighborhood because I'm transgender. I didn't want my then nine-year-old to be asked, "Why does your daddy wear a dress?"

On the other hand, I was nearing forty and my biological clock was ticking faster than ever. As I saw it, I was running out of time and options if I ever wanted to try and reach my dream of becoming female and finding inner peace.

When did my wants, needs, and desires take priority over those of my family? At the point when I began considering my options, I was so obsessed with becoming feminine that I developed tunnel vision and pretty much shut my family out of the decision loop. In hindsight, I wish I hadn't hidden so much from them and had allowed them to be more inclusive in my plans. Maybe then they'd have been more considerate and understanding. Maybe things would have worked out differently ... but in truth, I doubt it.

So, the answer to that question was: When I had come to <u>the end of my rope</u>. I either had to hang onto my feminine life, or just jump off the platform and let my male self be hung. If I did the latter, Gordon would be executed and forever exiled from my life. So would Shannon, as neither would truly exist.

The previous questions are tough and I wish that neither I nor any other trans-woman would have to address them, but alas, we must. Any trans-woman that is involved in a marital relationship and especially one that includes children will anguish over some extremely difficult questions before allowing her true self to go full-time. For that reason, many that are transgender choose not to transition. Instead, they bury the woman inside them and in most cases, they remain unhappy till the end of their days. If I was to guess, and that's all this is, based on my subjective observations from those at support group meetings and online, I'd wager that for every trans-woman that goes full-time, there are probably five or more that don't. The price is just too high and some just can't pay the toll. Nope! Being transgender is not for the meek, or for those who cannot commit to paying the ultimate costs.

In the end, only the trans-woman can make the tough decisions concerning how far they want to make their transition. For someone like me, that lived decades as a male, I needed to open both my eyes wide and realize going in what I was getting myself into ... and what the potential costs might be if I chose to transition. This entails, as it often does for all those like me, giving up the life, benefits, family, and everything of value that one has constructed over the years.

Trying to Explain Transition to Youngest Daughter - '96

This was the last full day I got to spend with her in the past 22 years. X2 made me out to be a threat to my daughter's psyche and the female judge would only allow chaperoned visits with a state-appointed counsel. (Have you seen the movie, Mrs. Doubtfire? Her fate was also mine, only I could not get X2 to waive that decree).

Rather than do that, I remained in Dallas and her in Abilene with X2. I did not wish to interfere with her happiness, so I made a difficult choice to allow her to live without me. So, I stayed out of her life, for it embarrassed her that her dad became a woman. That's part of the price a trans-woman sometimes has to pay.

Five years later, I offered to provide her with a kidney transplant, as her own was becoming worse and required her to have dialysis twice a week. When tested for a tissue match, mine did not qualify, so she had to use a cadaver kidney donor. That transplant didn't work, so they had to remove it. It took another nine years before she got a good kidney.

Chapter 11:
Counselor

I do believe a great deal of my success was due to locating and using the services of a very gifted, knowledgeable, and compassionate gender specialist here in the Ft. Worth, Texas area. As stated previously, she has a doctorate in psychology from New York University. She is a former member of the liturgical Catholic order and as such, she is an especially moral person with high integrity and before retiring was exceedingly active in the transgender community in this area, throughout Texas, and the nation. She is also the founder of the Ft. Worth P-FLAG (Parents and Friends of Gays and Lesbians). So far as I am concerned, I could not have been in better hands. I found her to be extraordinarily competent, non-gratifying, and yet compassionate and encouraging when dealing with someone that is transsexual or transgender. She was a role model for all of us who aspire to become female.

She was the facilitator of the Ft. Worth transgender support group (see photo above for "some" of the dozens of girls she counseled) that met once a month. The rapport built with the sisters (and brothers) in her support group and this fine woman did much to help me transition and become the person I am today. For the person that sees herself as being transgender, there exists a real need to secure the services of a competent counselor that one trusts and likes.

Transsexual or Transgender

Let me address the word <u>transsexual</u>, as opposed to the term, <u>transgender</u>. The transgender expression is usually attributed to having been coined by Virginia Prince back in the '80s. At first, it was used to describe people, like Prince, that lived 24-7 as a woman, but who did not seek GRS as a means to support her gender presentation. Rather, Ms. Prince chose the word to describe how one maintains a gender role without accomplishing it through surgical means.

Pink Heart

Over time, the term has evolved to become an all-encompassing umbrella to describe gender-variant people in varying stages of transition. As a result of the escalating utilization of the word, the term has become even more inclusive and is used to describe all manner of human diversity, including intersex people, effeminate men, butch lesbians, drag queens, and numerous others, as well as … the transvestite. For that reason, I am not always endeared when someone refers to me as being transgender. If they do, I hope it is applied within the proper context, but that is tough to determine these days.

I believe this term has been overused and for certain it no longer separates transsexuals from others that are not. The meaningful difference that abides between someone that is transsexual versus one that is transvestite is not illustrated when both are presented as being transgender. That equates to describing someone as being human. Sure, but is the human a black American, Hispanic, Caucasian, and are they male or female? See what I mean?

However, not everything about the word transgender has fostered negative developments. It has served to tie in a wider range of people under its banner, thus broadening the overall political effectiveness of those that seek affirmative amendments within gender diversity. Many who claim to be transgender are working to enhance the embodiment of the idiom, giving it a more powerful voice among those who seek positive change for those in our nation and world who experience life as a gender variant.

Only Cash Will Do

A personal regret for having to endure counseling and therapy was that my health insurance covered <u>none of the costs</u> for it. Few, if any, gender specialist accepts insurance for payment of services. Later on, I will address some aspects of why I believe this is an inequity, injustice, and that the condition of being a trans-woman should be more respected and recognized by those that solicit and provide health insurance policies. Not only is being transgender a psychosexual condition but the causes are based on <u>medical</u> and <u>biological</u> reasons as well. Thus, to me, the condition is worthy of being covered by medical health insurance. I understand that Medicare now covers part of the costs for GRS, which in itself is a major milestone. However, I doubt any private institutions that issue health policies shall ever voluntarily endorse GRS surgery unless they are forced to do by some legal ruling.

The trans-woman will be pulled in several directions, so know what your destination is, and then get sound, sage advice from a wise counselor on how to get there.

Although health insurance coverage will cover some expenses for most recognized mental diseases and alcoholism, it will probably not provide for any benefits for someone diagnosed as having gender dysphoria. To me, the law should amend this injustice. This exclusion of coverage directed at those who are transgender is but one more example of the flawed social systems in place within our society.

Chapter 12:
Everywhere I Turned … There She Was

In my studies of psychology, I found that when someone like me has these intense feelings and desires for their <u>feminine self</u> to take over that it is very difficult to suspend that sort of thinking. It is the quintessential path to which the psyche seeks to journey. As a male, I spent very little time seeking to improve upon my masculine image or attempting to make that part of me the dominant personality within. There were simply too many inescapable things in society that stimulated and triggered my desire to be a female.

In every magazine I picked up I saw the soft, lovely faces and bodies of beautiful women. In department stores, I bear witness to the vast array of cosmetics, jewelry, perfumes, and sexy lingerie luring me as if they were singing to Ulysses the "<u>Songs of the Sirens</u>" calling out incessantly to me.

They were everywhere, in every direction that I turned, on television, in movies, at the mall, the corner drug store, or just watching cheerleaders at a football game. I was exposed to and bombarded by <u>femininity</u>. I found myself drooling and swooning over the lithe young bodies I so acutely scrutinized and observed. It didn't seem like carnal desires, but it certainly stirred my imagination and made me covet what each of those girls had. Inside, I secretly wept that my fate, my own body, and life weren't like theirs. I very much desired what I hadn't acquired, but so desperately wanted.

The fantasies I endured were both sweet … and yet oh so bitter. I questioned that even if I could take hormones and have surgery, I wondered if I could ever craft myself to appear like these lovely, female human beings that I witnessed at every turn in life. Their feminine youth and beauty were intoxicating, yet for me was like a wisp of smoke that materialized before my vision when I cross-dressed, and then the image quickly vanished into oblivion, only to haunt me by refusing me the opportunity of being one of them. Yet, it was not them that denied me, but rather it was my "self". What

I didn't realize was that it was me and only me that held the power to change into that which I envied and desired.

Thus, all of my previous life I was preoccupied with the yearning to be young, attractive, and female. I somehow accomplished the latter of those two, and so I suppose, as Jack Nicholson referred in the movie, "Mars Attacks," two out of three isn't bad!

As stated, I lived as a male for several decades. Being youthful is one feminine longing that is no longer possible for me to appease. My mind shall always be comprised of a yearning for beauty and naturalistic feminism/ Now, I'm older than I've ever been ... and as young as I'll ever be. A lesson for all ... we all get older with time, like it or not. Save for someone discovering a time portal that I can use to travel back to the time of my conception or youth, I am resigned to live with what cards dealt me ... as are all those trans-sisters like me. Much of what I most love about being feminine is yet beyond the scope and current abilities of medical science, chemistry, or surgical interceding to accomplish the five-foot-six-inch-tall body I would have liked to have had. Still, being tall does have its advantages at times.

For a while in my young life, I survived, as does every trans-person by a process that is called <u>projective identification</u>. That is to say, I took photos of myself dressed in femme and I used those photos as confirming evidence that I could become reasonably feminine if I so desired. This too proved to be somewhat frustrating, unfulfilling, and a fantasy that left me only aching to take it all one step closer to my ultimate dream of becoming an actual female.

<u>Dressing as a woman</u> was not fetishism to me; it was always a matter of satisfying my intense and growing need to be female and express myself as a girl/woman. The feminine clothing was merely the means of achieving that process. In my mind, as I have stated, my female personality was polarized within me when I was very young. I did not always understand the implications of that and because of my personal and social circumstances, I grew up appearing to others to be a normal male. Nothing could have been farther from the truth, but then as I mentioned ... I was <u>perceived </u>by others to be a male.

Pre-Wired

As stated earlier in this book, in my case, I concluded that my being transgender is a condition whereby my <u>fetal brain</u> was somehow chemically pre-programmed to think in terms of being female, rather than being content with how nature made me. This is called psychogenesis, thus has biological reasons for one becoming transgender, even if those reasons are still debated. I for one believe that being transgender is a <u>predisposed condition</u>. One's childhood environment serves to either reinforce these feelings of incompatibility with their anatomical sex, or else it will serve as an impediment. In any case, it will not prevent the person whose brain was somehow <u>altered before birth</u> to respond to female stimuli and having a desire to act, behave, or even become female.

In some scientific studies, it has even been determined that there are discernable differences in the physical brain areas essential to the sexual behavior of a male to female trans-woman from that of a non-transgender male.

In one acknowledgment of this theory about predisposition that bed nucleus brain area known as the BSTc of a male to female trans-woman was shown to be female, rather than male in size and scope. It was further determined, for the first time that the size of the BSTc was not influenced by sex hormones and was independent of sexual orientation. ^ The resulting conclusion to this scenario was that the study showed a <u>female brain structure</u> in genetically trans-women. Therefore, this study supports the hypothesis that gender identity develops as a result of an interaction between the developing fetal brain and sex hormones.

Zhou J. -N, Hoffman M.A., Gooren L.J., Swaab D.F. (1997) "A Sex Difference in the brain and its relation to being transgender", IJT1, 1.

A Shannonism: After transition and working as a woman, I discovered something that does the work of ten men: … five women.

Chapter 13:
"Ve Haf Ways"

"Ve haf ways uf makinz you talk"! The heat from the intense light shining in her face made the sweat trickle down her forehead and run into her squinting eyes. She was tied to the cane chair, her arms and hands bound behind her. She felt a strong hand grab at the back of her hair. With a fierce tug, it pulled back her head, exposing her agonizing face to blinding light and the dark silhouette of her interrogator.

"Don't be a nincompoop! Cooperate, Fraulein Shannon. Tell uzz de truth. Vat happenze to Herr Gordon? Confess dat you makinz him go kaput." Through the tears, mixed with her perspiration, she grits her teeth, grimaces, and then whispers weakly, "I told you before. I am … or I was … Gordon! I did not kill him off. I only altered him; taking him to a higher, better place."

That somber answer only brought her a stern fist across the cheek, and then another backhanded swipe across her already bludgeoned and swelling right eye. She screamed out in pain, to no avail. "You're lying, fraulein! Confess! You drove him to committen de suicide, or else you smote him until he vuz kaput!"

This portrayal of a "third-degree interrogation" may seem like a scene out of a bad Nazi movie. Perhaps to you, the reader, it is far-fetched, but I can attest that in many ways it comes frighteningly close to an exacting depiction of the attitude some have had about the transition a trans-woman endures going from male to female. Among those cynics in families, some might consider what this person did to their son, husband, father, brother, or friend to be of the same consequence as if it were a homicidal offense. To those acquaintances, it was as if the male to
female trans-woman stuck a gun to "his" head and somehow blew out the brains of that being that once was known as a male.

In many cases, despite the appeals for these close relatives and friends to accept that their male relative or friend has instead now become a woman, the trans-woman is treated like a condemned criminal. To them, she is guilty of committing the most heinous of crimes. They care not to hear the trans-woman's testimony about how <u>she</u> is still that same person inside that they knew and loved.

To her critics, there is no way the feminine being she presents now is remotely similar to the person they knew before. To them, she has become like a murderess, and they want nothing to do with her. They look upon her with disdain, suspicion, and contempt. The woman she became took from them their loved one and close friend. It was she that drove him to commit suicide and it was she who made him <u>go away</u> and leave their presence forever. For that, they shall never forgive her and she must always bear up to their scrutiny and their criticisms.

In life's courtroom, this is not a case in which the prosecution is likely to get a conviction. There are several problems with the charges these folks bring against this new woman. It is their argument and accusation that she removed their son, husband, brother, or friend from their lives. There is no denying that she did exactly that. She sympathizes with their loss, but she has committed no crime.

However, if some believe she killed him off … where is his corpse? I think a more accurate question in this instance would be <u>what has happened to his body?</u> The obvious answer to that is his body is alive and well, yet now has been altered, improved, and feminized, but it is <u>not deceased</u>.

A trans-woman does not <u>steal away</u> or take the life of the person they used to be but instead allows the inevitable metamorphosis into womanhood to begin. The slow-moving, sluggish caterpillar spins the cocoon and emerges from the sarcophagus lifestyle he once leads to be converted into the blossoming butterfly. Thus, <u>she</u> bursts forth into the world, having transformed herself into a new identity, but one not devoid of the same loves, desires, hopes, or dreams as before.

In no way did the trans-woman become like one of the alien <u>pod-people</u> from the movie, "The Body Snatchers." She is not pilfering her male life and morphing into a completely different alien personality, nor leaving behind the spent, dead shell of the person she replaced. Altering her body to resemble that of a female is based upon chemical and scientific fact, not science fiction.

If she appeared to those relatives or friends dressed in a Halloween <u>costume,</u> they might think her eccentric and perhaps silly. Yet, so long as her character and her personality didn't radically alter, then I'd wager each would still consider her to be the same person, only with an outer costume covering her flesh.

Why then is it so big of a stretch for relatives or friends to imagine her as the same person, yet say … in a Woman costume? As ridiculous as that scenario is, it is closer to the truth than they realize. She is still the same individual inside that <u>womanly flesh costume</u>; only her gender presentation is different.

Therein lies the problem; as such a thing is so difficult for most of these skeptics to conceive. To them, it seems to be something surreal, weird, or even perverted. From their point of view, she is swimming upstream, or at best flying against the wind and the laws of nature and God Himself. To them, is it that she must be mentally ill or insane to conceive of such a bizarre thing as <u>changing her sex and gender</u>?

Those relatives and friends that think of their male relative or friend as being deceased and gone should rather look upon him as being well, safe, and happy only inside an altered costume of flesh. Her mind, soul, and heart still yearn for their affection and still have the same affection for them. The previous male has evolved into womanhood; rather it was the woman who shed the ill-fitting, old worn-out costume of the male and it is she that dwells now among them.

Imagine for a moment a person you know and love with all your heart and soul. They might be your beloved husband, wife, son, daughter a parent, or perhaps one of your closest friends. You've known this person for many years and this person has endeared themselves to you in many ways. This person is moral, has exhibited to you their love and trust and you have loved and trusted this person. Together, you have shared laughter, tears, hopes, dreams, and maybe even parenting. Now, imagine that this same beloved person is suddenly in a bad fire and their flesh suffers third-degree burns.

After many surgeries and healing, the person's face and body are still covered with hideous scars and that person then becomes <u>beyond physical recognition</u> to you. You listen to the voice of the person calling out your name and finally, it dawns upon you that this is that same person you loved so much before the accident, but whose body is now disfigured, misshapen, mangled, and whose flesh is a tangled mess of scars. One need only think of the war veterans on T.V. that suffered severe burns and scars from an IED explosion.

How do you feel <u>now</u> about this human being ... this human soul? Do you have a knot in your stomach? Do you feel a great deal of compassion and sympathy, or simply feel sick to your stomach? If you are honest, you are likely very uncomfortable seeing this person as they are now. Do you turn your face away from those loving eyes that you once knew so well? Those are the same eyes that before held such a comfort for you; eyes that held such promise for the future. Does the person's imperfect flesh now disgust you so much that you can no longer look upon it with the same affection that you once had for that person? Instead, you may feel pity, but also a feeling of repulsion.

That's a tough analogy to imagine, but is it so different than how others might look upon the male-to-female trans-woman and the female into which she develops? Rather, should we say they don't look upon her at all, but rather they turn away their heads, their hearts, and their lives ... sequestering her and leaving her to wander this world apart from them? Although to many of them, she may have become an unrecognizable modification, or perhaps a blemished abomination with whom they do not wish to have to deal. Inside she remains that same person they supposedly cared for, loved, admired, or respected. Sad isn't it that people only tend to look at or love that which they are comfortable being around. <u>Unconditional love</u> is a word that is easier to describe than it is to do.

What would you do if a son; your husband, brother, father, cousin, or a dear friend confesses to you that he is a transgender and seeks to transition into his true feminine self? How should you treat or deal with her? Recall when I wrote that one size doesn't fit all? This is what I meant, as here are a few suggestions on how to react:

1) Try not to judge her and don't turn her away. Being a trans-woman is not a perversion, a weakness, or a sign of bad character. Don't talk or

spread malicious rumors about her to others. Educate yourself on her condition and what can be done to help your loved one or friend.

2) Even if you don't understand her reasons, do acknowledge that you will be there for her if she needs to talk. Her desire to change genders is not a phase that she is going through.

3) Practice tolerance and encourage the trans-woman to seek counsel, but do not pretend that the condition does not exist. Talk to the person, try to remain patient, listen to what she seeks to do even if you don't condone her action. Try not to abandon her to make her journey alone.

4) Do not ignore your loved one or friend. This only serves to make you grieve, embitters you toward the person's new identity, and it serves as notice to the trans-woman that you no longer care about what happens to her.

5) Do treat the trans-woman with the same compassion, respect, or love that you would if they had contracted some deadly or crippling disease. Practicing the golden rule is always a good thing to do with anyone, much less someone you love or who has been a close friend that is enduring the trauma and experience of changing her gender.

6) Don't dwell in the past. Life is lived forward, not backward. What happened yesterday is but a memory today. The trans-woman must change and transition into her new self. She must adjust her thinking to accept the person she is today or will become tomorrow. Let not your memories of who she lingered on affect your relationship with her in the present or future.

Shannon's favorite poem: "The Road Not Taken,"
By: Robert Frost

Which road did he take? Hopefully, it was the one that took him where he wanted and needed to go. If not, then backtrack and maybe it will be more rewarding to take the other road to get to your preferred destination.

Chapter 14:
Thinking ... and Transgender Transgressions

Recently, I heard some schools in Mid-America touting to their students about a new combination of evolution based upon the assumption of "Intelligent Design," which implies the existence of a CREATOR ... and neither that humankind, nor the universe resulted from happenstance or random sequencing of altered genes.

To hearken back to quoting Henry Drummond, consider his words as he confronts the prosecutor, Mr. Brady, in the infamous Scopes (monkey) Trial, reenacted through the film "Inherit the Wind." He said, "Yes! The individual human mind in a child's ability to master the multiplication table, there is more holiness than all your shouted hosannas and holy of holies. An idea is more important than a monument and the advancement of Man's knowledge more miraculous than all the sticks turned into snakes and the parting of the waters."

Continuing, he stated, "Then why did God plague us with the capacity to think? Mr. Brady, why do you deny the one thing that sets us above the other animals? What other merit have we? The elephant is larger, the horse stronger and swifter, the butterfly more beautiful, the mosquito more prolific, even the sponge is more durable. Or does a sponge think?"

To paraphrase Mr. Brady, he answered, "If God wanted a sponge to think ... it would think!"

Indeed, it would be so, for I am more inclined to align my own beliefs with that of Mr. Brady, but I also see some credence in the words of Mr. Drummond. I agree with and those who tout Intelligent Design. Scientists can harp all they want to about the irrefutable evidence of evolution, but I think they are missing the real point here. Did our world; did we just evolve out of nothingness? Anyone that can think will have to answer that question ... NO!

This planet, this solar system, this massive universe in which we are but a speck has to have some origin that came about by Intelligent Design. Whether or not one believes the Biblical account of the creation and Adam and Eve, surely nobody can refute that some supernatural being or entity started it all and formed it from the void. Something ... cannot come from nothing.

Indeed, Mr. Drummond's words ring true, as the ability to <u>think</u> is what separates us from animals and other species. Still, I have seen many animals that do have intelligence, though not as sophisticated as that of a human. It is that infinite ability to think that also elevates our ability to conceive of an all-powerful, all-knowing, omniscient Creator. Thus, Mr. Darwin might be right about some things in his theories, but so too are those who worship and give notice and praise to the Almighty power that breathed life into all of us.

The ability of a sponge to think is debatable, but one thing a sponge does well is to <u>absorb</u>, to soak in that with which it comes into contact. So too, should the person that <u>thinks</u> she should have been born a female absorb the world around her and the thoughts and ideas of those with whom she comes into contact. She should use the mind God gives her and learn, study, and form her own opinions of the universe and this biological engine that gives her living mobility, carries her through a period in time, and allows her to create thought, to love, act, and react with others. We should all use our minds to formulate, calculate, and evaluate every aspect of our lives, but please base your assumptions and decisions about your life and the existence of your creator and soul upon <u>FAITH</u>. In science, you may discover the map, but only by walking the actual pathway to God are you able to achieve setting your feet upon solid ground. There is no better way to come to know God and this universe than to trust and obey the Lord God Almighty.

※ ※ ※

There is one question in this book about how being transgender affects one's status and beliefs about religion. I'll address that question a bit here and then also later in the <u>question-and-answer format</u>. Based upon the evidence of biological predisposition, then how do those of us who <u>THINK</u> ourselves transgender and profess ourselves to also be Christians respond to those criticisms from others or <u>within our own families</u>? What sort of

Pink Heart

<u>transgender transgressions</u> does one bring forth with this GENDER identity condition?

Other than Vern, I have another brother that's a minister. He and my sister (now deceased) made the argument and stated emphatically that God doesn't make mistakes. From their fundamental religious point of view ... I was born a male and <u>I should forever remain that way</u>. They refused to accept me as a woman and to them what I am now is an affront to God. My being a trans-woman seemed to them to be a sin of the highest religious magnitude.

How did I defend or answer such claims and explain to them and others that I am not just some poor misguided lost soul? Should I have even bothered attempting to explain myself, or simply ignore them, as they did me, and then leave them and others to live with their own opinions? I have done that for the most part. I did, but the question remained and for you, the reader deserves an attentive answer.

First of all, I agree with them in one respect. I agree that God does not make mistakes. Thus, I categorically deny that my being transgender is a <u>mistake</u> or an affront to God. I do not feel that God made an error with me; He <u>just made me ... a trans-woman</u>. For those that would think otherwise, I pose these questions:

1) What of children born into the world who are blind, have a port-wine stain on their face or body, a cleft palate, are born with Aids, deformed limbs, twins with conjoined bodies? What of those born like my youngest daughter, whom I mentioned has kidney problems and had two kidney transplants before she was grown? She was also born with congenital problems and ambiguous genitalia? Are she and others merely biological errors or misfits? Any sane, compassionate person would have to answer such a question, "NO"! Most people would merely view these unfortunate beings as having been born with a deformity that's considered a handicap. The afflicted are not considered affronts to God; rather they are those born with <u>birth defects</u>.

2) <u>Why then are trans-women viewed any differently?</u> If perhaps a trans-woman's brain was somehow feminized before their birth, would not that become <u>their birth defect?</u> That's it plain and simple! Such a thing

causes an acute gender incongruity and their gender identity becomes the opposite of that of their biological birth.

3) If our brain is female, but our body isn't, what are we supposed to do? How are we supposed to live with that? Do we just ignore it, as so many think we could and should? That's easy for them to say, but impossible for those trans-women to ignore.

In my opinion, transgender people are a genetic anomaly anyway, so to me being born this way is as much of a biological blunder as that child born with a clubfoot, one that is Autistic, or one born with Downs Syndrome. We are none of us, some cosmic garbage, nor unworthy children of a wrathful God. Rather, I see God as a loving parent who wants the best for "all" His children. Since other trans-women and I are just that, one of God's children, then He wants the best for all of us who happen to have been born transgender or with some other physical, psychological, or mental anomaly. Nobody will ever convince me otherwise.

Keep focused on the target, breathe, relax, and let life carry your arrow where you need to go.

Holy Opinions, Batman

So, what of the opinions of my Baptist minister brother and my sister? I saw their opinions as just that … their opinions. To me, they based them on fundamentalist subjective interpretations of a topic that the Bible does not address, and in whose text the question of one being transgender does not exist. To me, their opinions are assumptions based on bias, and solely on misinterpretation and misinformation. As a trans-woman, I told them my true self was formed within the womb. They acted like deer in the headlights when I said that.

Pink Heart

God also created at birth my very essence, **my soul**, which is that everlasting part of me that is of the most value to Him and me. Although on earth my body is born to house my soul, by itself that body is nothing but flesh and bone. When it dies away it reverts again into dust. Whatever goodness I have or morals I've acquired was done so not because I was either <u>male or female</u>. Thus, I am not willing to give up my soul to Satan merely because others think I have committed some unpardonable sin by being a trans-woman. With all my heart, I do not believe I have. Sure, for the first ten or so years as Shannon I went through my "boudoir phase", plus I wore low-cut blouses and sundresses. With age, I stopped doing that and went back to regularly attending church worship. Even though I did derive pleasure from exhibiting my twin treasures, I have never been a fornicator, nor compromised my morality. I didn't do drugs unless you count estrogens, progesterone, and androgen blockers.

※ ※ ※

As a child, my adoptive parents took me nearly every Sunday to a very small Methodist church in Waco. Like secondhand smoke, if one is exposed enough to religion, sooner or later there is the absorption of the process. Thus, at an early age, I absorbed enough that I became passionate about God. I have always considered this a blessed dependence. Even as a youngster, I grew up hearing Bible stories about Jesus' love and His sacrifices for my sins. <u>I saw God not only in the church or the Bible</u> but everywhere. I saw Him in the miracle of a rose, felt Him in the loving embrace of my adoptive parents, in the clouds and clear blue sky, the green grass, the laughter of my children, in the dogs I've had, and in the wisdom of my gray-haired old grandmother. The presence of God has been with me for most of my life and He was not just some abstract entity, but a reality that I firmly believed in then and now.

My only contention with God is that He seemed to turn a deaf ear to my childhood prayers as I pleaded to Him, "<u>Oh, Lord…please make me a girl</u>," Still, even though that one nightly prayer seemed to go unanswered, did it? If it did, then why am I now living as Shannon and not Gordon? As I write later in this book and as the saying goes, "God's delays are not always His denials".

As for my Baptist preacher brother and sister's spurning me, I did not condemn them. I simply think they are stubbornly blind fundamentalists that allowed bias, ignorance, and misunderstanding to slant their views of my being transgender. I comprehend their reasoning, but just don't agree with it. As I see it, they each tried to <u>save me</u> from what they acquaint to my rushing into a burning building. What they couldn't possibly understand is that particular building has been on fire my entire life. Thus, I think they saw it as their duty to attempt to dissuade me from entering what they <u>perceived</u> to be a dangerous realm that would threaten my eternal salvation.

To them, my attempts to become a woman were somewhat like I was diving off into a pool with no water in it. I suppose the problem is not with their reasoning or motivation but is more with their <u>lack of familiarity,</u> education, and understanding of exactly what my condition entails ... and what is gender dysphoria.

My ministerial brother, God bless him, is a good example of a man who uses the Bible like a man trimming a tree uses cropping shears. Like so many in the clergy, he chooses certain select verses, lopping off a branch here or there from Deuteronomy, or elsewhere, to use as fodder for his arguments to me about gender and sexuality. He states these points of view as rigid canonistic examples that what I sought to do (become a female) as being against God's will – and that I will be chastised for it.

Unfortunately, this approach is all too common and to me, there is something very fundamentally dangerous and inadequate about such an approach. From my perspective, it sounds to me as if my good brother believes that I am nothing more than a man wearing women's garments, or in other words, only a transvestite that gets a sexual thrill out of cross-dressing.

In defining my brother's claims as to what God says on this subject, to me ... <u>he couldn't be more wrong.</u> He is in essence making flippant the Bible's text and assuming it has only a solitary meaning. That is to say, it's as if his selected Deuteronomy verse speaks for or against this particular conception of human sexual and gender identity when it does not.

Pink Heart

Using the Bible in such a method gives the impression of it being fractured and composed of fragments or even contentious parts. The Bible is not a book to be discharged, but neither do I believe it addresses every contemporary gender issue that confronts those of us in the modern-day world ... and especially not about the transgender condition.

My ministerial brother is a fundamental loyalist, schooled under the tutelage of the "Moral Majority" minions who claim the Bible is literal, unerring, unfailing, and provides us all of life's answers. I do not deny that possibility, but who is he to translate or interpret to me what those answers are concerning trans-women? My query to him, or anyone is this: <u>Who says that God is through talking to me, or through me</u>? Did God write just this one epitaph for humankind, or is He still whispering to our souls, speaking to us and <u>through us</u> in today's modern world? Maybe God made me transgender because He desires me to be one so that He can speak <u>through me</u> to the remainder of the humanistic world in an attempt to inflict wisdom rather than supposition, suspicion, or condemnation upon other of His children.

For example, I have tried to show others that all trans-women aren't like those that one sees on the Jerry Springer show or on Maury. Although my first ten years as Shannon weren't pious and or as good an example as I would have liked, it did help me grow in getting to know where I wanted to be and who I wanted to become as a person. I have regrets and admit I was trying to be "too sexy" for years ... and was ... but age tempers a lot of that urge and I've become more conservative and more as I should be.

If God is <u>alive</u>, and I am certain that He is, are only those blessed by <u>being clergy or those who consider themselves good normal Christians</u> the <u>only ones</u> who are saved and can hear His call, or feel His presence ... and no other of us? If I am transgender, has the door to heaven been closed to other trans-people and me? I certainly don't think that, nor can my brother prove it to me with any verse or combination therein within the Bible.

Yet, from those with such visualization, he and they would seem to have me become a marginalized human being, oppressed by sin and confused by Satan into believing that I should have been a female. How Christ-like is it to judge or condemn those who are transgender, or for that matter to judge anyone, even those who are bi, gay, and lesbian? Why must he or other Christians become anyone's moral or spiritual moderator?

God knows I love him, but that dear brother of mine, the whole of the world does not fit one image that you seem to have for it. Like I've written before, LIFE is not a one-size-fits-all in this world. We don't all act alike; we do not all look alike. We do not worship alike, we are not all thin or tall, and we are not all of one race or one nationality. We don't all speak the same language, we're not one ethnic group, we're not all rich or poor, not all of us are of one age group, nor are we all one sex ... or for that matter ... even TWO! We're all human beings with a soul and are a multi-cultured tapestry of God's creation.

Those who often proclaim themselves to be Christians speak a lot about having tolerance and understanding in this world and even our own nation decrees us a land of equality and justice. However, in reality, does the nation or its individuals practice it among every group of humans? More and more the American lifestyle seems to be drifting away from an affiliation with any formal church or religion.

Jesus saw us all as "Children of God." Sinners yes, and yet He spoke of unity and oneness with the Lord. Thus, we all have ready access to God through Jesus, and NOBODY will ever say anything to me to take that access away, despite my wilder days and more exotic ways.

Jesus tells us that we did not choose Him, but rather He chose us and He continues to care for us even now, in this dangerous and violent contemporary world. Unfortunately, the questions of truths in the Bible will remain interpretive. As long as scriptures are used as a *sound bite* off the evening news to validate such arguments against us who are transgender, then the possibilities for disagreement are almost endless.

Let Our Wounds Heal

Now that I am Shannon, I tried to put aside old wounds and let the scars heal as they may with the passing sands of time. Using a Bible verse of my own, I cannot forget, Matt. 5:44, that says, "I say unto you to love your enemies, bless them that curse you, do good to them that hate you, and pray

Pink Heart

<u>for them which despitefully use you and persecute you</u>." My beloved brother, my sister now in heaven, my ex-spouses, kids, and those others of my family or friends who have been critical or turned away from me shall receive my blessings, <u>not my curses</u>. Forget I must any transgressions that I thought they might have sent my way or any harmful, false judgments, as they too are human and make mistakes. I shall simply allow them to live their life and I attempt to live the remainder of mine.

The best things I can do are stay my course, remain faithful to my Lord, and serve Him, by example, as best I can. I live my life as Shannon and do so; by being a witness to others that one <u>can</u> still <u>be Christian</u> and transgender. As Jesus said, in Matthew 7:8-11, (Changing a few appropriate pronouns), "<u>For everyone who asks receives, and she who seeks finds, and to her who knocks the door will be opened. Or what parent is there among you, if his daughter asks for bread will give her a stone? Or if she asks for a fish will be given a serpent? If you then, being human know how to give good gifts to your children, how much more will your Father in heaven give good things to those who ask Him!</u>"

I asked and received not a stone, nor a serpent, but from His infinite mercy, I have been given the joyous gift and opportunity to live my life as a woman. I shall never take that gift for granted.

<u>I do not believe that God condemns me for wanting to become myself.</u> God is not shallow and He, above all others, knows my intentions are honest, pure, and that I have never meant to harm anyone. His love is unending and I find my spiritual comfort and solace in His promises.

Chapter 15:
Where to Now?

As a confessed trans-woman, the bottom-line question is: What should we who are transgender expect from the non-trans populace of this world and nation? As I see it, we transgender deserve no special concessions, no more or less; no better or worse treatment than you would give to anyone else. Simply put, we would like to be permitted to live our lives as we wish, to pursue our dreams of womanhood, and to be treated with respect and dignity. We do not wish to become a morbid curiosity nor a target for suspicion, accusation, or the victim of some hate crime.

From personal experience, I know that nothing anyone else can do to us even comes close to the self-inflicted persecution that most of us endure. We are different, but we don't deserve to be seen as outcasts or faux women. We too deserve the same chances for happiness that other females get without being looked at with reservation and mistrust.

Truthfully, I would guess most of us that are transgender don't expect the General Public to ever truly understand us, and there is a lot about ourselves that even we don't understand. Trans-people are unique, but we should not expect special privileges, nor should we make unreasonable demands on our society or government. All we should ask is for fair treatment and to be liberated from national, state, or local antiquated discriminatory laws.

As for me, I do whatever I can and do as I say ... I live now by example. Few trans-women I know would like being pointed out as being activists. In that regard, I'm also not like some that actively seek notoriety. Yet, neither should I turn away from the need to make known my point of view, which is why I wrote this memoir. All of us that are transgender can display integrity, dignity, candor, and strive to be one in our communities that make known our views without confrontation or disrespecting others.

Make our voices heard, and attempt to bring about positive change.

Pontificating

We transgender are not a threat to society, although I think some men look upon us (those of us who are male to female trans-women) with an

Pink Heart

indifferent and suspicious eye. Their fears of <u>castration</u> bewilder them as they question why any <u>man</u> would want to remove his penis and testicles, much less ingest hormones to make his bust and body-shape feminine, or dress and act feminine. Still, we who <u>are</u> consumed with this desire to become female do exactly that. So, the question is … WHY? Why go about seeking a course of action that will perhaps lead us to humiliation, ridicule, or financial ruin?

<u>That question is a key one</u>, and it has many answers depending on whatever person you are asking. We come from all walks of life, just as anyone could. Some trans-women I know are doctors, lawyers, salespeople, clerks, educators, computer technicians, athletes, booksellers, and musicians; just about any profession under the sun. Yes, sadly, some too are in the <u>oldest profession</u> and that deeply saddens and concerns me. By my rather open, low-cut blouses and tops, I feared others might think that of me, which is one reason I became more conservative as I aged. Growing older has that effect on many women.

I believe numerous people among the general public associate every trans-woman with this latter type of person and look upon our condition as being one of <u>sexual perversion</u> or immorality instead of a legitimate gender identity crisis with psychological reasons. But as I stated, who knows? Some of us just might be your husband, your brother, your neighbor, your co-worker, or in some cases even your boss!

Perhaps those who do mistakenly categorize and associate an MTF trans-woman as being a <u>loose woman</u> are due to the connotation of the word itself…<u>trans-sexual</u>. With the ending suffix being <u>sexual</u>, I believe this suggests astigmatic. All those who are ignorant as to what that word encompasses think it portrays only men having "sex changes," rather than as it is a legitimate psychological problem known more properly as gender dysphoria. As I pointed out before, it also involves those of both sexes and not just those that are males. Few, if any of the general public <u>perceive</u> or conceive that the word can also be attributed to females changing their gender to that of a male.

When some laypeople contemplate the word transsexual, they might attribute it in a comical sense to someone zany, with loose morals, and lurid, extreme dressing. For the most part, the TS condition has become a misunderstood phenomenon that is debated even today among members of the psychological and medical communities.

As a trans-woman, when you go <u>digging around</u> trying to create a new identity and life, it's a good bet that your old one is going to get buried in the process. If that's what you want, then power up, and start your engine.

In a male-to-female trans-woman's life, she might build a <u>dam</u> to hold back the bitter waters of <u>lies and deceit</u>, which she hides from those she loves. Not that she wants to, but it's her only way to live the life <u>expected</u> of him/her.

More Shannonisms:

If you're transgender, you're bound to get into more hot water than a teabag.

As a former "guy", my sage wisdom to all men: It's easy to figure out how to understand a woman. The only problem is … no man can figure out how. I hear two men in the world understand women. One is dead and the other went

Chapter 16:
One Step at a Time

As you might imagine, for the most part, our journey is one of solitude and is potholed with many obstacles and barriers. Yes, some of it is of our own making. For a trans-woman, a gender identity disorder is ever-enduring and it will follow her to the grave, unrelenting in the magnitude of its influence on her. In between, she will likely have denied it, attempted to purge it, and in due course ... if she's lucky, comes to accept it.

Ultimately, the trans-woman will seek to better <u>understand it.</u> With a compelling sense of wonder, she will have to learn that it is not a curse. Many see it as <u>an inevitable challenge to accept or deny</u>. I suppose it is an obsession one learns is eternal. At some point in a trans-woman's life, she learns to no longer fight the <u>woman</u> within her ... instead to embrace her with all her heart.

As is the case with all that has gender dysphoria, we came forth from <u>two separate</u> and distinct identities, each remarkably present within us. One was from having been <u>male</u>, the other one now from being <u>female</u>. Both have had the misfortune to share but one physical body. For me, I have been Shannon full-time for almost 24 years now. Living my life 24-7 as a woman has cured the sensation that I once had of feeling schizoid.

In this story, is a great deal of introspection and reflections from within my psyche. Why? As with a car's engine, only by lifting the hood, tinkering, and entering inside it, in this case, the mind of the trans-woman, can you truly begin to understand what it is that drives the car ... or in my case ... the trans-woman.

As noted, we are all dependent on so many others to help us get us to where we want to be. We receive help from numerous sources, not the least of which is our <u>peers</u>. We seek and obtain their advice and learn from their experiences or even more so from <u>their mistakes</u>. They often provide us with a mountain of information about which health and counseling professionals might best serve our needs.

Perhaps we who are transgender are a novelty of sort, perhaps even a curiosity to some, a quandary, and a conundrum to others. In the past, in my wigged-out, cross-dressing bad hair days, and far too much make-up, I often wondered if there were times when the gender signals that I projected confused some people and left them questioning if I were indeed a true female. Almost all who are transgender at one time or other during the transition process have produced mixed gender signals, which are doused in sexual ambiguity and androgyny. Some remain androgynous in many ways for the entire length of their transition. However, most trans-people seek to <u>blend</u> not just bend their gender, and draw attention to themselves.

Although most of us would prefer not to stick out in a crowd, for some that is tough not to do. I blend in and would have been more comfortable if I were shorter, but I can't help being the height I am. Still, I seek to impress on everyone who sees me that I am without a doubt a woman. If someone is <u>obvious</u> and <u>read as a being male</u> instead of the female they are dressed and desire to be, then they are not accomplishing their need to be identified with the female role. No one likes being laughed at, ridiculed, embarrassed, hassled by the law, or worse … arrested.

Even as feminine as I look; I have not always been a vault of confident womanhood. Via hormone therapy, rhinoplasty, a brow lift, breast augmentation and few other minor tweaks to my face (that's all I'll admit to) I became quite feminine. At the start of my journey. when attempting to pass in public, I often wondered how well I could blend into the masses when out among others. I worried that being my height as a female could be detrimental and a handicap. In truth though, it only became a barrier if I let it be one. Mostly it was just a mental thing that I had to overcome. In time, I did and paid little heed to what others might be thinking when I was exposed to the public. After I developed via HRT, no one ever doubted I was female, for I certainly didn't look male anymore.

Time, hormones, and surgery generally made me much more confident and impervious to attention. Now, when I am ready to go someplace, I simply go. I pass without any problems. As a younger woman, I'd toss back my hair, stick out my D cups, and strut out with feminine pride into the world as the **woman** I am, which is far more important. My gay friends and trans-sisters were very supportive and encouraging about my development as a woman. Without their love, friendship, compassion, and

Pink Heart

understanding, all this would have been a much more difficult process. Looking back on life when I first stepped out, I don't recall a single excess of my responsive first days of exposing myself as a female. My only regret over the years is certain occasions when I had possibilities that I didn't embrace. For the most part, though, I am a virtuous lady that enjoyed my opportunities, even though they came later in life.

Some trans-women are like that poor homeless man standing on the corner with his crude sign saying, "Will work for food. Please help, I'm hungry!" When folks who drive automobiles are confronted at a stop sign or red light by some poor soul proclaiming he or she is homeless and hungry, some drivers will help with a token donation (a kindness). However, as many others do ... they simply choose to <u>ignore</u> the panhandler and <u>avoid eye contact</u>. This lack of personal connection signals to the panhandler that the person driving or their passenger is apathetic and uncaring about the panhandler's problems. The driver and passenger just don't want to become involved. They are either disinterested, too stingy, or haven't the time or the inclination to help this person in any way. They choose instead to drive away as quickly as possible leaving the panhandler and his problems behind. Then too, in today's world, who knows if it is safe to do such a thing in the first place?

I believe that to some people, trans-women do indeed become sort of invisible to the general public's scrutiny. I can't say I've ever felt invisible, and I've gotten more than my share of lustful glances from men. Some of that likely because of the cleavage I displayed in my earlier exotic wear. Still, such feelings by a trans-woman are partly because trans-women don't want to be seen as being transgender and the same reasons drivers avoid eye contact and look the other way with that hungry, homeless man. Some people are too concerned with their own lives and problems to care about involving themselves with what they may perceive to be some derelict, outlandish, or even dangerous stranger. Thus, they turn a blind and indifferent eye toward those they see as insignificant or perhaps not needy. Such a plight is also shared by the ever-increasing homeless population plaguing large urban cities in the U.S.

Some folks may be filled with good intentions, but they do not always act on those intentions. Except for others thinking her attractive, the trans-woman seeks to be transparent as cellophane. I noticed (read) at all, she may only receive "the look" from a normal, and then simply collect a token glance or a snicker from a stranger that hasn't the time to bother with her.

Other Obstacles

This brings up another significant, yet disturbing question that post-op trans-women may face. What happens after GRS? Will she be attracted to males and desire to be with one? It is human nature to be curious, so most trans-women post-ops likely question what their reaction will be toward men. After surgery, men do become the opposite sex to the trans-woman. What were and are my reactions toward men? Did I become more attracted to men than women? The answer is simple … somewhat, but still more attracted to women. Does that make me bisexual? Perhaps, I suppose. I admit my being involved in an intimate session with a couple of men, but in truth, I am no more attracted to males as a sexual partner than I was as a man. I do now see things in some men that I find … attractive and engaging like a strong sense of machoism confidence. That is attractive.

Let me interject something here. I have made some foolish mistakes and bad relationship decisions in my past, some of which I will elaborate on later, but now I will not be untrue to Nicole and our domestic partner relationship. She is post-op herself and doesn't need to have to worry about me being unfaithful, or bedding down with someone else, then, now, or in the future. With the risks of contracting Covid, HIV, and AIDS, such a lifestyle would be foolish and dangerous anyway. If I expect her to remain faithful, then I must do the same. I pledged to her all my love and she shall receive no less than that. If that's unexciting to some of you, so be it, for even if I am a woman, I have learned that it's my responsibility to first and foremost be a "good" and descent person and loyal mate. Even when married to and living with the two women I loved, I was faithful, nor did I get involved in an affair of infidelity. I did have a brief affair with a man after divorce, but it never led to any commitment on my part.

In my life as Shannon, I have gone through various stages of existence. From the frilly, sexy boa stage, as is witnessed in some of my more explicit and exotic photos, to my sincere, conceived attempts at being femme and sexy. Since those early years of my transition, I have come full circle. At my present age, at long last, I leveled off into being a woman who lives a life synchronized by my better comprehension of being female, by a sense of conscience, common sense, and by my spiritual and moral values. If I had to describe where I am now and hope to be, I'd quote my counselor and say, I became a woman from the <u>inside out.</u> By that, I mean I am more concerned now with what it's like to <u>be</u> a woman than merely to just give the visual impression of looking like one. I attempt to exhibit class and dignity, not just the frivolity and exotic veneer that others saw when I first began my journey. Do I miss being younger and sexier? Sure, but life is a one way street and we all age and mature.

Hormonal Therapy

Some have asked me about my hormonal therapy. How did estrogen and progesterone physically or mentally alter me? I should explain at this point that endocrinology doctors in Ohio had me tested after my youngest daughter was born with ambiguous genitalia. I discovered my chromosomes are XXY. In truth, I've never quite accepted that but how does one explain that in my late twenties my nipples enlarged and my breasts began to swell. I developed, what was known as gynecomastia. Whatever the reason, hormone therapy and androgen blockers seem to have been very effective on me.

Although declared someone with <u>Klinefelter's Syndrome</u> (XXY), somehow, I was not rendered sterile. From all I've read, that is not typical, so something didn't seem Kosher. No physician or clinician has been able to explain to me why I can be XXY and yet was not sterile. By siring three kids by two women, I was not. The evidence of this fact is their existence; at least I think they are mine. :o) They look and act too much like me not to be, plus X1 and X2 were devoted and loving women who themselves were loyal mates. Also, unlike most with this condition, I am not mentally retarded; yet some might also argue that point as well.

After being on a female hormonal regimen for about three years, my male libido became virtually nonexistent. I mostly took an oral estrogen called, Estrace, progesterone, and an anti-androgen product known as Proscar, which oddly enough is a strong version of Finasteride, which is a drug used to counter the effects of prostate problems and is the core ingredient for Propecia, a hair re-growth formula for men. I did take Spironolactone (Aldactone), but it gave me too many leg cramps and I couldn't pass up a toilet, so I ceased taking it. It is a mild diuretic and will help prevent fluid retention and thwarts body hair growth as well in some.

My original gynecologist (a very kind man) who prescribed for me retired, so I found a new lady doctor that prescribed for me. In the past, I have been on Premarin and Estinyl. I took 60 mg per day of progesterone, which greatly helped with breast growth. I have also taken Estradiol valerate injections once every two weeks. The oil-based estrogen did not pass through the liver, so it is easier on the system, but harder on the rump or thigh where you must inject a syringe. One downside of doing the injections was that I reacted to the oil base and my face sometimes broke out in a reddish, scaly rash. Yuck!

I used to think I could never self-inject, but the promise of the benefits from the estrogens outweighed any trepidation that I had of needles. The Estradiol worked extremely well as an enhancing hormone, especially for a post-operative, and my female secondary-sex characteristics and physical development topped out after about three years of regular hormonal dosage.

Physical changes from hormone therapy come subtly and slowly, but surely. The key is to remain patient and not to overdose. For a pre-op trans-woman, the desired effect is one known as being chemically castrated, so that feminine blood levels and female sex characteristics develop.

Some trans-women despise their genitals so much that they elect to have an orchiectomy (castration) even before having GRS. Nicole and I have a good friend that did this and nine months later had her GRS. My question is, why bother? If GRS is the goal, then plan for that and be patient. I do understand the desire, but a basic castration can lead to future problems with vaginal depth at the time of GRS and constructing a neo-vagina. It is best, I think, to endure and tolerate one's genitals until GRS.

My ministerial brother says my <u>penis was not</u> some <u>birth defect</u> and that it had functioned well, as is evidenced by the existence of my children. Duh!

Pink Heart

I cannot deny the obvious fact that it did operate and that I did sire my children via the prior appendage between my thighs. Yep, my babies got here via the fruit of my loins. Yet, to him, I would say, at that time in my life it was my only physical option and outlet for sexual pleasure. Keep in mind, we are transgender, but we too need to express pleasure by what nature provides us. We can continue doing so even after GRS if we later have a skilled GRS surgeon that fashions nerves onto a clitoral like a tiny appendage and creates a sensitive vaginal canal. Estrogen intake greatly increases the pleasures and arousal a trans-woman derives from breast and nipple manipulation during sex. I can attest that there is such a thing as breast orgasms … and wow!

The alternative I had was that science and surgery can and do modify an MTF trans-woman's penis and the testicles and reconstruct them into female appearing genitalia. In that respect, the trans-woman needs the tissue components within those genitals, even though after a lengthy period of hormone therapy, the penis is likely used only as a funnel for urination and is of little to no further use.

Once I accepted what I am, I could then plan to correct what I considered to be a physical abnormality from my birth. With the advances in modern surgery, it's as I stated, for it's certainly possible that a trans-woman can experience genital pleasure as a woman, or as near as we can become to a woman. Unfortunately, there is no surgical procedure that can alter my chromosomes to lop away that Y chromosome and have me become XX or afford me a working genetic uterus. I should point out, that merely having a vagina does not make one appear to be or to act like a woman. People do not see our genitals when we walk down a street. They see the whole package; attire, make-up, hairstyle, mannerisms, feminine figure, etc. That is how they perceive our gender and sex, not whether or not we have a penis or vagina, for that is assumed and hidden beneath our panties. Appearing, as a female is superficial, yet, as I stated before, the book that is seen is judged by its cover. So, we that are MTF trans-women should attempt to be as feminine as we can be!

The female hormones helped stimulate my breast growth. With the help of adding progesterone (started later), I became better than a B cup before having implants years ago. I became a full D cup, and it looks nice on me. Unfortunately, there has for me been an unwanted effect of the hormones … that being a struggle to control my weight I aged. I developed hypertension ten years ago and was taken off hormone therapy a couple of years ago because of it. I've lost the excess weight, but it's been a struggle. I had mild depression because of that and especially when my breasts went from a D cup to around a large C cup. It's not that big a deal, but it was disconcerting. If I am ever in a car wreck and drift into a coma, I've instructed Nicole and all relatives to not let them awaken me <u>until I'm a size 7</u>. With my height, I'd look absolutely like a living skeleton. I've back on estrogen again for years now and back to my D-cup. Like all transwomen, I shall be on hormones the rest of my days.

My male muscles all disappeared. My skin on hormones became soft as a baby's behind, albeit now I'm an older <u>baby</u>. Hey! You'll age too if you live that long. I gained girth in my hips and my buttocks became rounder and plumper, to the point of being able to sit a tray of drinks on the ledge without spilling a drop. ;o)

Like most females my age, I have to exercise to fight off cellulite. My hands, forearms, and feet are about the same, but my arms and wrists are noticeably thinner. I suppose it's from the <u>hormones</u>. In the beginning, I was somewhat self-conscious of my hands and forearms, but in time they too softened, got smaller, and became more feminine; wearing longer nails helps a lot. I keep my nails long and often polished, but these days mostly I wear a French gel unpolished style. That helps with the overall feminine appearance I seek to display.

I've no body hair left, not even under my arms, nor on my legs. On hormones, my face became much more attractive and feminine than before estrogens. I found it to be amazing. It is subtle and took about a year to slowly soften and transform. There is no great change in the tone of my voice, except I do have more range, which I notice when I sing. I sound very femme when I make a conscious effort to do so. However, holding that pattern takes concentration and there are times I don't do enough of concentrating. No big deal! People don't judge me by the tone of my voice; rather they do so by my appearance, which is completely female. Talking

Pink Heart

as a woman is mostly second nature to me, but it may never become natural and will always require effort. I am a high tenor anyway, so with practice, I've managed to be more of an alto and to sound feminine. My blood pressure meds have kept me stable now, and my PSA is as low as anyone my gynecologist has ever seen, as is my cholesterol. My pituitary, though once inflamed by overdosing on "Mexican" estrogens and my liver are both fine now. In the past six years, I developed chronic kidney disease, although I am not at a stage where I need dialysis. I must be careful of my diet and be certain to stay hydrated.

Observing your life through a magnifying glass may seem to make things clearer and in focus, but ... be sure it doesn't just amplify your problems. Have a "my" exam and correct any vision of transition being like looking through rose colored glasses. It is a life-changing decsion and "nothing" will ever be the same. Yet, going through "The Change" is and can be amazing if you do things the right way.

I would caution anyone that is transgender to not self-administer hormones without being monitored by a physician. That can prove to be lethal or at least lead to other physical complications.

The hormones won't make me shorter or younger either. I have tried to repeal the law of gravity, but alas I cannot.

Looking at your reflection in a mirror will show you the reality of your your soul. physical being, but you must look from within if you are to see the essence of your soul.

Doctors demand, "Show me the money!" If you truly desire to have GRS, get breast implants, do hours and hours of electrolysis (Ouch-Couch), and then have facial feminization surgery ... save lots of cash, for you'll need it, as insurances probably won't cover elective surgeries. Feminizing your voice takes practice or surgery for those that choose it.

As for how estrogen therapy affects a trans-woman's mental and emotional state ... I can only tell you that it did not have any effect at all on me. That's right! I said it, so you can believe it or not. No, don't argue with me, and those are not tears in my eyes ... I just didn't get enough sleep last night. Darn that romantic show, "An Affair to Remember." I mean, who could sleep with all those dogs barking outside. If I see my neighbor today, I'm going to choke him and his dogs. Ahem! Excuse me; I suppose I did seem a bit emotional and unhinged there for a few moments ... didn't I? So, why are you asking me silly questions like did hormones make me emotional? Yes, of course, they do ... err did ... silly-willy. I still like sports and other things that I enjoyed as a male.

Huh # 2: Chihuahua Dreams:

Here's a funny doggone tale. When I was in high school my adopted dad developed a bad case of insomnia. He visited his doctor, who prescribed some strong sedative-type sleeping pills.

In the meantime, we had a small Chihuahua that was getting on in age and developed a skin condition causing her hair to thin and fall out. It wasn't a skin disease, but it made her look awful. The condition also made her listless and she had no energy. My adopted mom took her to the vet, who prescribed a bottle of special vitamin pills that would help raise the dog's energy level, correct the iron deficiency that caused its skin rash, and help restore its thinning hair.

One hot day I came in from school and dad was outside sweating like a pig as he mowed the lawn in his undershirt. Mom was inside busily cooking dinner and taking a meatloaf out of the oven. I tossed my books down, while the other of our dogs, a small Pekinese came running up to greet me. I waited for a second or two, expecting to see "Tina", our Chihuahua come running up as well, for it was the way she greeted me each afternoon. She did not. I looked through our house and called her by name.

Mom heard me calling and stopped her kitchen chores to help me look for Tina. I pulled up the dust cover on their bed and there under the bed lay little Tina, all stretched out and not moving a muscle. Her tongue hung from her mouth and her eyes were closed. Mom reached in, shook her, and then dragged her out from under the bed. She lifted poor Tina, but the dog was limp and unresponsive. Mom's face went ashen and she tossed the dog about a foot into the air and screamed, "Oh my Lord, she's dead!"

Tina hit the hardwood floor with a limp thud and I too thought she was dead. I looked closely at Tina and saw something puzzling. I placed my head close to her mouth where I felt and heard her breathe. The dog was snoring. She wasn't dead, she was asleep.

Here's what happened. Mom got the meds mixed up and instead of giving dad his correct pill; she gave him the dog's vitamin pills and gave Tina one of dad's sleeping pills. We rushed Tina to the vet and they pumped out her stomach and kept her till the next morning. When we brought her home, that poor dog couldn't walk straight for a week. However, dad was a bundle of energy for weeks, He claimed he'd never felt better, and he finally grew two hairs on his chest. I think mom asked the vet for a year of refills.

Another Shannonism:

All you want-to-be trans-girls … don't go through life camping at the complaint counter. If you're living a "double life," it just means that you're getting nowhere fast.

Some trans-girls I knew that would self-medicate bought into bogus products that they found pitched on the Internet. They wasted their time and money placing their hopes on fake estrogens, bust creams that don't work, or some other quick method of becoming feminine. Only legitimate exams, hormonal prescriptions, and monitoring by certified physicians, labs, and endocrinologists will work and be safe for a trans-woman. One should also be cautious and carefully decide on which surgeons you allow to modify anything on your body.

Chapter 17:
Responsibilities

One contention that others and I that are gender dysphoric wrestle with is the claim that our motives are selfish and not Christian. We who were once married are often criticized for shirking our familial responsibilities to pursue our self-interests. These same critics proclaim we have a foremost duty to tend to our children's needs, and then to be the spouse we pledged ourselves to be to our betrothed.

I cannot deny that as a parent and as a spouse, that I had duties and responsibilities that must be addressed. Those responsibilities, including a strong loving bond with my mate, were a major factor in my having delayed so long in doing something about my transgender nature.

It was not my intent to forego any such responsibilities, but neither could I any longer deny seeking my true self or this one last opportunity to find exacting peace and self-contentment. The goal of <u>attempting to find my proper self</u> was <u>never</u> based on an endeavor to <u>alienate my family</u> and friends in the process ... or to separate myself from Christ and God. I simply sought to establish <u>rightness</u> in my life and I never felt right as a male. Realize this, if nothing else some things in life <u>just are</u> and my being transgender is one of those cases.

My need to reconcile my <u>body image</u> with that of my gender identity truly haunted and hounded me 24 hours a day, 7 days a week, and 365 days a year. This obsession would not go away. Self-denial, sacrifice, and service to my family were important issues to me, but in the end, Gordon could not win the conflict going on within him. For my sanity and self-preservation, I had little choice but to seek self-actualization. In the end, I could not refuse myself this one last chance at feminine fulfillment and peace of soul.

If my following this path in life was a selfish sin, then I am just as certain now that God has forgiven me. I pray that somehow, so too will my ex-wives, children, siblings, and former friends.

Bless the Dear Children

The one issue that has bothered me as much as anything with my transition was in having to reveal myself to my children, most especially to my youngest daughter and my son. Telling them was in many ways more difficult for me and harbored as much concern as it was telling my spouse. I worried that I might taint them in some way, embarrass them to their peers, and create in them some emotional or psychological problem. I was even concerned that they might harbor resentment and come to hate this new me. As it turns out, that concern proved to be legitimate. I don't think they hate me, but their absence in my life then and now does not exhibit their endearment for what I am or what I did in becoming Shannon.

Even though my youngest daughter became more at ease around me, none of my children embrace me as Shannon, even though I once thought they both had come to accept me. That was a ruse on their part, as each harbored their grudge toward me as Shannon for leaving them fatherless. My son is grown, married, and has his kids and still has serious problems in dealing with the demise of his father. My youngest daughter married three years ago and she too now avoids me. As for understanding, they each had their conceptions of what I was doing. They did not, nor could they completely comprehend the reasons why I did it. I wrote to each of them several times to explain my motives, but they did not respond.

From the start, I never made it my intention to, nor did I harbor any false hopes of getting custody of my youngest daughter. I knew she would be better off away from me. That would afford her time to adjust to the idea of my being a woman and it would give me time to become one. At this writing, she is but thirty-one years of age, so those maturing years and learning more about my condition have not positively affected her in our now non-relationship. She's still bitter about my divorcing her mom.

She has many health issues, including two kidney transplants, plus being born without a bladder had radical surgery at the age of five. In an eight-hour operation where surgeons created an internal pouch out of a portion of her intestines so that she could catheterize through her navel (now a valve for urinating). I have had some, but little contact with her, and I have tried not to be intrusive into hers, her brother's, or either of my ex-spouse's lives.

Pink Heart

<u>I do not see their concerns as trivial or unimportant</u>. My transition placed a lot of grief, personal and financial burden upon all of them. I love them too much to want to see them hurt more. I hoped that their mother would not paint me in too bad a light and rather would leave it to my daughter to decide for herself in a few years what the future of our relationship would entail. In retrospect, my ex did nothing to encourage my daughter's relationship with me. On the contrary, she did all she could to dissolve it.

My son is a remarkably resilient young man, so I am confident his heart is pure and that he wishes me no malice. He fell in love with a young girl and married her. I believe it was best for me to just bow out and let them both live their own lives as they wish. I desire that both my daughters and he shall one day reunite and that they will see that I am more comfortable and congruent with myself now that I am Shannon. If that never happens, then I will pray that their lives are happy, even without me in them. I can only attest to the fact that I love each of my children and I miss them tremendously.

Oddly enough, of those I raised, only my X-2's daughter keeps tabs on me, tells me she loves me, and we email back and forth regularly. She thanked me for all I did when she was a child and knows that I love her.

Chapter 18:
Eye of the Beholder

Too often the tendency is to overlook the inherent worth of humans. In the text, I noted that people still judge the book by its cover. Our society today is obsessed with youth and beauty and one cannot pass by a magazine rack or watch television without being bombarded by ads that display scantily clad, young, curvy, and beautiful female models that emphasize ways to improve your looks or make you feel better.

As an aging female, I look for products to help me reduce wrinkles or some magical new diet aid. Thank goodness for my "Retinol to help keep wrinkles to a minimum. Then there comes some new supplement drink or potion that will keep us from aging or some herb that will make us more immune to contracting Covid-19, or even kidney disease and cancer. Let's not forget those extreme makeovers we've seen on television using some new cosmetic surgery procedure that will peel away years of aging from your face or body. The bottom line is the pursuit of staying young and the possibilities of improving our physical selves captivate all of us. The possibilities achieved via cosmetic surgery are admittedly tempting and amazing. Many trans-women have what is called "facial Feminization Surgery," which does amazing things to their profile, noses, brows, chins, and eyes.

At my age, I find that I now look through eyes made wiser by life's experiences and have learned much from my own mistakes. Although I too have sought methods, means, and wouldn't mind something like a face-lift to improve my physical appearance as I age, there are far more other things of interest to me that also prove to be rewarding. The internal and external pressures I had when I was younger and the responsibilities of raising a family are behind me now. I still provided child support for my youngest daughter up until she was twenty-six years old, but my life is much less complicated now and I find more time to relax and just be me.

Pink Heart

The valuable things in life are not just those material possessions we all crave or the superficiality that we assign to beauty. Rather I think that each individual must seek their definition of what beautiful is to them and within themselves. Truly, one's <u>perspective</u> of themselves and others lies in the values we place on one's inner beauty. Some of the most physically beautiful women I've ever known were also some of the most shallow, arrogant, and self-centered. There is nothing I envy more than a woman who is symmetrical and aesthetically beautiful in every way, and yet also exudes with that persona inner confidence, intelligence, enthusiasm, and compassion for herself and others.

Pretend You Don't See Her

The following analogies contain more in-depth introspection and illustration of the psychological aspects of being transgender:

A trans-sister of mine once sent me copies of two books, signed by their authors. If you read a lot of books and novels you probably know these two distinguished individuals. One book was written by Mary Higgins Clark entitled, <u>"Pretend You Don't See </u>Her." The other book is by one of my favorite macho actors, Charlton Heston, entitled <u>"To Be A Man</u>." My friend worked in the bookstore that hosted this book signing, and she simply randomly sent me these out of the goodness of her heart because she knew I liked these authors. I was intrigued and began to consider their titles. After a brief hesitation, I began to chuckle and reflect on the irony of each one. No unknown can match the one I have lived on. So, the mystery, "Pretend You Don't See Her," grabbed me by my psyche.

That book title was a perfect description of how we trans-women often react to being gender dysphoric. Much of the time in my male life, I pretended <u>not</u> to <u>see her</u>; sort of like that homeless man I described earlier whom everyone ignores. Essentially, I sprayed OFF Pest Repellent on my psyche hoping to rid myself of her. I wanted her to leave me alone, to stop bothering me … but knew that wasn't going to happen. Yet, the other side of my mirror is where she lurked, and no matter how hard I tried to imagine she wasn't there, she always lingered.

If the eyes are the windows to the soul, then the mind is the doorway. For all those years the door to my mind was neither open nor shut, rather I'd describe that it was left ajar. I was neither inside, nor outside, simply caught somewhere in between. In a way, Shannon was locked inside a padded cell inside my mind. However, at some point, Shannon firmly wedged her foot therein and she came forth through that doorway and into the open room inside my mind. At long last, I could see her, and better yet…yearned to become her.

Before, I often closed my eyes to the truth and then turned away from this obsession deeming it unfit and possibly aberrant. I guess I listened to one too many Baptist preachers.

One consistency I've noticed in most trans-women is that we are our own worst critics. This <u>self-condemnation</u> led me into depression and paranoia of sorts. In many ways I felt I was a split personality, (there's that reference to being schizoid again) feeling slighted, cheated by birth, and that my whole male existence was some sort of a bad dream; a cosmic joke pulled on me by my creator. My correct nature could never truly exert itself because of excuses and my sense of guilt. As a result, my male personality became prevalent, for it was far easier to deny my accurate nature than to face it. Yet, no matter how hard I pretended not to see her, she was always there ... waiting, hoping, growing in strength, and her existence undeniable!

More than twenty years ago, after being brutally honest with myself, I confessed my transgender desires to myself and others. I received the confirmation I already knew was true. No one had to <u>tell me what I was</u>. I simply admitted the obvious! I came to terms with my gender identity disorder. (If you want to call it a disorder…I don't!) With this revelation, came purpose and direction to my muddled life. I discussed my future with my wife and others of my family, my counselor, and other doctors. The challenges were evident, yet I had a new mindset and a new vision of what I was and wanted to be. Instead of <u>pretending she wasn't there</u> in my mind's mirror, I chose instead to accept and become her. All these years, I've not seen anyone else therein except her! I came to find a sense of peace within me, and the beginnings of true happiness. With acceptance came peace…at long last! Also, there was anticipation for the future.

Pink Heart

Certainly, though I tried for over forty-four years to be a man, I am not, nor never was adept at doing so. My heart just wasn't in it. However, I do hope Mr. Heston's grandson and my son can achieve such status. I no longer had the desire to be a man and I am satisfied with my choice of becoming a woman. As I've heard it said, an MTF trans-woman has to prove her dedication by being man enough ... to become a woman. The once-divided mental complex has to become melded into but one feminine personality. For me, there was no more confusion or delusion on the matter. By the way, my heart and prayers go out to Mrs. Heston for Mr. Heston passed away from the ravages of time and Alzheimer's disease. Truly, I loved his acting and charisma. That terrible dementia also took the life of my sister that was a little over three years older than me.

As I expressed it to one trans-sister, if I now walked out my door in drab (dressed as a male), I'd feel as though I were cross-dressing and being sort of a reverse transvestite. Male clothing no longer fits nor feels right. I wear women's clothes because I am a woman in every sense of the word. I will never again have any desire to dress in any way but feminine. Therefore, I exist in a somewhat contradictory realm, part of a historical separation of human male and female. We all bring with us through life dualistic modes of thought influenced by our past and our society. The dichotomy of being male or female has always existed and resonates throughout the eons whereby each sex articulates itself by certain ways of thinking.

However, the roles and nature of women are shifting, especially in this country. Career women, lesbian couples, and many of today's modern women defy the logic of our patriarchal-dominated society. The true definition of female is more multifaceted and diverse today than ever before. The sexual segregation that once reigned and consigned women to sub-ordinate roles and fewer responsibilities, thus less money has evolved into greater opportunities and more open minds by employers, some of whom are in women-dominated companies. The chief operating officer of the last company I worked for is a woman. She got her Master's degree from SMU in business and is a bright and shining example of the success women can and do achieve in today's world.

Achievement, not which sex and gender one is determines the true measure of human definition ... not whether one is male, female, or transgender. Prejudices still exist, as was evident when a former employer released me when I tried to transition from Gordon to become Shannon. A trans-woman does not suddenly become stupid or unlearn all those skills and things she acquired as her male counterpart. Estrogens did not dim my brain cells. On the contrary, they freed me from many distractions that before, as a male, kept me from fully concentrating on the job I tried to do.

I would tell all trans-women that you too can succeed and that even if it is a man's world, they can and do recognize achievement and ability. Still, you have to become like them in so many ways. I suppose one could say I had an advantage because I once was a male. Maybe there's some truth to that, for I know how the game was played, yet we still have to perform and prove our worth by doing. Even an inept manager will usually recognize skill, value, and worth in an employee, so go the extra mile and you'll more often than not be rewarded. Like Shannon, I was a woman at work, but I never used any sexist remark or flirtatious come on to advance my cause. Well, except for my wearing low-cut blouses. Maybe that stirred some loins, but if it did, the men I worked with knew better than to come on to me about it. I simply showed up, was dependable, and exhibited to everyone that I can perform. Management told me they appreciated my professional attitude and willingness to do whatever it took to do the job right. We trans-women can ask for acceptance, but the best way to get it at work is to earn it.

Pink Heart

My "Boa" stage - Many girls go through this. I did too.

A Shannonism Question / Answer:

How can she assert to be so unsoiled, when at times looking so exotic? Well, I mellowed with age and cleaned up my act, so now I put my best foot forward ... when walking in the dark. And after I finish this "Huh." you'll understand why when I bend over now ... it's only to put on my shoes.

Another Boudoir Moment

Now There's No Man in The Mirror

Pink Heart

Even if a trans-woman doesn't think she "measures up" to genetic cis-women, she should learn to be the "ruler" of her own life.

The right timing is important when the trans-woman plans to transition. Recognize the opportunity and turn off the alarm.

Many trans-women wish there was a magic fountain or waters to soak in to become true females. Instead, we brave the seas of challenge and do what we can.

Huh #3: <u>Flop Shot</u>:

This is about a real "<u>coming out</u>" party. My roommate and best friend, Nicole, and I had some dear gay male friends that lived near downtown Dallas in a ritzy, high-rise condo <u>penthouse</u>. When I lived in Dallas, they often had me over for parties, which the one I'm about to mention was about a year before a couple of femme procedures I had before going 24 / 7 as Shannon. One night, I attended one of their festive occasions at their lavish residence.

Also in attendance were several women lesbian friends of theirs, plus many others, all of whom were gathered in our friends' living room and having cocktails before dinner. Back then, I had been on estrogens for almost two years and had developed about a small C-cup bosom. Like many women, I preferred that my bosom was rounder and fuller. Because of my height, I felt such a "fuller" look would make me better proportionally ... and sexier. Therefore, I padded my bra with a pair of soft silicone breast forms that I'd bought in an expensive department store. They were known as "<u>Curves</u>" and fit nicely inside a bra, tucking under whatever natural assets I had to push them upwards, increasing my <u>cleavage</u> and making it appear my bosom was at least a fell cup sizes larger.

I remember wearing a summer dress, casual, but low-cut in front, yet in a classy way to reveal just the right amount of bosom. I had somewhat darker blond hair then and got some stares and smiles from the women. From the men, most of whom were gay, I got only an occasional glance below my shoulders or neck.

The stately furnished condo had beautiful dark oak hardwood floors and its living area was spacious, with the furniture arranged in a manner way so that we could mingle close together. A half-hour after arriving, I stood sipping my drink while I small talk with a few of the guests.

Pink Heart

My Lord! I'm Glad I Don't Need Falsies Anymore

    As I was sipping my cocktail, I took the little umbrella out and meant to suck on the cherry stuck to it. Instead, I dropped the cherry from my drink to the floor. When I went to pick it up, to my horror and surprise, one of my "Curves" popped out from under my right bosom and fell towards the floor. I watched in startled disbelief as the soft, <u>skin-colored silicone gel boob</u> tumbled to the floor. The Earth and time seemed to slow as I stared frozen and in dismay while the fake boob fell in slow motion before my eyes and slapped loudly upon the floor like a limp carcass. The dull "thud" echoed through the condo and my somewhat dull mind.

    Almost instantly, about a dozen pairs of eyes diverted to the floor and the lifeless, non-moving skin-colored jelly-fished-shaped object lying there before them. At first, I grabbed at the bosom from which it fell, and then as I saw the shocked looks on the faces of those present, even that of my two gay male hosts, I had to react quickly and perform "damage control." I'd already suffered embarrassment enough.

    I casually bent down, picked up the squishy wad of silicone-pink jello, quickly tucked it back inside under my bra, and then retrieved and ate the cherry down in a swift gulp. I turned to all the crowd and said, "Darn thing has a mind of its own sometimes. I suppose it doesn't like cherries." The women snickered, the men laughed, and then the party continued and I had to step out on the balcony for some fresh air.

A year later, I'd saved enough to nearly get my breast implants. Nicole helped and paid some of the fees, teasingly claiming afterward that my right boob belongs to her. So, I gladly assigned the retired "Ethyl" and "Cherry" Curves to the bottom drawer of my vanity and forever out of circulation at any more parties. No, you may not borrow them!

Section 2:
Questions Along the Way

QUOTE: APOLLINAIRE
"Come to the edge, he said. They said ... we're afraid! Come to the edge, he said ... and so they did. He pushed them ... and they FLEW."

* * *

Throughout my decades upon this planet, many have asked me some very interesting personal questions, seeking my input, ideas, and thoughts concerning this odyssey I call my life; about direction, and where I think life's journey will eventually lead.

My written responses herein are the results of pondering and contemplation; thus, they are less spontaneous than my vocal answers would be. Nevertheless, these thoughts came from legitimate questions asked me by peers, family, friends, or professionals who counsel trans-women. We are all the <u>sum</u> of our life experiences. Therefore, I call upon remembrance, topics of interest, research, and issues that I've learned over the years to shape this section into my thoughts and phraseology.

This type of subjective format will hopefully clarify to both non-trans-people and those like myself about the many obstacles trans-women may face. It will chronicle some of the enormous challenges and costs that are incurred along the way. Hopefully, it will also bring enlightenment about the other side of the gender coin. More often than not, most relatives or friends think more of their loss; they generally fail to comprehend the enrichment and satisfaction derived by the trans-woman from facing and dealing with this life-altering obsession. Perhaps too, my opinions and perspective may provide useful insights to these third parties whose lives are or were touched and affected, whether positively or negatively by knowing someone who is transgender.

In this section, I would present to the reader more circumspection about the psychological aspects of this gender dysphoric condition. From that perspective, the digression of mental issues covered herein will from time to time be presented in a **third-person** scenario. Perhaps that may seem a bit more schizoid, (Dang! There's that word yet again…am I trying to tell you something? No, but I am! Shut up, you'll confuse them all! Hey, if they aren't confused by now, you haven't been trying hard enough. Close your pie-hole, dummy, and just explain ourselves!) Ahem! Ignore them! Let us go on then.

Anyway, it is but a format style that allows me to describe a point of reference between my past <u>male</u> personality and <u>she</u> that has always been there inside me; that being my <u>Shannon</u> identity. Perhaps some of the following answers and comments may seem mentally redundant, but I assure you it is as expected, for being trans is a redundant obsession. It's a way of allowing you, the reader, to crawl around some more inside the mind of a trans-woman in ways that <u>Normals</u> are not often privy to doing.

all my kaleidoscope of opinions and comments about this pink continuum expressed as best I know-how.

Working as a woman in a corporate environment, you should be sure you understand that sometimes … the higher up the ladder you get, the longer the fall. Ambition is a good thing if tempered with common sense and being smart about how you handle those above you on the ladder.

PART 1

Question 1: How did you come by the name Shannon and did you ever go by any other names?

As stated, my male name was Gordon. As for my femme name, <u>Shannon Leigh O'Shea</u>, that came about from taking my youngest daughter's middle name (Shannon). I chose Leigh as my middle name because of the female star of "Gone With The Wind." <u>Vivian Leigh</u>. Over the years, before legally taking on the name of Shannon Leigh, I had called myself <u>Sabra</u> and <u>Michelle</u>. I loved the name Sabra, but Shannon was a name I liked and one I could go by if forced to remain in my male role for an extended period. That's <u>a hint</u> to those who may consider changing their name before going full-time. There are unisex names like Pat, Sean / Shawn, Billy / Billie, Tony / Toni, Gene / Jean, Jesse, etc. that can be applied to either the feminine or masculine gender.

Before going full-time as a woman, I had legally changed my name to Shannon. I still worked in drab as a guy, so I needed a male name a bit longer. A trans-woman may also choose to take out a DBA (Doing Business As) with the county in their previous male's name to use until it is no longer needed. I did that. That way, it avoided any charges of fraud and was legal for banking needs, or until all credit cards; utilities, etc. got changed over.

The key to changing names is timing. The Trans-woman must decide to switch over the whole of her gender identity at the time of her name change or to merely get the paperwork out of the way before she decides to change her entire identity. Either way can be risky if one is not prepared to counter the possible objections to be raised. Needless to say, any male going to change his name and gender should appear as feminine as possible before the court judge. Those who don't will regret it.

Question 2: What sort of person are you, Shannon? What are some of your best characteristics?

This is a question my gender counselor asked of those attending her support group meetings. I believe she attempted to make us more cognizant of the positive things we each think of ourselves. How we view ourselves is often how others perceive us. For me, I know that I am a far happier person as a female than I ever was as a guy, so for that reason as much as any other I believe others perceive me as being a nicer person. Truly, I attempt to not judge people and to let them live their lives as they see fit. I would hope and expect that they would give me the same considerations. I know the people with whom I know and interact at my church all treat me fairly and without any bias.

I think it's important for every human being, transgender or not to have a <u>sense of humor</u>. As you can probably gather by my accounts of past incidents in the "Huh?" sections of this story that I love laughing and making people smile. I admit that I have sometimes used humor to mask my self-doubt as a mechanism not to reveal my true thoughts, much as a circus clown does when he applies his greasepaint and clown nose. Remember in the beginning when I spoke of wearing masks. Laughter is often just such a mask.

Still, for the most part, my sense of humor is genuine and I often find I must rely on my wits and be adept at spontaneity. Hopefully, I have several redeeming qualities, but most of all I am proud of the fact that I am loyal, loving, a respectable parent, friend, and now more than in my past I am a moral person. I do try to be compassionate and show temperance with those who might not agree with my way of thinking but won't hesitate to give you my opinion on matters that are important to me.

Nicole, my dearest friend, and mate know I can be stubborn as a mule, but in the end, more often than not I can discern right from wrong and weigh out a scenario. I believe in accountability, seeking to avoid being overly defensive and as I've matured, I've learned better how to admit it when I think I've been wrong. I try not to gloat (too much) if I am right. That is, except where Nicole is concerned. ;o)

If I am right…and I always am when it comes to reasoning or arguing with her, then I stay the course and egg her on until I get my way. She's a great gal but has a fiery temper. When she blows up, I just smile, go quiet on her, and then give her space. In time, she'll come around, and then I get my way. Besides, she realizes the futility of trying to argue with someone who has a far superior intellect. Is she reading this? She is! Gad! Is she smiling? Someone else please see if she's smiling! Good grief…I'm in trouble now!

Question 3: Who is the real-world Shannon and how did she come to be?

People have asked me that for years now. When I was barely three years old, I was bitten by a dog that later proved to have hydrophobia (rabies). Some folks, seeking answers, have even attributed my being transgender to some sort of reaction I must have had to those long series of shots I took for several days in my young abdomen. Perhaps, they suggested, I suffered some sort of adverse mental response to the rabies shots and that it was them that turned me MAD! What? Me worry?

I would tell you all right off that such a theory is absurd and those who would suggest such nonsense are only grasping at straws by those who don't comprehend that this condition is predisposed and something that was established before my birth. It is a unique condition in that no physician can find a grouping of cells that will define where this strange feminine desire came from. The fact that it is so corporeal elusive and non-definitive in its cause is what makes it so difficult for those that don't have it to understand how an otherwise biologically normal male could evolve into a trans-person.

Nicole's elderly mother commented to me, "I just don't get it, for William showed no signs of any feminine nature the whole time he was growing up. How can something like this be hidden for so long and not even a mother be aware of it?" Her question deserves an explanation and is easy to answer. Nicole and so many others like her can attest that we each hid, what was back then … our dark secret from those we loved most. As mentioned, for those who were the dearest to us, we buried our true selves deep within because we felt shame, guilt, and as if we were indeed mentally unstable and inferior. We did not wish to cause those we loved grief or to bear the brunt of the humiliation that would come if we revealed our true natures. Thus, we became masters of deception and <u>overcompensated</u> with our <u>masculinity</u> to divert or distract others from even the remotest possibility of thinking of us as feminine. As transgender people, we are at that time in our life's journey in denial!

Still don't get it? Okay, brace yourself, for you're about to fall off the edge of the map and into the mindset of a trans-woman. What follows is intensely psychological, introspective, and will at times seem like repetitive rambling, but actually, it is exactly what the trans-person goes through. By now, I have to assume you want to be here or else that you'd have not gotten off at the last stop. <u>So, here goes</u>!

Ahem! Giving This My Best Bob Dole <u>Third-Person Imitation</u> ... God Rest His Soul:

Though she didn't realize it at the time, Shannon took her initial breath of life's oxygen at the same moment in time that Gordon did. As stated several times before, at the risk of sounding schizoid, she'd have to declare that the part of her that is now Shannon has <u>always</u> been present within her psyche. You know that already!

For most of her life, <u>she</u> seemed to gasp for oxygen. Her life wheezed and inhaled from her early years and on into adulthood when she was limited to experiencing microseconds, minutes, hours, or perhaps even days of the sweet sensory, fragrant air of femininity. She exhaled and the remnants of her alter ego Gordon converted that into the by-products of his life's experiences. As pointed out, from as far back as memory serves her, she cannot recall an instance when she did not wish that she was a female.

However, Shannon as an actual and identifiable entity complete with a moniker to designate and define her did not come about until almost a half-century after Gordon's birth. Therefore, Shannon accrued like accounts payable and accumulated within Gordon each day of his existence, eventually tipping the ballast and spilling Shannon over into the real world. Gordon spent all those many years of frustration trying to comprehend who he was while she tried to refine her presence from within. In a strange sense, it was a <u>tug of war</u> for control of her psyche. <u>War</u> is an appropriate word when describing what goes on inside the mind and body of someone transgender.

Sometimes, in this storm called life, Shannon existed like hurling and churning within her. Even into adulthood, Gordon's existence seemed vague and somewhat a mass of confusion. In many ways, Shannon became like a forbidden abstraction. She could heal, touch her soul and braid her life together into something that made sense far better than could ever be done in the uncomfortable role of Gordon and what others thought her to be.

<u>What Gordon did never quite mirror what he truly was</u>. Sometimes, Shannon moved through his psyche like the slow solemn fingers of the blind, maneuvering her way through life with vigilance, attempting to decipher the codes of the flesh and spirit, thus, transmitting the feedback to her brain. To those she introduced to her inner secret, it must have seemed to them that she indeed was insane, schizoid, or just plain weird and goofy. At times, she seemed at odds with herself and two distinct and separate personality entities; one a discernible female, the other a reluctant male. The tug of war that went on inside her was incessant and unrelenting, as it is with anyone that is truly transgender. The anatomical evidence of her maleness was indisputable, as she had the penis and two "<u>test-tickles</u>" to prove it (Yeah, I can spell them, but this way is more fun). However, the essence of her <u>identity</u> was most definite that of a female.

Shannon's male body seemed foreign, sort of like ill-fitting clothing. She was completely incongruent with the gender role and genitals that were physically bestowed upon her at birth. That part of her that was openly visible to everyone else was but a <u>shell</u>, the outer wrapping on a package. Shannon wept because Gordon was denying her and not allowing her to exist. Shannon was an integral part of <u>her</u> and as if by roots in the soil, she and Gordon were connected. Though on opposite poles in the scheme of identifiable sexuality and gender the accurate depiction was that two were one body, yet sharing two lives. Gordon lived the external life and became the visible driving force. His life was the normal one that became the one everyone would judge him by and the life that would exemplify by example the masculine existence others expected of him. After all, wasn't he a man? Wasn't he born a male? To his parents, his mate, his children, and employers, plus to all his friends he lived the type of life and did the things they expected of him as a man.

Expectations and Illusions

Someone once asked her, "If you believe only in what you see, why do you pay your electric bill?" Similarly, expectations can be dangerous and elusive things and are in many ways illusionary. The question became, what would happen to poor Gordon if Shannon became the dominant force within him? Life was pretty simple and straightforward for him as the man he was expected to be. What if all of Shannon's fears were vanquished and the feminine personality came forth? Was this a betrayal of Gordon to compromise all that he had done, put at risk his career, jeopardize all his relationships with friends and family; to ultimately risk losing the respect and love of all those he held dear?

Gordon lived a safe existence, one that was comfortable in so many ways. Though his economic situation never became quite as stable as he would have liked, when based upon the status of many other citizens he had it pretty easy and was living a life of leisure. His relationship with his kids and his beloved second wife were strained, but he could pass among society with ease as the male he appeared to be. Nevertheless, in a manner of speaking, to Gordon there was in the blink of an eye, a half an inch of difference between existing in heaven or hell ... for both he and Shannon.

All those years that Shannon was denied and left in the dark reaches of Gordon's mind were certainly like being cast into hell. Shannon became as a promise from heaven, though she lingered always, she would only come out if Gordon released the controls and she was willing to walk through hell to achieve the Promised Land. Gordon was always distracted by the desires within him, but he knew no peace would ever come to him unless one day

Pink Heart

Shannon was given a chance to come forth. This undeniable fact frightened him, yet excited him and made him anxious.

He once reasoned that if he simply denied Shannon access to femme clothes, make-up, lingerie, etc. that he'd be able to control her. Thus, he reasoned he could cure himself! Wrong! Nor was he simply going to <u>get over this thing</u> and get rid of those femme feelings inside him. In time, even his marriages seemed to become a sham, for he had failed miserably at being a husband and a man. Still, he was <u>safe</u> and comfortable being a guy. However, soon after his forty-fifth birthday, the air to life would begin to become dry, stale, and choppy as a river.

I suppose me writing this about me in the <u>third person</u> is somewhat <u>Bob Dole-ish</u>, but please bear with me longer, as it is an accurate means of conveying my message.

Giving Shannon CPR

Shannon moved from room to room amongst Gordon's soul and being. One day she had the <u>Aha</u> moment. In that poignant, yet nervous instant … her revelation and self-confession forever awakened her and she knew it would soon become her time to drive the flesh-covered vehicle known as <u>the body and the life</u>. Gordon found himself stepping aside to let her behind the wheel and he knew that eventually she would stop and tell him to get out. She would pass him by. Since that moment, Shannon has but caught only a fleeting glimpse of him from time to time in her rearview mirror. Only then did her life-enhancing changes begin. She saw this moment as both a sad and glorious one.

Over the years, she had floated in softly, silently, slowly like an early morning mist creeping ever onward. Eventually, her emerging spirit covered Gordon like a warm blanket. Her angelic wings touched and brushed against him. It was as if to tempt him with her femininity and yet taunt him at the same time to let go and to give in to her. Her presence unfolded within him, and then <u>Shannon</u> sighed and **She** was…at long last <u>born</u>. Gordon knew when he had made that first trip over the border there at El Paso into Juarez to pick up that first supply of estrogens that Shannon was never going to remain complacent or silent again.

He was returning from his birth mother's funeral in Oregon. She had been his last living parent and her death, as much as anything, triggered within him a sense of urgency unlike any other he'd ever experienced. Shannon recognized this key moment and knew that for her ... it was <u>now ... or never</u>! As she ingested the first of those estrogenic pills, she felt from <u>one eye a tear rolls down her cheek</u>. No doubt, it was due to both relief and elation, but it was also due to Gordon's realization that his end was at hand and that the life of comfort, respect, property, and probably even his love and marriage was threatened and in jeopardy. Later on, those fears and dread proved to be well-founded.

In a way, he'd used his life as Gordon like a <u>shield,</u> a means in which to deny and divert his mind from facing the truth about <u>she</u> who is. Indeed, like Gordon, she was consigned to the dungeons within his psyche. His memories forever emblazoned in her mind became like precious artifacts that made up the very essence of his past being. Still, the negative things about life as Gordon were the lies and hypocrisies, he invented to cover up the fears and depression in his own heart. As Gordon, deceit filled him with regret for he knew that his family and the life he had created would suffer from his revelation and the future course of action Shannon was planning. Whew! Even I feel schizoid after reading that paragraph. Yeah, me too!

Anyway, Shannon's life entered her <u>infancy</u> with a physical body far too tall for her liking, but it was the only one she had with which to work. The sobering truth of the challenge before **her**, like Shannon, was that beneath the hulking male exterior she'd somehow had to remold and remake herself into the image of a woman. She knew that skilled surgeons could meticulously cut away the undesirable appendage that she had between her legs, but that could not lay bare the heartwood of her soul. She knew that exercise and diet would take off pounds and inches from her manly body. Her true self would have to be defined in the afterglow of the decision to become Shannon. She would have to attempt to reconstruct the debris of her male existence into a thing of grace and beauty ... not just physically, but also mentally and spiritually. Thankfully, she accomplished this ... with some help.

Pink Heart

Therefore, even after years of estrogen, progesterone, and anti-androgen therapy, breast augmentation surgery, electrolysis, nasal septum surgery, and GRS, she became the woman she'd sought all her life. To all who know her …she is Shannon, a lofty woman but certainly … no longer a male.

Gad! Even as I wrote these words, Shannon is still blossoming and defining her indisputable self. She was in a state of flux and learned more about herself each day as she aged. Though rescued from the ashes of that knurled, twisted, and uncut pulp that was once Gordon, she would be cast into the fire to be forged and fashioned into a new feminine image to become like a jubilant ornament. Her boughs, that once stood naked and waiting to be caressed by the patient artist, would come to reveal by her skills and imagination as a <u>newly decorated life</u>. Her life would be reshaped and whittled into a new labor of love. Gee, after reading this paragraph, I sound like a Christmas tree. Hmmm! I suppose I am ornamented, but being able to accessorize is one of the things I enjoy most about being a woman.

Me Playing with Puppy Poodles – '97
This Was Before I Had Breast Implants

Shannon became like a line carved somewhere in his / her brain. Gordon has since <u>abdicated </u>his throne and given way to Shannon and there's the beginning of a new line of my heritage. That last sentence was strictly used as an analogy and not as an attempt to exhibit any majestic arrogance.

Gordon's search for happiness that had always seemed to elude him, was centered now on her / my new life and comprehension that <u>life as Shannon ... really does seem to fit her / me better</u>. Why is that? I think it is because <u>she is me</u>. My attitude has improved and my behavior became a clear barometer that I am a better person today than I was back when I was Gordon. Why are my attitude and behavior better now? Simple! I don't have to hide who or what I am anymore. No, I don't stand on some street corner and decry to the world that I am a trans-woman; I mean that I am honest to myself now, which results in being more open and honest with others.

I should make it plain though that I am not happier because I'm divorced from a family I loved and cherished, nor of those responsibilities; that is something I truly miss. Nicole knows that, as do my closest friends, but that is part of my past and I can't turn back time. Rather, I am happier because of the <u>lack of inner conflict</u> and the sense of satisfaction I receive now from knowing when I look into a mirror, the person I see therein reflected is at long last ... me. I see a feminine woman now. Peeled away is the stratum of that which had been hidden within me. The shrine I'd built to my feminine self that was once entombed in a closely guarded sarcophagus arose and came forth into the light. However, I would also point out that it hasn't all been the proverbial bed of roses. The travails of my life as Gordon paled when compared to those I would face as a woman.

Pink Heart

As a woman, I no longer fell into the ravines of purge and denial. My final rebirth was and is permanent. In this realm, Shannon is real. She is the quintessence of my life. I cannot exist apart from her now. No more is she relegated to a segregated existence of solitude. Some have told me that I have a mental affliction. Anyone in transition must deflect such comment and insulate herself from criticism and censure. Rather than preparing myself to suffer, I prepared myself to heal. As I noted, I now have many friends and loved ones that know me and accept me as a female. There is no vestige of Gordon left within me. Shannon radiates within me now, her life at long last casting its own shadow. She is a pure vessel, and a condiment that without I could no longer live.

Whatever strength I needed to face this challenge came forth from my Creator. As Gordon, my life seemed in some ways to be profane. Sexual urges or sheer curiosity misled me, especially during the early experimental days of my female existence. However, when I became Shannon, I developed a solitaire mind. Fears, doubts, urges, and temptations that Gordon faced became less important than living the truth. I sought to make my life become one not based on anyone's expectations other than my own. For the most part, I have succeeded in doing so.

Daily, I reclaim my sanity from having lived in what to me was such an insane male world for so many years of my life. Like Thelma said to Louise, "Something crossed over in me." Nope! Once the genie was out of the bottle, there was indeed no putting her back inside. I crossed the bridge and there was no turning around. It should be noted that I paid my toll … and I can attest that it was a very costly one, as it always is for anyone that is transgender. As Shannon, the daily ingestion of estrogens was my physical nutrition, but the psychological nirvana and the greatest satisfaction came in just knowing I was accepted as a female. A full-time transitional trans-woman sings a new rhapsody and the melody of life, as Shannon was as yet back then only in the first verse. I hadn't reached the chorus, but I went through my second puberty willingly … and this time it was right and much more fun.

The mind is an extraordinary instrument, which can conjure, create, or manifest through conscious or unconscious thought amazing things. Before

Gordon finally acted upon his fantasies and dreams, he was but a mental voyager. His mind had often created its drama; its fantastic fantasies in which he would become transformed into the beautiful female creature that beckoned him. His imaginative intellect would fabricate his allegory, burlesque, and entertainment via his self-stimulation, which sometimes would lead to surreal sexual encounters with carnal entities that would derive their pleasures from the freshly created woman in his mind's fantasies. Was that a means of diversion, masturbatory fantasy, or perversion? It might seem so to some, but everyone has fantasies, only Gordon's involved switching genders. Sadly, Gordon lived in the expanse of a castle in the sky existence and could never fully concentrate on getting his life on track. His career suffered because of this and his distractions only got worse in time. Wow! This does get schizoid, doesn't it?

Even the devotion and love of his family, his mate, and his friends could not suffice to bring him peace of mind. Often his moods would erupt like an angry abscess with him snapping at friends or family, or with him bursting into tears at the slightest of things. For no apparent reason, often he'd bark or snarl at his children as if to take out his frustrations upon them. The next moment he'd regret his actions and throw his arms around them, contrite for having been so emotional. His life was a roller coaster of raw emotions and he never liked himself as a son, dad, or husband.

Shannon was always there, like a hand on his shoulder trying to calm him and the rage of testosterone that she considered poison to his / her system. She was like a cooling breath of wind, an itch that came on strong, and then would quietly retreat. However, one day, as we've seen, she did not go away. Gordon's life came to be like a ten-story fall to the street below, a tumbling act of sorts. However, it would not be the fall that killed him, but the <u>sudden stop</u> that Shannon inflicted upon him. His demise would leave many others saddened and in mourning; and leave him longing for lost friends and loved ones.

Dueling Banjos

The fact is Shannon came to be only because Gordon gave up and gave in to her dreams ... that, by the way ... he shared in as well. The floor that

Pink Heart

Gordon walked upon was also Shannon's ceiling and ultimately the two joined and became but one plane. Indeed, Shannon touched a door inside Gordon's mind, and then swung it open and lingered inside. For years, she had been breaking and entering his heart, and then one day in El Paso, she entered his soul as well ... and they <u>merged.</u> Where before Shannon had been in hiding; crouched inside Gordon's head, she came forth from the shadows and from where she dwelled and would never again retreat.

I've said this many times when describing what life was like before I became Shannon 24 - 7. At times, I felt like I was an actress inhabiting a frail costume of flesh. Its seamless fabric impermeably stretched out upon me, shaping my thoughts and me into my metaphysical self. As Gordon, I knew not my spot up on the stage or the proper dialogue from the play. Others directed my life and I was but a puppet of their expectations for me. As I wrote earlier, expectations are dangerous things and are sometimes illusory. The rules of Gordon's life demanded he be a man. They declared he was a normal heterosexual male and to everyone around him he was.

Though he had hidden his secrets deep within, they would one day burst forth, like a malevolent volcano. For far too many years, like those of his wasted youth and young adulthood, Gordon languished in his cross-dressing state ... never quite able to accept what he was, or who he was. He and his <u>inner trans-sister,</u> Shannon, were like two constituents of a primitive age self-taught as to what was the semblance of womanhood. He would often hide her embellished and fragrant body in a sequestered rented residence whereby he would rejoice in every minute and occurrence that he could spend as his sister half. He would, at every convenience vest himself in the arraignments of femininity, donning himself with ceremonial paints and doing his all to make the illusion of Shannon real.

Gordon heard the laughter of Shannon trickle down the stairwells of his mind like a musical scale and finally came to realize that this incessant longing to become her would never cease. However, any music without its pauses and silences is only noise. In effect, Shannon was but unruly noise in Gordon's life. She somehow survived the inner war, the shrapnel, and flak of life as Gordon, a male, and emerged from his mind's darkest tunnel as a shimmering hope for the future. Her progression was remarkable and she accomplished far more than she ever dreamed possible. Her existence is like a sachet of sweet scents, and her fragrance lingers on, creating a syntax and reality that she adores.

Okay, that's enough **third-person** analogies. I wrote it that way because it best reflects the duality in all us trans-women. Take a deep breath and continue at your leisure.

Nicole and Me Out and About in Dallas

Question 4: Even as a child you wanted to be female?

That's an easy and quick answer. Yes! As I wrote in my previous one, I've known I was different from as far back as I can recall. Even as a child, I always knew that I wanted to be a girl ... not a boy. Early on, it wasn't a sexual thing, but a matter of identity and relating to being feminine, which of course is what being transgender is all about anyway. My first moment to live out that fantasy was when I began dressing in my sister and mom's clothing at around the age of six. From that first silk scarf and nylons slipped over my legs I was hooked. There's no denying it. As a child, I did not comprehend the distinctive differences in genitals between boys and girls, or that there were such things as hormones that influenced secondary-sex-characteristics. I only knew that I felt more congruent to being a girl than I did a boy, but I had no idea why that was the case. My genitals didn't bother me so much back then, for I was pre-pubescent and unaware of what a female vagina was like.

I believe that this strong instinctual desire to be female was deeply ingrained in my mind. What other explanation could there be? I was mentally <u>pre-programmed</u> to feel female from the get-go. Perhaps as a fetus in the womb, my mind was flushed with an excessive dose of estrogens, dopamine, or some other chemical/enzyme that caused an imbalance that imprinted upon my brain forever that I should be female. Your guess is as good as mine, but I have never been able to think of a more reasonable assumption.

Still Crazy After 10 years Together

Slow down and enjoy the journey. When you get there isn't as important as that you arrive at your destination safe and intact.

Huh # 4:
<u>The Neighborly Thing to Do:</u>

I once had a neighbor that prided himself in his gardening abilities. One spring, he had a bumper crop of cherry tomatoes, so he gave us some of his bounties, and we enjoyed them in our salads. They were red, ripe, and delicious.

The next spring, he had even a bigger garden, and one day in late February I saw him out there planting his prized cherry tomato plants. By then, my ex taunted me into planting a garden as well, and I went into the same town nursery to buy several plants that day.

When returning home, I got blessed out because I'd bought the "Big Boy" variety of tomato instead of the smaller, juicy cherry tomatoes that she liked. I grumbled, but instead of taking them back or planting them, the devil got in me and spawned a devious idea.

Late that night, I sneaked out of bed, and up the hill to my neighbor's garden, removed all his cherry tomato plants, and replaced them with the Big Boy tomatoes, which at that point were about the same sized plants as his cherry ones. I put his plants in my containers, and the next day planted those in my garden, not explaining to my wife what I'd done.

As time passed that summer, I saw my neighbor one day and he told me, "Wow! I knew I had a green thumb, but you've got to come to see how big my cherry tomato plants are this year."

That spring and summer, we supplied our neighbor with many cherry tomatoes for their salads, and he provided us with plenty of his prized "Giant Cherry Tomatoes" that he displayed to every neighbor who'd come listen to his story. I suppose "size" really does matter in some things.

Question 5: After all that time living as a male, why did you choose to take action and begin your transition?

Forty-five years is a long time to repress something and keep it a secret, but for the most part, I managed to do exactly that, at least with my friends, employers, and most of my family. I revealed to very few people my true nature and femme desires. Up until then, I divulged only bits and pieces of the real puzzle, even to those who thought they knew me best. The first four decades of my life were spent in what I consider to be a state of <u>self-enforced hibernation</u>. As stated earlier, I was in a <u>feminine depravation</u> stage, and Shannon only existed in my dreams and the farthest reaches of my mind. Thus, I never let her fully develop as a real entity until a few years ago.

To all of you that may have cross-dressed at one time or another, you know what it is like to open that closet door and let your feminine side peek out at the world for a few brief moments. Afterward, most of you would wind up shoving <u>her</u> back inside and throwing the deadbolt, vowing never again to let her out. With me, I could no longer hold back the tide, for Shannon was too entrenched inside me. I know now that it was a naive and repulsive slumber and I learned, as do all that are trans-women that to live my dreams, one must first awake to face the new dawn. However, as does anyone with a goal, before I could ride my dreams, I had to saddle them.

We all have a vision of some sort, a heart's desire. As you know by now, mine was to <u>be a woman.</u> After my birth mother died, that's when I had my <u>Aha</u> moment and decided to do something about my inner feminine feelings. Until then, I had only toyed with the idea and never gave it my full attention or consideration. I used every conceivable excuse I could muster, burdened by fears, guilt, and denial as my reasons for the delay. As a result, I allowed the years to accumulate one on top of the other until my youth was gone and the pursuit of my dream seemed only an illusion. Instead, I spent my time and abilities pursuing things I thought would make me happy, things I believed would bring me fulfillment: a new house, new cars, a fish and ski boat, a camping trailer, big-screen televisions, and yes ... even two marriages. I couldn't get enough of what I didn't require to make me happy.

When that new car didn't make me happy, I blamed it on the car. "I just need another new one." I'd say to myself, "Surely <u>THAT</u> will make me happy!" In some ways, I even applied that same type of reasoning when I divorced my first spouse. Although I was single for a year or two, I would later remarry a second time, thinking that a <u>fresh love</u> and soul mate would distract me enough that I could find happiness. It worked for a while, but after X2 proved to be disappointingly human with her faults, disillusionment set in, and <u>the dream</u> beckoned stronger than ever.

During that time, I was so far away from living my dream that I'd almost forgotten what my dream was. I abandoned my heart's desire, deep down I knew it, and it ate at me like <u>cancer</u>. Why wasn't I living my dream? Because there was something back then that I was trained to honor more than my dreams: <u>Love</u> ... and <u>the comfort zone.</u>

Being a <u>MAN</u> was the <u>comfortable choice</u> ... causing no conflicts or rocking no boats. In contemplating leaving this comfort zone, stepping outside the barrier, I felt a cold-blooded <u>FEAR,</u> more guilt and unworthiness, hurt feelings, and anger. Those were things I considered <u>Uncomfortable</u>. The irony of it is, those things I labeled as uncomfortable were, in fact, among the very tools necessary to overcome and fulfill my dreams. I also feared <u>losing the love</u> and adoration of my spouse and children, which pretty much happened after I left that comfort zone and decided to pursue my dreams of becoming Shannon.

Another Shannonism: In my first years full-time as Shannon, I found I spent more and more on clothes that covered less and less. Thank goodness time cured that see-level habit and now I'm slack-happy, decent, and have a larger bank account. Still, I did look pretty dang good in those tight, sexy, low-cut styles.

Pink Heart

Pausing a moment, I'd like to present you with this realization. I served my nation in the military and I am a staunch patriot and defender of our Flag and of those who served. I object to the moral indignation of "WAR," and pray to God no more of our American sons and daughters will become the "Silent Soldiers" of future embattlements. Though the Wars are over ... for now ... the following poem is my tribute to those who gave their all to defend our freedoms:

Silent Soldiers – God Has Called Them Home

The Sentinel

By: Shannon O'Shea

In vigilance ... on a gloomy runway ... his watch he now does stand,
A steadfast soldier ... of his country ... a defender of his land.
Through this night ... his solemn duty ... he does quietly perform,
Hoping to prevent ... for other brothers ... any further harm.
In the aircraft are ... flag-draped caskets ... of ones who were friends,
He's glad ... they're going home ... where their Earth journey ends.

***

In his mind ... he sees faces ... of "Silent Soldiers" ... he once knew,
By whose side ... he once fought ... protecting many ... with the few.
He was spared ... but these fair ... brave ones ... they were taken,
God now ... calls them home ... and their souls ... are not forsaken.
This lone sentinel ... sheds a tear ... it rolls slowly ... down his cheek,
He brushes it aside ... not wanting others ... to think perhaps he's weak.

***

Now, the dawn is breaking ... the sun rises ... higher in the sky,
Relieved of duty ... he salutes ... and then whispers his good-bye.
Moments later ... the aircraft lifts ... into a firmament of blue,
He hopes all Americans ... will know ... they gave their lives for you!

***

For duty, honor... and country ... they faced ... the enemy,
And paid the price ... by sacrifice ... for God ... and liberty.
Answering the call ...they gave their all ... for freedom ... to survive,
So, terrorists ... won't win and ... bravery's ... still alive.
This sentinel ... will never forget ... the soldiers ... that did fall,
Who like our Savior ... they too shed ... their blood for one and all.

Thank You! May God bless your souls!

PART 2

Question 6: What about feeling transgender?

I had to challenge that comfort zone and step over the boundaries, completely waking up from my slumbering, lumbering, and going nowhere life. If someone is indeed a trans-woman, she has but two choices. she can:

1. **Do something about it**   2. **Do nothing about it**

Either way, they must live with their choice and attempt to make the best of whatever comes from their decision. Ultimately, NOBODY is lashed in place unless you choose to be. Simply ignoring that one is transgender will not make those inner feminine urges and desires vanish. From my perspective, as I've displayed, for anyone truly an MTF trans-woman there is no escaping the woman within. Neither is there some magic cure for the condition. Only by shifting the body (physical) to match the feminine image (mental) in the mind shall an MTF trans-woman find real solace or mental balance. The trans-woman must adapt and persevere against all odds to overcome the fear, doubt, and circumstances that she shall face in her transition. By being true to herself, with self-recognition and acknowledgment, she can endure and learn to fly into the wind, climb the mountains and locate her destiny.

I would caution anyone going forth into such a blinding blizzard to insulate your psyche or be prepared to suffer severe frostbite. Expect the unexpected and be prepared to face all types of adverse reactions from those you think YOU knew. I was fueled by the promise of perhaps catching a glimpse of the treasure at the rainbow's end, of the feminine lifestyle and that true self-identity I had sought from my earliest childhood. This endeavor to discover my feminine self would not be because of coercion, but by my own volition. Hearts would be broken, including my own, but I had been forever shaken from the nest of complacency and cast upon the winds to either fly of my own accord or else to fall into the crevices of broken dreams below.

Question 7: Where are you right now ... today ... with your transition and being transgender?

Farther than I was yesterday and maybe not as far as I will be tomorrow! Every day presents new challenges and new opportunities, especially for older trans-women. Oh, and by the way ... I do not live life as a transgender but as a woman. I've been 24 - 7 now for over twenty-four years, so the physical was taken care of by hormones and planned surgeries years ago. I've had to assimilate quite a lot, as in some ways I became like an <u>infant</u> and was <u>being reborn</u>.

In many ways, a trans-woman must become an involved and astute <u>observer</u>, watching how women move, sit, how they use their hands to gesture, how they laugh, plus how "we" flirt and present coy and subtly demure signals. It should become the goal of an MTF trans-woman to <u>mimic</u> those traits and to make them her own. If one is to spend every waking hour in the role of a female, then one had best develop the natural rhythms that exhibit to others in society that indeed <u>she...is a she!</u> Being female should become second nature and the trans-woman should disregard that she is a trans-woman and just be the <u>woman</u> she always wished and thought herself to be.

I struggled with some issues, including my economic situation. If I had to judge it though, I'd say I made many strides and accomplishments in my journey through womanhood. Since I'm still alive, I guess God is not done with me yet. I compare where I am by stating that after all these years ... I tossed off my training wheels quickly and no longer seem just a few feet away from my desired destination. I made it to the Promised Land at the edge of the horizon and hopefully will keep breathing even though I have reached it. I'm confident my home in heaven awaits me when my days on Earth are done. However, as I've often said to others, it's where I'm going that's important, not how fast I get there. You should always remember ... <u>it's your choice and only .... your choice</u> as to what you do with your life. Others may influence your decisions, but ultimately, it comes down to <u>Y.O.U.</u>! I heard one young trans-woman say, "Slay your own dragons."

Pink Heart

Nicole and I attended Cher's farewell concert here in Dallas a few years ago. One thing she said in a video interview stuck with me and applies to everyone. She told an interviewer that Singers don't consider her to be a singer, that actors don't consider her to be an actress, that Gay men think she's their best friend, and truthfully, she doesn't care what anyone thinks, for her life is her own to live and … it's nobody's business but hers!

Reading my answers won't change YOU, the reader's life, just as reading a guidebook to England won't truly show you England. It may give you a sense of what it is like, but England is England and can only be experienced by action and <u>being there</u> in person. So, it is that way with being TRANSGENDER. If one <u>only talks or reads about it</u>, then that person will never actually know what it's truly like. One must act on his dreams if they are to become reality. No matter how much empathy a family member or friend has towards one who is transgender, they can never truly comprehend what in reality it's like to be transgender. At best, we who are MTF trans-women can only hope for some degree of compassion and sympathy from those of you that are not.

Those of us who are trans-women should not judge some <u>normal</u> harshly for that; rather we should seek to embrace patience with them and be thankful for any acceptance we receive. To those who direct their prejudice and bias toward us, shun us, or shut us out of their lives, we can only hope that for them some future enlightenment will occur and that they will come to learn … and one day accept who we are and what we are.

Who's That Lady?

Although we can all learn the art of persuasion and attempt to influence others, long ago I learned that ultimately the only mind and body I could control is <u>my own</u> … and even doing that has been tough at times. To be realistic, the MTF trans-woman might wish for equal treatment, but should possibly not expect to retain the same degree of respect, love, or admiration that they once had in their male career or identity. However, a carry-over of such things to their new gender role and identity is possible, as I have seen in some cases involving other of my trans-sisters. Nonetheless, in many other instances, including my own, that love and respect for the most part faded away when I terminated the identity of him whose life I lived before becoming Shannon.

I have pointed out and learned from experience that when one is transgender, your children, ex-spouses, parents, past co-workers, employers, and even old friends may become indifferent and choose to avoid you like you have a contagion or an affliction. In truth, I believe some haven't the inclination or the courage to face you.

No More the Husband, Brother, or … Father

For certain, most of my family has not been endeared to my being Shannon. Other than my oldest brother, Vern, some nieces, and my stepdaughter, others of my kinfolk have shown no interest in getting to know me as Shannon or being with me in person. They pre-judged me in that role and could not adjust to the idea of my being female. It simply did not seem feasible or possible to them. Thus, to some of my past friends and family, I've become the burdensome pink sheep, someone to be pitied or even despised for having taken away their husband, brother, friend, or father.

Pink Heart

As I mentioned, in some ways, being a trans-woman truly is like being reborn, resurrected, and having to reprove me to everyone else again. Thankfully, in time I have established myself as a female and there are many now that know me only as Shannon. For those friends and co-workers with whom I share my time and new life ... I am eternally grateful.

I have been challenged every day to create, exist and persevere in the personae and role of Shannon O'Shea. My two jobs as Shannon were a blessing as they afforded me several opportunities for acid tests whereby, I stood before groups of managers, sales managers, and men numbering upwards of two hundred in which I had to give updates on our plant or do detailed production presentations. Not one person was ever inconsiderate to me and all treated me fairly. If they knew I was transgender, they did not make a point of calling me out about it, nor were there any created rifts between them or me. In truth, in some I detected lust in their eyes.

I have had acquaintances from my past pop in and show up after several years apart. Within one ex- company as a customer, manager, or a vendor I met and saw people from my past that never suspected I was once Gordon. In each case, those people did not connect me with having been the male they once knew. My appearance was then and is no doubt different, but I think this failure to connect was mainly due to their belief and perception of me as a female, and by not expecting me to remind them of some guy that they knew from their past. They didn't suspect or question that I was ever someone else, other than the woman they saw. I found this aspect of my transition to be as pleasing as anything I've experienced. With my last inside sales position, most of my customers were contacted via the phone or Internet. I was careful not to slip out of my fem mode or being slack. None mistook my voice or called me "sir." If there had been Zoom back then, I'm sure none of them would have ever doubted I am female.

Nicole and I even took road trips to my hometown of Waco, whereby I mustered the courage for us to go to Baylor basketball games, familiar old restaurants where I used to eat, and to the one regional shopping mall that they have there. In one instance, at a Baylor game, a guy I used to play golf with sat directly next to me with his family and friends. He looked at me, but never once winced or got a puzzled look. If anything, his glance was one of desire and common interest revealed to any attractive (ahem!) woman by a man. We made eye contact several times, and I caught him sniffing the air and inhaling the scent of my perfume, but he presented me with no indication of recognition.

I was a bit nervous but relieved that this man, in whose golf foursome I was often included in the past, did not have the slightest clue who the woman was that sat next to him. He was polite and with his wife next to him I didn't flirt or try to embarrass him. This was sort of the acid test for me and proved that few if anyone I knew in my hometown would ever suspect that I was once male ... and once was enough. Since then, I've been to many Baylor games in basketball, baseball, and football ... all without a single person questioning my gender.

Pink Heart

Huh # 5: CRaZY MoVie NiGhT:

Between my first and last marriage, as a once again forty-year-old newbie bachelor, I dated a lovely lady and took her to see a horror movie at a Dallas cinema. It was a weekend and the place was very crowded. About fifteen minutes into the flick, I wanted some popcorn. I asked her if she wanted anything and then excused myself as I went up to the concession stand to get us a large bag.

I soon re-entered the dark theater, found my seat beside the long hair brunette, and sat down. The movie was at a tense point as I offered her some popcorn and we shared the treat. After finishing the bag, I settled in, put my arm around her shoulder to comfort her during the intense scenes, and then she often grabbed my other arm and squeezed during the scary parts of the movie. I heard her scream and managed to get to first base once, enjoying the few brief moments when my hand glanced and then landed sensually on her thigh.

After the movie was over and the lights began to illuminate the theater, I stood and turned towards the aisle. I called her name, "Well, that chainsaw killer was some weird psycho. Let's go, Linda, I'll treat you to a nice dinner."

I turned slowly and took her hand when to my complete surprise I discovered a bad mistake I'd made. The young girl said, "Okay, but my name's not Linda, I'm Betty. My mom is picking me up, so I'll have to ask her if it's all right for me to go."

This not more than <u>sixteen-year-old girl</u> I'd sat by the entire movie was <u>not my date</u>, but a cute, young teenager. In the dim light, I quickly saw my error and scanned the audience for Linda. She was a few aisles back, still sitting with her arms crossed and a sneer on her lips. I sheepishly excused myself from Betty and made my way back to Linda, who needless to say was not happy that I'd bailed on her, even if it was an accident. After she doused me with a few choice words and a "Take me Home" directive, I did so, and then seriously considered investing in some night-vision glasses before my next movie date. Years later, I imagine that young girl still fantasizes about our dark, but brief horror movie love affair.

A Favorite saying: By Oscar Hammerstein

A bell is not a bell until you ring it. A song is not a song until you sing it. Love in the heart is not meant to stay. Love is not love… until you give it away.

A Favorite saying: There might be many folks in life that cause you to hurt. It's up to you to figure out which people are worth the pain.

A Favorite saying: At my age now, I have more medicine in my cabinet than I do food or utensils.

Into a Tempest Cast
By: Shannon O'Shea

The essence of America isn't found in buildings of concrete.

It is fashioned by the courage of the citizens on the street.

In every heart dwells a universal dream waiting to unfold.

Seeking truth and justice for all, that is liberty taking hold.

We should all make the effort to keep the dream alive,

To not philander freedom, and may our sovereignty survive.

We must not govern like a spindrift, or into a tempest cast.

Let us focus on the future, but not forget about our past.

Pink Heart

Wise Quotes:

"Be yourself, everyone else is already taken."
Oscar Wilde

"Peace begins with a smile."
Mother Teresa

"What lies behind us and what lies before us are tiny matters compared to what lies within us."
Ralph Waldo Emerson

"When you arise in the morning think of what a privilege it is to be alive, to think, to enjoy, to love."
Marcus Aurelias

"Our greatest glory is not in never falling, but in rising every time we fall."
Confucius

And my Favorite:

"You have brains in your head. You have feet in your shoes. You can steer yourself any direction you choose. You're on your own. And you know what you know. And you are the one who'll decide where to go."
Dr. Seuss

Question 8: What advice would you offer to other trans-women to help them live their dreams?

Good question. I state my convictions herein and let those who read them decide if they are worthy of being considered good advice or not. To me, I think all of us have the worst enemy ... and for many of us, it's ourselves. We tend to let negative thoughts enter our mind and we think of a thousand reasons why we can't, instead of the equal number of reasons why we can... and should. I think I heard Dr. Malcolm say that about reanimating dinosaurs in the movie, Jurassic Park."

Some trans-woman I know say they can't become female when what they mean is they won't! They aren't willing to do whatever it takes to make that transition to find their true self. I've mentioned it several times already, but it's worth repeating: Though the costs can be tremendous for many of us, denying this femme urge and obsession within will only lead one to an unhappy end in life.

I believe there are many stages in the life of a trans-woman. I know I went through a few myself. That is also why some never have GRS, and others do. Circumstance, be it economical or simply degrees of desire for absolute physiological and psychological change determines which stage of this journey each will attain. Each of us is unique, but we all seem to have a very close bond to others like us who share our love of femininity. It's a known fact that horses in a field will gather by bloodline, so too then do many transgender folks recognize their own. In a way, we are a special rare breed that tends to gather within a close-knit grouping of those with like interests and challenges. An example of that is group meetings conducted by a gender counselor or open meetings with those like I had in that hotel where the soccer girls hung out.

I can't adequately explain it, but in an often rather rare and fascinating trans subculture, we tend to act as birds of a feather. Some actively seek out other trans-sisters or brothers, and then tax them for information, compare experiences, and confirm our own identities among those who walk the same paths as we.

Pink Heart

This interacting with those who are <u>traveling companions</u> is essential I think to maintain a healthy outlook on our progress or a lack of it. I believe that talking and sharing ideas with another <u>trans-sister</u> is vital. To a trans-woman, I think this sort of relationship is a very effective method of therapy and of understanding her own life. Comprehension and empathy toward and from a sister traveler are some of the very best ways to learn about her challenges, reaching her own goals, hopes, and desires, and learning more about the direction her own life is headed. I've been blessed with many wonderful transgender friends, plus an empathetic, bright, and compassionate counselor who wisely guided my feet down a proper pathway to womanhood.

My counselor said to me, "<u>If you're going to be a woman, be a good one</u>." At first, I thought she meant physically, but later on realized she meant good, as is moral and loving. I never forgot that advice. After spending my youthful 50's and early sixties being rather risqué with my wardrobes, I mellowed and tapered my wardrobe to more conservative clothes.

Think Positive

I believe we should all spend less time thinking negative thoughts and spend more time focusing on the positive things we learn from life. We should not take the time or any precious moment for granted and should enjoy each day that God gives us. I believe each trans-woman should <u>forgive herself</u> and let go of the past and the rage within her. As with any other human being, you may one day find your rose garden, but you should still expect there to be thorns. True happiness is always our choice; it's the reality of life. There will inevitably be pain, but suffering is an option you choose! Far too many of us don't know what we want and it seems we are killing ourselves to get it.

We may not all be able to become activists or vocal advocates for the rights to live in our chosen gender roles, but we all can be heard … and must be heard. As I stated earlier, we can call, visit, or write letters to those lawmakers, judges, city council members, members of congress, or anyone who may affect positive change concerning laws that now discriminate or affect a trans person in negative ways.

Can <u>You</u> Hear <u>Me</u> Now?

Often, I feel like I'm in a bad television commercial. In one such commercial done by a mobile phone provider, a nerdy guy walked around in all sorts of remote areas with a mobile phone to his ear. In a droning voice, he spoke into the phone and asks, "<u>Can you hear me now</u>?" Then he pauses, smiles, and says, "<u>Good</u>"! This response is presumed to indicate to the caller on the other end of his phone line that they can hear his words clearly and precisely.

To me, a lot of those oppressed outcasts of society, such as transgender, gays, lesbians, and those bisexuals have shouted out unto the rest of the world, "<u>Can you hear me now</u>?" The answer they more often receive back is to hear nothingness in return save for the faint echo of apathy and their own timid and hollow voices. As trans-women, we need to quit striving and <u>start arriving</u>. We must somehow find the right frequency, locate the tallest towers amongst us; tapping into the source that lets our voices be heard in every region of the world and universe.

Although the LBGT and their factions have made many strides to correct the inequity, many other prejudicial and biased laws still exist which were specifically targeted at those who are transgender. I mentioned before that over the past decade, Texas courts created a travesty of injustice and discrimination aimed at defining what, <u>to them</u>, is how to derive and define someone's true sex, which also determines their gender. Those court decisions have come down in which judges have come to interpret and point out that there is but one obvious conclusion; <u>that one is</u> the <u>anatomical sex that one is born</u>, no matter what psychological, mental, chemical, or surgical corrective alterations are made. Thus, all trans-women are being voided of their perceptions of which sex/gender they are.

"Hello! Can <u>you</u> hear <u>me</u> now?" all of you judges and legislators who don't have to live even one second of a day within the scope of this conception need to wake up, remove your blinders, and put down your

Pink Heart

unjust, unfair gavels. As I see it, one of the most basic of human rights is now denied to those who are classified as being transgender.

Even after years of intense therapy and diagnosis of being transgender. Even after years of medically monitored hormonal treatments and obtaining all the legal documents to prove their new identities, plus living full-time as a female. Even after being employed full-time in their new chosen gender role. Even <u>after</u> having completed gender reassignment surgery to become either anatomically correct a female or male, as the choice may be, to the august group of legislators in the <u>state of Texas</u>, that person is still <u>legally</u> deemed to be of the defined sex specified unto them at birth … <u>PERIOD</u>! Pardon me sirs, but what a crock!

To those lawmakers or judges, in the context of numbers, such rulings affect very few and thus the resulting backlash is little or nothing when compared to other LBGT issues or those of the majority … the considered <u>normal</u> constituents. By doing the right thing, such unjust laws should be repealed, merely because they are wicked, WRONG, and target specific groups of humans who have done nothing criminal or deserving of such intense prejudice and bias. I won't even dignify the skewed interpretations that they place upon the post-operative trans-woman that <u>attempts to marry a male</u>. That ludicrous decision is so ridiculous it deserves no comment except for the one just made.

Such narrow-minded decisions are <u>now</u> in place and have set into motion a dangerous precedent within our Texas and U.S. legal systems. The Texas <u>Littleton</u> case and other biased national landmark cases have only served to smirch the truth, and have not solved any of the complicated issues of human rights concerning those that are transgender. To me, many of the current verdicts handed down were contemptible decisions, unwarranted cop-outs, and as I pointed out earlier were made by judges who do not have to live under the severe restrictions of their judgments. Perhaps, those same judges simply sought their own fifteen minutes of fame. Hopefully, in the future, these simplistic, gross unreasonable types of adjudication will be overturned. In the meantime, what small voice we all have should continue to cry <u>foul</u> and point out the changes that need to be made. "<u>Can you all…hear me now?</u>"

<u>Fundamental definitions</u> of the sex of a person should take into consideration the circumstances of being transgender and what all that entails. As I've shown, exceptions do exist to anything biological and to have any trans-woman declared <u>legally bound</u> to her birth sex is simply cruel and preposterous.

What if a person was born blind or paralyzed by no choice of his or her own and could have an operation to restore his or her sight and mobility to walk? From such a forum of justice by definition and reason, those persons would still be considered <u>legally blind and immobile</u> ... for that's how they were born. The point being, it makes no sense to not take into consideration that philosophy mentioned earlier ... that one size does not fit all and that the biology of birth <u>does not cast into stone</u> that which is repairable or achievable by today's science or medical technologies. Seeking to do the <u>right thing</u> should entail doing so <u>for everyone</u>, not just the <u>voices or votes</u> that are the most numerous. Sometimes the right thing to do is the most unpopular.

Another example would be the conjoined twins that were in the news. Their heads were fused at birth and miraculously, surgeons managed to separate their heads and bodies and make it possible for each to live a life free of that horrible birth defect. However, using that same illogical judicial reasoning above, they would be recognized not as <u>two individuals</u>, but only the <u>one</u> in body ... <u>as God made them</u>! Absurd as these crude analogies might seem, they make about as much sense as that decision handed down in the Littleton case and other nonsensical puritanical decisions aimed at pleasing the majority at the expense of those affected by being transgender. And you who are normal wonder why we rage or <u>voice our contempt about injustice</u>! I believe that local, county, or even state courts will not have the final say on this matter. I believe that ultimately our nation's Supreme Court or federal legislators will one day be forced to rule on defining these complexes, yet simple to solve contemporary issues confronting this small segment of the world's populace.

Just as a recent court ruling declared that the words "<u>Under God</u>" be stricken from our nation's Pledge of Allegiance, those placed in judicial roles <u>must learn to rule with their hearts as well as their heads</u>, and with

<u>plain old common sense and logic</u>. Thankfully, that did happen in this incident and the state rights "Under God" in our pledge are restored. I doubt the founding fathers had a trans-person in mind when it wrote that pledge, but its words ring as true today as then: "One nation, under God, indivisible, with liberty and "justice for all"! "<u>Justice ... for all</u>." I wish that it was indeed a perfect world.

Besides, in the past few years, another issue has come to the forefront in Texas, as well as states like North Carolina and others. It's an issue to regulate bathroom use and keep transgender Texans from using bathrooms that align with their gender identity. In 2017, the Bill came up for a vote to make that directive into state law. This legislative effort, backed by the state's Lt. Governor, would have required transgender people like me to use bathrooms in public schools, government buildings, and public universities based on "biological sex.

The measure would have preempted local nondiscrimination ordinances that allow transgender Texans to use the bathroom that corresponds with their gender identity. This call to action prompted school board meetings across the state to listen to why such a law would be necessary. It was noted that the legislators touting the Bill claimed that they wanted to protect their wives and children from "pedophiles that target restrooms, especially men pretending to be women.

Mind you, trans-women are not pedophiles, nor are we men "pretending" to be women. Ours is an identity related to gender, not a sexual perversion. What are we that have lived full-time, worked full-time, dressed as women, and do all medical science can do to give us the appearance and bodies related to women? Are we to venture into a public restroom in our dresses and prance up to a urinal before men and squat? It's ridiculous to assume or consider that such an idea is feasible, much less ethical. Besides, who would enforce such a law? Is there to be bathroom police at our schools, libraries, sports stadiums, colleges that blow the whistle and declare a foul each time one of us "ladies" ventures into a restroom? As President Biden would say, "Come on man!"

My resulting action was to go before open school board meetings and present the case for trans-women and men, plus the case of trans-children in our schools. I had but three minutes in each meeting, but as you might imagine, I politely scolded those parents or others that agreed there should be such a law. I agreed that if the school system administrators know of a child with transgender tendencies, or one that has come out into the open and declared her / himself transgender, then the school needs to alert the parents, and then do all they can to accommodate and protect that trans-child from discrimination and bathroom facilities; to not deny them their dignity by telling them they'll have to use the restroom of their biological sex.

The Texas Legislature failed to pass a bathroom bill during the 2017 regular legislative session, or during a summer special session. One of the reasons for the failure was there was absolutely no evidence presented that transgender people are a threat to anyone, much fewer children or the wives and other women entering female bathroom facilities. The trans-woman goes there for the same reasons anyone would … probably too relieve their bladders … in a private stall to finish their business, then wash their hands, and leave peacefully as the others do.

Question 9: What are your greatest fears? What worries you the most?

Worrying ... worries me the most. What purpose does it serve? None I suppose, but that doesn't mean any of us can stop doing it. What do I fear most? I try not to be afraid … only cautious. I did have trepidations that I would come home one day and find my closet again full of male attire, discovering this has all been just a delicious dream. As if! Though I always dreamed that one day I'd be known and accepted by others as a woman, it took many years of effort before I made it happen or believed it could be done. Well, it is real, I found my fears have in a large part been overcome and for the most part they no longer exist. Like anyone, I don't wish to die, but I know that physical death is inevitable, but it is well with my soul.

For quite some time, I've had no thought that perhaps this too is an illusion, or that I am only dreaming. The joys of my life as Shannon have

Pink Heart

exceeded even my wildest expectations. I've not been a beauty queen or that darling little petite Scarlet O'Hara type woman, but I still enjoy life as a reasonably attractive, tall, mature woman who possesses integrity and a strong sense of pride. A very wise trans-sister once told me, "A life lived in fear ... is a life half lived." That was very good advice, for everyone to follow.

I pray that my journey will not end before I want. I had no desire to be resigned to death in a body declaring me a male, even though female in appearance. I do not want my obituary to read: Male, nor have the coroner because some judge decided to proclaim me to be that way. It is okay if he knows and states, "She has had some upgrades, breast augmentation, GRS surgery, nasal septum surgery" ... but if he declares me male ... I'll swear I'll come back to haunt him forever. ;o)

A trans-woman can only mold the clay just so much. God's hand still guides us every day and though we stumble and fall at times, our faith and our love for life should always pull us through. Nicole and my oldest brother have been my own biggest supporters and have been a Godsend to me in so many ways. Not only is Nicole my soul mate and roommate, but also, she's there every day to help keep me focused and on the straight and narrow. Neither of us shall ever be twenty-one again, but what life we share today and what we will have together promises to be a grand adventure.

I regret falling short of some goals I had for my life. I may never accomplish professionally that which I desire, but I am content in knowing that I've lived and worked as a woman. I also have the goal of writing and selling some successful, marketable novels and songs before my worldly demise. Thus far, Nicole and I have published several books. As for being an author, though I am writing this book, I can tell you I'd much rather be penning a work of fiction for my next novel. Nicole and I have written nine screenplays, seven novels, and have more coming. Writing a non-fictional account about oneself does become tedious, redundant, and much more self-revealing than I first imagined.

I believe that anyone can conquer their fears by doing that which they are most afraid to do. Once you've done that, fear won't happen. Aim for success, not perfection, for if that were the case, I'd aim at being twenty-one again. Now, I'm sort of a hybrid between Dolly Parton and Jane Lynch. Life itself is an experiment, and we should all gain strength and courage from the fact that we learn from every experience and choice we make. In life, we have to face fear head-on and deal with it. I firmly believe in the saying that if we do that which we fear ... then the death of fear is imminent within us.

If you're a trans-woman and becoming a female doesn't ring your bell, then your clapper is broken.

Question 10: Is being transgender truly a duality of the mind and a condition of being schizoid?

Not Really! Yet, as I remarked earlier, I do believe it is somewhat of a schizoid condition. Being transgender may seem to those that are like one person with split personalities, sort of <u>twin souls</u> inside them. Thus, the layman might view the trans-condition as one having a severe case of schizophrenia. In reality, though, there is <u>but one mind</u>, <u>one body</u> ... and <u>one soul</u>. Granted, the trans-woman is obsessed with becoming the gender they prefer themselves to be. Some, as I've pointed out, decide to do something about that, and thus they choose to follow a difficult path that will alter their physical to match that, which is their <u>primary core identity</u> deep inside them.

The idea of two personalities inhabiting one body may seem more logical to some normal laypersons, but it isn't the case at all. Trans-women are, as I've pointed out, <u>not possessed</u>, rather they are <u>obsessed</u>. From whatever mental source it is that compels the MTF trans-woman to think of herself in the gender opposite that of her anatomical sex, it isn't because of two separate entities inside her mind. To a certain extent, it is due to that

Pink Heart

<u>dominant</u> thought process that surreptitiously, or perhaps openly, seeks to right that which feels so wrong about the person's physical body. Until it is properly feminized, she is incomplete and out of synchronization with her female mind. Realize that the trans-woman has but <u>one</u> brain, so whatever thoughts transpire within it about gender incongruity is not the result of schizophrenia.

A Trans-woman is continually drawn to that gender which is the dominant one of their core identities. If that is <u>female,</u> as is the case in that of trans-women, then it is as a moth drawn to a flame. No matter what diversion or illusion of male normalcy the person may present outwardly to others in the guise of that anatomical sex that one <u>was assigned</u> at <u>birth</u>, inside them is a female desperately seeking and desiring to come forth into the light. Whether that happens or not, the interior base mind/soul is not split into <u>two entities</u>, it is but one fractured, <u>unfinished mind/soul</u>, that seeks to heal itself by becoming that which <u>she</u> dreams about every waking hour of every day ... becoming <u>a woman</u>. If denied that, then indeed to others and perhaps even herself, the trans-woman might at times seem schizoid, but in truth, she is not. I would explain it in James Bond type terms...or as if the trans-woman has become a double agent.

The trans-woman often finds herself flung into a deep perplexing calamity and remains ignorant, blind, or in denial as to whom she is or where she is heading. She becomes like a ship without a rudder or a sea captain without a compass.

Regrettably, the trans-woman may even become <u>self-argumentative</u> with that female side of her personality that is in opposition to that which exists openly as a male. I know, because it happened to me all the time. Thus, the MTF trans-woman may submerge that which she hopes, dreams, and prefers to be as the male side of her personality resists removing the mask of falsity and unveiling the real person inside the shell.

Referring once again to the tug of war concept, I believe, the <u>mind</u> merely becomes <u>an arena of conflict</u> whereby the confusing, rough-textured degrees of separation from the <u>adulation of a female</u> to <u>become one</u> are part of the mind/body relationship and the eventual process of transition. The true MTF trans-woman at some point will not succumb to the will of her male counterpart and the farce imposed upon her by society, nor self-restraint that prevented her from being her. Thus, she forces her other side to the surface, and the physiological, neurological, and psychological find a <u>harmonization</u> within her that evolves into a solitary sense of purpose. It must be considered that males and females are not simply linear opposites. This concept is somewhat akin to body parts being interconnected; just as our lungs engage in a perpetual adjustment, first filling bit by bit, and then steadily emptying. In a trans-woman, this inter-relatedness never assumes a completely stationary state of being.

I would also offer this one caveat. A MTF who cannot claim their female side, may find their indecision leading to his or her self-undoing. Those whom I have witnessed that believe they are MTF trans-women and make no strides in reality to achieve their dream, often wind up with a fractured personality and a longing for that which they can never seem to achieve.

"She Lives"

By: Shannon O'Shea

From the start ... when I was born,
As a dismal male ... I'd felt her scorn,
But as I grew ... and went life's way,
She grew too ... more every day!
She was like a bird ... that seldom sings,
For I'd grounded her... with somber wings.
Harnessed, halting ... self-denial,
Condemned before ... she'd had her trial.
Yet still, she whispered ... to my mind,
No peace from her ... was I to find.
Laid-open my heart ... my soul to bare,
Naught but faint pulse ... was stirring there.
Then in the evening ... of my life,
She came to me ... one clear, dark night.
I dreamt of dancing ... ladies fair,
With billowing skirts ... and golden hair.
They twirled and whirled ... in ecstasy.
I dreamt that ... one of them ... was ME!
In beauty, I drifted ... with style and grace,
Then she appeared ... and WE embraced.
Knew I then ... that she'd always stay,
Even when the night ... gave into a day.
That next new morn ... I heard HER sing,
Stood tall did she ... to unfurl her wings.
Lilting and free ... she began to fly,
WE soared together ... through the endless sky.
As two became one ... in dawn's new light,
And so ... SHE LIVES ... in pure delight

PART 3

Question 11: How do you feel about same-sex marriages?

Before I attempt to answer that, permit me to impart to you, the reader a rather unique scenario of which I wage you have never considered. What I am about to reveal to you is not some imaginative or farcical whim that I dreamt up to make this story more interesting. Nope! It is indeed a <u>real-life incident</u> that has come about due to certain circumstances and … as you might imagine, it involves a post-op trans-person. For my illustration, I shall mention no real names, but in their stead shall call the pre-op trans, Michael, and the legally married spouse to Michael being called, Jane.

Michael and Jane have been married for over 20 years and have by marriage, several children and grandchildren. Michael retired from a successful military career and began working for a contractor that supplies aircraft for the federal government. During this time, Michael decided to become, Michelle. Jane did not particularly enjoy the prospect, but went along anyway and supported Michael's efforts to become Michelle. Sometime last year, Michael legally became Michelle. She had her gender reassignment surgery and afterward because she was born in Indiana, was able to change her birth certificate, which now amended identifies her sex and gender as being <u>female</u>.

Now comes the conundrum. Although Michael and Jane were husband and wife, male and female before the surgery, what happens now that Michelle has been legally recognized by the state of her birth as being female? They still live together and plan to remain that way. One can only assume that the reason has to do with love, devotion, and the willingness to compromise.

The questions that arise from this scenario, as it applies to their situation are numerous. If they are now two females living together, as spouses, does not that imply a same-sex union? This brings up many issues of concern for those that declare a legal marriage is only between a male and a female. Therefore, what about this marriage? Does it even exist any longer, or does the state they reside in (Texas) have the right to absolve or now to simply ignore their marriage? Would the state use as its basis that from the moment of the alteration of the <u>birth certificate</u> proclaiming Michelle is a female that there was no longer a basis for the state to recognize their union as a legal marriage? Hey, wait a minute! I've already brought out that in Texas the law states once a male ... always a male, no matter what is done to the physical body to alter it. Therefore, in Texas law, a post-op trans-woman is merely considered a <u>castrated, mutilated, surgically-altered male</u>.

However, Texas is compelled to accept the legal declaration of a person's designated sex upon a birth certificate. So, if her birth state and its official documentation of birth declare Michelle's female ... then she is indeed legally female in the eyes of the federal government. Confused yet? Wait it gets better.

Is the next national movement for an amendment to our U.S. constitution going to carry this absurdity a step further and proclaim that a marriage can only be between a double XX chromosome person and an XY chromosome person? Has anyone that's reading this ever seen a dang chromosome anyway? When was the last time you saw a guy whistle at a pretty girl and remark, "Hey check out the chromosomes on that babe"! The last thing we need is more legalese added to an already bewildering and controversial situation.

Marriages that were legal when they began might, under such scrutiny as those listed above become dissolved. A marriage that society acknowledged as being legitimate and constitutional before now is mired in semantics and interpretations that are being forced onto the trans-person by those that are not. Reverend Louis Sheldon started a lobby group that clamored for a constitutional amendment proclaiming a ban on all same-sex marriages ... including civil unions. He dared to proclaim "Absolutely! We don't want the roof to leak in any place. We must make sure that marriage is protected." Protected from what reverend ... and from whom?

As with the Littleton case in Texas, when a transgender female that was married to a male died under questionable circumstances, the trans-woman brought suit for wrongful death and attempted to collect from the hospital's insurance. It was likely she would have won her case for a large sum of money had she not been transgender. The next thing that transpired was that the insurance company brought to the court's attention the fact that she is a trans-woman.

The court then ruled that the marriage was dissolved, as there was never a legal marriage. The court also stated that she has no claim for damages, as she has no legal right to damages ensuing from the death of the man, she claimed was her husband ... even though the couple had obtained a legal marriage license and lived together for many years. On the spot, that court nullified that marriage and the judges' bigoted decision stated that Ms. Littleton was born male and that, despite gender reassignment surgery, the state would not recognize that <u>his</u> sex had indeed been altered. Thus, to the court, no marriage ever existed.

What was this case all about? Simple really; it was about <u>M O N E Y</u> and devising legal loopholes for an insurance entity to save paying it to Ms. Littleton. However, this one case set precedent, and all future trans-persons in the states of Texas, Tennessee, Ohio, and Kansas all now must suffer and face having their state of origin refuse to amend birth certificates even after GRS has been performed. Even though the individual has accomplished the process of changing genders and taking on an entirely new identity, these states refuse to update or recognize their new gender. They accomplished this unfair ruling to introduce more bias into the minds of everyone that deals with those that are transgender.

In over half of the remaining states of the country, a trans-woman <u>can</u> have her birth certificate amended, and thus continues the enigma. No firm policy on this issue leaves those of us that are MTF trans-women in a state all right ... a <u>state of confusion and frustration like I pointed out earlier</u>. We're in a state of flux and once more finding ourselves the victims of prejudice, discrimination, fear, and misunderstanding. Is this America or is it Nazi land? Do the moral majority and religious right hold in its heart a bible, but wear a swastika on its shoulder? Michelle and Jane aren't looking for legal loopholes. They only seek to continue in a loving, legal partnership that began for them decades ago. Since they do not wish to separate, no court can yet issue a divorce. Why then should a law be made to force them to lose all that they acquired together, or all that they hope to share with the other in this life and after one is gone from this Earth? What power on earth can state to them their love and devotion is a travesty or a ruse?

If Congress chooses to bow to the pressures of the religious majority, what happens then? Are trans-women then not to be able to marry anyone of either sex? What if congress adopted such an amendment that would restrict, nullify, or define who can be married, unified, or legally partnered to whom? Would not our nation then become one … <u>of</u> the <u>most people</u>, <u>for</u> the <u>most people</u> … by the <u>most people</u>, and not one whereby there is liberty and justice for all!

Conclusion: <u>Do I approve of Same-Sex Marriage?</u>

I would tell the reader not to conclude that because I share my life with another trans-woman of the same sex, that I agree with those that sanction a marriage between two people that are of the same sex. I would remind the reader that Nicole and I are roommates, mates, or whatever you wish to call us. If we marry, then it is no concern to anyone except ourselves. So, are we? I'm not telling! All I know is I love the dang lady and she loves me. We've been together for over twenty years now, so I suppose a common-law marriage is an appropriate description of our union. Whether our relationship is an intimate one or merely that of a platonic nature, is as I stated a private matter and of no importance to anyone except the two of us. I will tell you, that in my opinion, we share <u>love</u>, and we have a civil union certificate from the state of Vermont.

I would agree with the notion that the <u>traditional institution</u> of <u>marriage</u> is indeed a bonding between <u>one man</u> and <u>one woman</u>. That's not a definition; it is just how marriage has been viewed and perceived.

Nicole and I are together <u>because we want to be</u>! When we said our vows of love in Vermont, those were for a <u>Civil Union</u> and not a legal marriage. Since same-sex marriage has been declared constitutionally legal in all states, we may tie the knot, so to speak, mainly because of inheritance and other legal issues.

We knew in Vermont and we know it now that a Civil Union in Vermont is not legal in Texas. That does not mean we both wouldn't like to have some of the legal restraints lifted by our government that would sanction such things as tax breaks, rights of inheritance, combined income verification, and insurance coverage for those of us in same-sex unions. It would also be nice to receive some of the general societal support given to married heterosexual couples.

I do, however, agree that the foundation of marriage has served our nation and the world well, and I for one present no dissent to have that sacred institution trivialized or degraded in any way. Most all of us are the by-products of marriages and most of us have parents that consisted of a mother and a father, be they biological, or in my case were acquired by adoption.

If the Supreme Court had not ruled for legal same-sex marriages and that came to a vote, then the majority would likely win and the remainder of those left in the minority of being gay or lesbian would have become even more divided and bitter at the heterosexual, religious factions that attempted to sanctify something that is already sanctified. To me, there are far more worthy issues with which to concern our congress and us. This distraction has already caused a furor within the nation's masses and especially sparked a passionate outcry by those within the religious community to whom the code of laws governing marriage is a holy sacrament blessed by God. Of course, it is, as it should be. Still, those same religious fundamentalists can't imagine that perhaps God also has joined together this woman to this woman … or this man to this man. Doesn't the vow go, "What God has joined together, let no one put asunder?"

As I see it, we seek a conforming answer to this problem within society and the world that has become very non-conformist. For those who would presume that the very succession and permanence of our society and nation rests upon our conserving and interpreting by a legal measure that which constitutes a legal marriage, I would declare that such an amendment would violate more citizens' rights than it would be designed to protect. I do not believe that gays or lesbians that are in loving, monogamous relationships are a threat to anyone's way of life or society. None of the gays or lesbians I know actively tries to recruit heterosexuals to become gay. None of them are child molesters, none have a contagious gay disease, and as I see it …

Pink Heart

none of their relationships are inherently sinful. Most of the gays and lesbians I know that are <u>partnered</u> off segregate themselves voluntarily from their heterosexual counterparts and pursue their life interests.

My biological parents were divorced, and they like many males and females who enter into such heterosexual unions, wound up separated and eventually divorced. The nation's divorce rate now states that over 50% of all heterosexual marriages end in divorce. Many heterosexual adults have been married more than once or even twice. I spent over 30 years in two marriages that eventually failed. I contend, then that in today's world, the climate is changing for heterosexual marriages. Some marriages seem to no longer be thought of as permanent relationships, but rather some have become serial monogamy and a succession of marital unions. Marriage has enough problems and challenges, but I am pleased that the need to be contested or redefined by those that are domestic partners in the same-sex union occurred by the <u>Supreme Court</u> judges. As well, I contend that those gays and lesbians who make up only two to five percent of the population pose no threat to bring moral destruction to our country or way of life? They and we that are <u>transgender</u> that are partnered with another trans-person, seek mainly <u>legal recognition</u> of our union and to achieve some of the same <u>legal rights</u>, protections, and exemptions as those that are heterosexual couples. Why is that so difficult for others to comprehend?

Would a Constitutional amendment create and place bias into our nation's laws making it only possible for <u>one man</u> and <u>one woman</u> to ever become legal partners? Yes, I most certainly do believe that would be the outcome. To me, those who would spur it on are those whose religious beliefs seek as much to punish homosexuality as they do to vindicate the marriage vows between a man and woman. That, I see as being not God's will, but rather a plurality of homophobic folks that take it upon themselves to solidify their war against homosexuality, or folks different than they. Discrimination by any other word or means is still discrimination.

Gays, lesbians, or <u>transbians</u> deserve the dignity of being given legal recognition for their chosen union and for the love they share with their life partners. If religious factions can place into law a definition limiting any legal union, and let's face it, that is what the religious fundamentalists wish to do, then that leaves that two to five percent of the populous living under even more rigid, discriminatory and unfair biased laws. That isn't going to build bridges between the two segments of society. Rather, it would only serve to deepen the chasms and crevices of hate and misunderstanding.

Divorce, infidelity, spousal abuse, and the dissolution of homes invalidate the argument about protecting traditional family values. What family values is it that produces broken homes, separates children from one parent or the other, and a custodial parent or an ex-spouse who finds him or herself confronting financial hardship or ruin?

Adoption issues affect both married couples, those that are single, and also same-sex couples. I know of several parents whereby either two mothers or two fathers have raised the child or children. Though not traditional, there is no proof that a child automatically becomes gay or lesbian just because both parents are of the same sex. I'm told that children that are raised in same-sex unions more often than not turn out to be heterosexual. Love is the basis of parenthood for a child and should not be of what gender are the parents.

In the process, the Supreme Court has re-enforced the civil rights of bi, gay, lesbian, or transgender citizens. This decision by President Biden to reinstate the rights of transgender soldiers to again serve in our military is a major step forward and reduces the indignities that primarily happen because of the fear and misunderstanding by the majority who does not agree with the life choices or lifestyles of those different than their own. Thus, I absolutely do believe a same-sex union and marriage (based on love) is acceptable and should be honored and legal.

Question 12: Explain your feelings for Nicole and how you envision your future together?

I do look forward to living out my days as her mate and I thank God for sending her into my life. She came to me at a point at which I was at a critical crossroads. I was floundering and had not made the final commitment necessary to become Shannon. With her as inspiration and with her support, I found the courage it took to make those bold physical steps needed to become a woman 24 / 7. I could never have accomplished that monumental feat without her love, compassion, and … gentle nudges.

Get out … and go do … what makes you the happiest. Take some friends and have some fun.

I dated a few guys up until she and I became roommates. That was okay I suppose, but eventually I stopped doing that and she and I eventually became life mates. I never considered that I was gay or lesbian. I still don't think of our love as being that way. Laughingly, we call ourselves "Transbians." In no way did I ever once consider that I'd wind up with a mate who is also transgender, but upon looking closer, the outcome just makes good sense. In retrospect, I have no regrets at all about the decision to take on Nicole as a life mate. My heart has guided me throughout our relationship and as I see it, she is a lovely woman and a dear sweet soul. I am privileged and honored to share with her my life and my love. I pledge to her my undying devotion. I had and have many men that are my friends and are certainly attractive, but when I committed … I did so for life.

In May of 2001, we took a trip up to Vermont and exchanged our vows of celibacy and love in a beautiful, simplistic Civil Union ceremony. A very thoughtful, compassionate lady that is also the Justice of the Peace in a quaint little town called Bennington, Vermont performed the ceremony. Such a civil union, though legal in Vermont, is not recognized in redneck Texas or many other states throughout the country. Vermont's pioneering liberalism for this type of service is now legendary amongst gays, lesbians, and even those that are transgender. Vermont was seen as a positive first step toward legal recognition of same-sex unions throughout the United States.

Do I fret that Nicole will one day desire more from me than I can physically give her? She too is post-op and I know that she loves me with all her heart. I admit I have to wonder if she won't someday regret not having had the opportunity to take her new equipment out for a test drive... as most of us have done with a potent male driver on board. However, I also know she would never do that, for she knows it would not be right and would break a vow that she and I made to each other. Yet, as one of our dearest friends so aptly put it, "It's sort of like owning a Ferrari and keeping it locked up in the garage, only being able to dust it off with a damp cloth now and then." ;o)

Question 13: Is it common for a trans-woman to seek out another trans-woman as a mate?

Nicole and Me Sharing Laughter

I am not privy to any comprised figures of such unions, but personally speaking, I know of several other couples in which both partners are trans-people. Is that an accurate indication that more and more of us are inclined to locate and hook up with another trans-person? That would be presumptive and foolish to assume. Rather I think, these folks are simply "individuals" who found, as I do in Nicole, another human being that they feel close to and one whom they come to love; one that stirs passion for companionship and bestows compassion upon them. Many trans-women I know are attracted to men and have had meaningful relationships with the same. There are MTF trans-women I know who are married to a CIS female and their union remains intact even after they have been through a transition.

To give an opinionated answer, I'd say no, I do not think that there is a trend toward all trans-women becoming transbians. I can certainly understand the motivations when some do decide that path. There are many legal obstacles placed upon any same-sex couple, even if it is a platonic relationship ... and it's even more so for a transgender couple. Nicole and I made living trusts giving each of us a power of attorney or naming the other as the trustee. That way, we each have a legal right to make health care decisions for each other, even if one of us was incapacitated in an accident or incapable of making her own life or death assessment. We have to go through legal steps for us to have a say in what treatment the other would receive. If I were to inherit any of her possessions or she mine, then making out a will or living trust designating such is an absolute necessity. Otherwise, everything goes to her or my heirs and our wishes become as muted a voice as that of one crying in the wilderness.

The bottom line is when in a close relationship with someone you love, be sure to cover all the "legal" bases and protect both parties.

Question 14: What did you learn about your condition by studying psychology and what do you hope to attain from it?

"Open your mind...and say ... Ahhhhh!"

The science of psychology is sometimes a paradox: As I pointed out in the beginning, we know the remotest galaxies and invisible particles of matter better than we know ourselves, often even better than we know those closest to us. Of all the wonders that man has probed on Earth, in the sea, and in the sky, the most interesting of all seems to be humankind itself. We all seek a better self-understanding.

Rather than worrying about what Mother Nature did or didn't do, my intense curiosity and probing of the mysteries of human nature is what motivated me to study the desires of the human condition. I reasoned that if I could learn more about what causes one to become transgender, in the process perhaps I'd come to better understand what beneficial solutions there might be to helping those who are trans-women…myself included. Human nature is a trait of the species and not just of some culture.

In the future, through efforts like this book, I hope to be able to pass along some of what I've learned to others and those like me. If I can give back something to those behind me in this journey, I will feel I've accomplished something productive. Writing this text then is my attempt to present ideas and explain my perspectives and ideas to other trans-sisters that might come after me. I've observed and experienced valuable life lessons from those others that were ahead of me in this journey and I've learned from their successes and failures. I owe a great debt of gratitude to those sisters who have shown me with their lives the example of how to triumph at being a woman, and not just as a trans-lady.

The human mind is a fascinating, vastly complex apparatus that I find intriguing. By studying things such as dreams, aspiration, suspicion, phobias, and the thought processes of why we humans do certain things, how we act and react to conditional stimulus, one cannot help but be provided with a much clearer view of one's situation in life. I have been a witness to the many mysteries of thought and I am awed by the conundrum whereby each of us attempts to maintain our rationality, attempting to keep ourselves in synch and in that balance, I referred to earlier.

Like others, sometimes I too stray off course. Through the study of psychology, I sought the ability to recognize and find solutions for what needs to be said or done to maintain the right course and a wholesome outlook. My quest has been to help others and myself, perhaps to assist some other friends or trans-person obtain a qualified therapist and receive treatment that would aid them in their endeavor to find the correct answers. Every trans-woman should attempt to support her sisters with encouragement in hopes of returning their lives, as well as our own, to the proper balance for which we all are looking.

At one time, I aspired to become a gender counselor for those considering treatment for gender dysphoria. Was that some measure of transference from my sessions with my gender counselor? I didn't think so at first, but upon further review perhaps it was. At any rate, I truly believed I could empathize with those who would come to me seeking answers. I believed in my insight and knew I would express empathy and compassion for others if allowed to counsel. However, in time, I found that I do not have the same passion for counseling. Nor have I possessed the confidence that counseling others were my calling. Thus, my desire to take on such a challenge waned. That does not mean I have no opinions or guidance to give, only that I did not do so in a formalized setting or seek my license to counsel. I prefer at this time to entrust other sisters and my well-being to those more qualified and experienced counselors. If I have an opportunity in life to help with transition matters of another trans-woman, then I shall do what I can to assist that individual to become a better person and to have a more complete understanding of herself as a woman. The problems and challenges which they shall face in their journey are likely not too different from my own.

My opinion concerning this transgender condition is just that ... <u>an opinion</u>., and merely my viewpoint to express. I can only hope that I present it with a degree of intelligence and honesty that will be beneficial and not counterproductive. For sure, my views are not the science of psychology, even if I base them upon scientific fact. Nor do I pretend to have all the answers, even for my own life. More often than not, my laboratory has been life itself. Most of what I've learned has been self-taught, as well as in a classroom.

Over the years, I would note that I became an accomplished and effective salesperson. I know human nature enough that I can usually discern what motivates people to buy or not buy some product, idea, or service. I am very good at pointing out added value and stressing benefits, but even better at asking for the sale. I am even adept at discerning personality types and forming my impressions as to the profiles of those with whom I come into contact. Still, that hardly qualifies me to conduct formal therapy sessions for those in need of them.

Like any human, I have those to whom I feel closer and that I enjoy being around more than I do others. That too is human nature. Those with whom I am friendlier and who are friendlier to me are those to which I'm more likely to offer my opinions and help. As Freud concentrated his efforts on the study of the term he coined, libido, Jung concluded that the one motive that embraced us all is the <u>desire to belong</u>. I do seek to make all those trans-sisters I come into contact with who believe they are transgender feel <u>worthy to belong</u> in that group who call themselves <u>women</u>. I want them to understand that they are all still God's children and that as such, they deserve the blessings of God and abundant life. Just because we are trans-women, we need not resign from the human race or pigeonhole all our hopes or dreams. On the contrary, theirs and my dreams are simply changed and become more focused on reality and thus are amplified in so many positive ways.

> PANIC! undo Escape! delete

Don't look for the above keyboard buttons after you make a mistake in life. You won't find them.

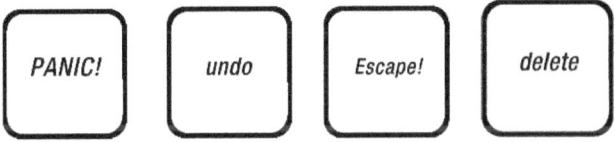

Life can only be lived forward. They say life begins at 40 … or in my case 46, but you'll miss a lot of fun if you wait that long.

WELCOME If grandpa becomes Aunt Minnie, and dad becomes Miss Elaneous, it may be that you won't find a welcome mat at every relative's front door. I sure didn't.

The yin and yang of it are...the only one that likes change is the baby with a wet **diaper.**

Question 15: What real value do you see from counseling/therapy for those who are transgender?

As I see it, the first thing to establish must be <u>why</u> a person is seeking professional help in the first place. The gender counselor should be adept at interviewing and a capable interpreter of the client/patient's reactions. Even if the person seeking help thinks he or she is transgender, the counselor must somehow assure that person of their fundamental normalcy and then decide how to guide the person toward possible alternate courses of action and responses. A wise counselor will also inform the client/patient of the realities of life and direct them toward a rewarding experience (going out in public with other trans-sisters, which is reinforcing.

For a novice trans-woman, it is paramount the counselor train them in feminine social graces and social behavior suggesting ways in which their lives can be stabilized and enriched. A big step is re-conditioning away the novice trans-woman's fears, and for some, I would suggest a change in environment.

My counselor encouraged all those she counsels to join her and their trans-sister peers in a monthly support group meeting. For a transgender person in transition, I found these meetings to be very beneficial, in that the exchange of information, ideas, and friendships made are priceless. The counselor told others and me that she had people come to her offering to pay her to tell them they are transgender. Like any good therapist, she did not gratify and she did not tell her client what she thinks that person is but drew out of her/him what the individual believed they were. If one is indeed transgender that fact came to light on its own.

Like every journey, at some point, therapy also needs to come to an end. None of us graduated with degrees or expertise at becoming females, but we did progress, through stages in a process toward our personal goals. It's up to each individual to determine when they are at a certain point in their life that they became comfortable and confident enough with who they are and of making the rest of the journey on their own, without the need of counsel or the support of others. I found that to be a major step in the process.

Some elect to have cosmetic surgical changes done to their face or body. This will require the services of a skilled and affordable cosmetic surgeon. The ultimate gender reassignment surgery will also require the skills and service of a qualified and expert GRS surgeon. The bottom line is, this is a long, arduous journey filled with pain, major expense, and one which precludes the need for several professionals to help one attain their goal of living in their chosen gender role.

All trans-women may have some issues that they are never quite confident about, and some may keep seeing counselors/therapists the rest of their days. For me, I reached a pinnacle and point in my life whereby I thought it was time I flew with my own wings. Thus, I chose to have less therapy after I became 24 / 7. My counselor never insisted that I continue in private sessions, but there were times when I'm sure she would prefer I had for her sake as well as my own. Yet, she left it to each of us she counseled one on one with to decide what direction they took in their lives.

We knew she was there if we needed her, or if we needed someone of authority to speak to and guide us back onto the proper paths. I know that

Pink Heart

for post-ops, this desire for direction seemed to become less acute after GRS. Until someone goes 24 / 7 and experiences a woman's life happening to them personally, I truly don't think they fully understand the need and desire to blend into society.

In the course of her life, a trans-woman often finds a few people she can talk to about her condition. If she is ruled by fear and as a result, she represses being transgender, it becomes her closely guarded secret. Her world can be uncharted and seemingly a hodge-podge of purges and denial cycles that lead her into confusion, frustration, anger, depression, and even self-degradation. Instead of controlling her destiny, she lets it control her. Like too many of her trans-sisters, she travels where others think she <u>should go</u>, her life is miserable, and she becomes very bitter. What changes her fate and makes her wake up to what she must do then?

It isn't just one thing, but a combination of many. She wasn't meant to be a withdrawn and bitter man, but rather an open and gentle-hearted woman. There is no such thing as wasted steps when your final destination is discovering true self-transformation. All those tough roads she journeys down should teach her where she desires to be. Never mind how difficult the task before her appears, if she'll seek to accomplish one thing at a time, then another and another ... one day she will find she's arrived at her chosen destination. Take things one day and one step at a time.

Counseling was for me a true blessing and exhilarating experience. It helped play an important part in my reaching many of my personal goals. In seeking answers and a new direction, I sought and found my counselor, recognizing immediately that I liked her. She listened and I could tell she genuinely cared. She respected me and exhibited compassion toward what I was going through.

I advise against anyone using the services of a counselor that does not display similar qualities. For the person who thinks she is a trans-woman, counseling should be something that does not instill apprehension, but rather a time when you can be straightforward and entirely honest and open. It should become an interval of eager anticipation where you can free your mind and confess and discuss those things that have been withheld from yourself or others ... perhaps for many years. Your gender counselor and you might be of a different opinion about certain things, but if he or she is upsetting or argumentative and makes the situation unpleasant then the experience will be counterproductive. If he or she is sympathetic and has worked with other transgender folks before, then that's all the better!

In sessions or out, we did not discuss other transgender folks, nor use their specific names, as each counselor should adhere to their vows of ethics and client / patient confidentiality. Rather, we only discussed my gender identity condition itself and how it affects those of us who have it.

Don't be the world's punching bag. Gather your courage, your purse, and throw a few punches of your own at life and the world in which you want to live.

Question 16: In your previous marriages to women, how were your children affected by your being transgender?

That time of my life imbedded many precious moments in my memory, and yet it was also frustrating and traumatic. It was a private period of my life that in many ways I cherish, but one that I knew could not continue if Shannon were ever to exist. I consider both my ex-wives (X1 and X2) and all my kids as being blameless beings in this whole scenario. They were not in the wrong, nor did they do anything that caused me to take the action I did. They were merely being their selves and expected me to do the same.

That meant, to my kids ... I was to be a father and provider, plus to my wives ... to be a husband. I tried very hard to accomplish those roles and to maintain that image. However, as time proved out, that was a familial status in which I was ultimately a miserable failure and one I could not accomplish.

Pink Heart

X1 came to know about my true nature many years after we were married. I explained my fem desires to X2 before marriage. One night in privacy, when we were still dating, I told X2 of my past and cross-dressing. I even emphasized that I wished I'd been born a girl. I was so afraid of losing her, that I didn't tell her everything I felt, but it was enough that she could have ended it right there, but she didn't. Better for us both if she had. She either did not understand what I had said to her, or else she blocked it out of her mind and merely considered it to be a phase that would later vanish. It was not just a passing phase, but an ever-growing obsession.

For the most part, I had hidden all evidence of my true desires from my first spouse. I was angry with X1 for quite some time for some things she accused me of and how she reacted to finding out I had fem desires. She claimed I was mentally sick, as in being a pervert, for she could not grasp the concept of my being feminine in any way. It appalled and angered her. Though, I never accentuated enough to her or X2 where I wanted or expected my transgender nature to take me. Back then, I suppose even I was not certain of what path I'd take.

X2 was a sweet distraction and she somehow made it easier for me to retract the tentacles of my trans-tendencies and desires, and then to put them on hold. For many years, my love for X2 sustained me and seemed to keep my fem side and Shannon at bay. For most of my years married to her, I didn't even cross-dress. As I stated, I believe that she considered this side of me to be merely a fetish and never considered my feminine nature to be a serious threat to our relationship or marriage. She simply forgot about it over the years and I suppressed all of my fem instincts and never exhibited <u>any</u> feminine desires openly to her until after we'd been married for over eleven years. I did that was after my birth mother died.

My fem nature then came out in the waning days of my marriage to X2, bursting forth with a pent-up attitude and a vengeance, all of which transpired after my birth mother's funeral. It became increasingly difficult for both of us, for as Shannon grew stronger within me, the signs of her impending emergence grew also. In time, X2's resolve also faded, and eventually, she too lost hope that I would ever relent or turn back toward ever again being her husband and her man.

We had some difficult decisions ahead and I recall periodic discussions between us as to what our future together ... if any would be like. Never did I desire to lose her as a mate, for I loved her dearly, but I also knew I was doing her no favors by staying around in the role of her lame-duck husband. Though my love for her was genuine, there was always this huge question mark on tomorrow's calendar. Somewhere in time, I quit making her promises I knew I couldn't keep, and she began to see there was little ground to be gained from flogging a dead horse. The writing was on the wall and the end was rapidly approaching.

As the days and months passed, it came down to a time and point where I suggested that she may be better off if she and I folded our cards and just moved on with our lives, before we both got hurt more by my impending decision to transition. I was reluctant to use the word divorce, but we each knew that such an end was the probable final alternative.

Our kids were involved in the schools, so X2 had no aspirations to leave the home we had there in Abilene, Texas. I decided that it was best if I sought and took a job in Dallas to put some time and distance between the two of us, giving her and me the occasion to think, breathe, and ponder our future.

I found and accepted a job in Dallas and moved there from our new 3600 square foot home on seven acres in Abilene (that I contracted and built) into a 600 square foot one-bedroom apartment in big "D". I left Abilene in the spring of '97 and left behind all that was dear to me, including almost every material possession I owned of any value. Yet, those were just things. By then, I was self-absorbed with the overwhelming compulsion and desire to explore life anew and to attempt to put into focus where I was going and what I was trying to accomplish. I needed time to embellish and expand the feminine within me.

This process would not come easily, instantly, nor without many challenges to my physical, financial, and mental psyche. Not only would I fight the melancholy of missing my beloved wife, children, and the home we'd made together, but the economics of my situation only got worse over the next few years. During this especially emotional and testing transitional

Pink Heart

period, I would learn if I truly had the resolve to carry out my life's dreams, or if this too were a mere illusion.

During this <u>alone time</u>, Shannon tasted freedom from the restrictions I'd placed upon her by the years of commitments to marriage. However, as I've noted throughout this text, such freedom would come with a very steep price tag and leave in its wake the residual lives of those I most cherished in this world.

Though I doubt it would have worked, I confess to you that more than once I gave serious thought about abandoning my desires to become Shannon, to seek and ask for a return to the life I'd lived before with X2 and my kids. If, during those first clumsy months in Dallas when my psyche was struggling to seek its own identity, if X2 had called and asked me, perhaps I would have laid down my dreams of becoming Shannon forevermore and returned to her arms without reservation. Why would I have done such a thing? My answer to that was because of my self-doubts, plus the love for her and my children. It was the same catalyst that prevented me from pursuing my dreams earlier on in my life.

As it turned out, X2 made her own choices and desired not to remain married to me. She already decided that such a state of affairs would return no happiness to her or my children, but rather only perhaps beget more problems in the future. I believe she was right about that. She questioned and or worried that I might relent later on and again renew my decision to seek my fem self. While I was in Dallas, she was already dating and seeing another man, whom she eventually would marry. Do I blame her? If things were reversed, I might have done the same as she.

My biggest opponent during this time in my life was <u>loneliness and depression</u>. I found the best and only tonic for this was a distraction. By that, I mean I had to occupy my mind, not with the ghosts of my past, but with the challenges and promise of the future. I needed to focus on the tasks before me and with becoming involved in some other outside interests that would afford me some relief from the feelings of <u>self-exile</u> and being alone in the world. I knew early on that I could not segregate myself from others and that I had to seek out other trans-sisters and anyone who could help me defeat those down in the dumps blues that I had during that isolated, lonely period in my fem life's journey.

Using the resources of the Internet, I sought and became friends with other trans-women online. In the process, I also happened upon chat rooms and forums whereby some <u>men</u> began to contact me. After some initial online communication and cyber foreplay, a few became interested and willing to date me. At that stage of my journey, I was more curious than I was smart and did some foolish things when meeting some of these guys. Though I was intrigued with the prospects of actual alive, breathing males being attracted to me, I wasn't sure about how I would react, nor how I should react to their flirtations. Admittedly, I was flattered and did find myself being inquisitive about them. A few of them I did meet during those first few years in Dallas.

Being a Woman ... Music That Sirs My Soul

I read how other male-to-female trans-women, though totally heterosexual before, had become interested and attracted to men after they went 24 / 7, or became post-op. For the life of me, I never thought that I

Pink Heart

would ever be the slightest bit attracted sexually to a male. As a trans-woman, I considered it a slim possibility, but in reality, it never was an issue of concern. In time, I found it surprising that the more feminine I became, the more I seemed to notice attractive things about guys. Maybe it was the effect of the estrogens, but at any rate, at some point, it began to seem more natural to consider a male for a sexual partner. In many ways I found this idea repulsive ... and yet it was odd, for it also seemed an accepted (for many trans-women ... and expected) progression for my becoming a female.

I acknowledge that in my dreams, as I fantasized about being a woman and having a man make love to me. <u>That was fantasy</u> and daily life was reality. However, my responses to the attractions males had for me, or I for them were never as joyous as I'd imagined. The outcome was never what I wanted, nor as rewarding as I had hoped. On many of my dates with men, I found them to be self-centered, shallow, and none seemed interested in any sort of a long-term relationship. All they seemed interested in was having sex. Some candidly confessed they only wanted to date me for <u>sex</u> ... if that were the case, they <u>did not</u> get it from me; others were far too short, were married, or themselves closeted crossdressers who were simply curious about me.

I never began a date with the anticipation or preconception that the liaison would lead to a sexual one. I was not naive, for I knew the risks I was taking by going out alone with these guys, but I was firm and avoided the issue of having sex unless I felt they were serious about a relationship. Some of the guys were gentlemen who respected my right of denial and they simply enjoyed my company. For the most part, I wanted companionship and to be <u>treated like a lady</u> by a man. There was heavy petting and hugs and kissing ... leading to what men and women do. Still, I found no intense sexual passion for those I dated there that first year in Dallas. Perhaps, the reason for those stems from a <u>Pre-Dallas incident</u> that sort of ruined it for me and made me set my expectations and sights a bit too high.

I had made some stupid, terrible, and serious mistakes before my leaving Abilene for Dallas. At this point, I could just skip on by this section and complete this book, but if this story is to be a true confessional, then I must, in all honesty, admit to you the error of my ways and reveal to you my humanity and the weaknesses of the flesh. Only by doing this shall I include to you my bleak experiences, as well as my good.

As I pointed out, my desire to become a female became so intense that in the beginning, I self-administered my hormones via stealth business trips to Juarez, Mexico. I protected and hid my hormonal bounty from X2 and my kids, much like a mother hen protecting her young; including my ever-growing feminine wardrobe, which I stashed amongst the darkened recesses and corners of my car's trunk, or else in some local storage facility. My mind became a clutter, filled with fem possibilities ... and yet it had no order or chronology. I didn't seem to have the courage to act upon most of my impetuous desires, much less have a clue on how to properly proceed with my transition.

In retrospect, I was ill-prepared in dealing with the psychological aspects of becoming Shannon. As a result, I caused myself and my spouse a great deal of anguish in the process. At home back then, though a novice with a computer, I became obsessed with the Internet and the chat rooms which afforded me opportunities to live out my feminine fantasies, even if only in a cyber world of virtual unreality. In those chat rooms, to those other sister cyber travelers that lurked and joined my surreal femme adventures, I was young, vibrant, and above all ... female. I became obsessed with this medium and the opportunities to chat, in real-time, to my peers and to others whose interests mirrored my own. As stated earlier, I managed to make some contacts with Texas area trans-sisters, mostly in Dallas and other towns in Texas where I traveled on business. Many of these girls would become close friends. Most, I no longer have contact with, as we all went our ways after a few years.

More and more, I had come to drift from favor with my children, all save my youngest daughter. She and I seemed to remain close, even up till the time I was last with her in Dallas and introduced her to me as Shannon. That reality happened several months before her mother filed for divorce, and it wound up being a point of contention with X2 during the court hearing.

Pink Heart

Though I intended to introduce my daughter to my true nature and femme side, in retrospect, I came to realize that the incident was ill-conceived, ill-timed, and served as a catalyst to confuse my young daughter even more. Unknowingly and unintentionally, the incident caused her undue mental anguish by exposing her too soon to that side of me that is Shannon. She was but nine years old and I should have known better. I desired to be honest with her, but instead, her young mind became confused and bitter about losing her Dah Dah (father).

My son had graduated high school and he and X2's teenaged daughter appeared to be so absorbed in their own lives, the trauma occurring in my life was of little concern to them. For the most part, I suppose it appeared I showed marginal interest in their lives as well. I worked hard in my career but was bitter because my family did not seem to notice or care. They and X2 had their problems and agendas with which to deal. Back then, I was a road warrior and traveled a great deal in my job, and I'm certain my absence at home contributed to this sort of apathy. X2 was left to discipline and teach them, and I was the weekend stranger that came for a few days, and then was off on the road again. None of them, X2 included, ever really grasped all the work, loneliness, and effort I put in to get them <u>the things</u> they all took for granted. The problem was, they could have done without the things, for <u>they needed me</u> instead and I was too often not there. I scarcely mentioned my work or brought the job-related problems I had into my home, but in truth the position I had created a lot of stress and caused me lots of angst.

My traveling manufacturer's rep position also was a factor in contributing to Shannon's growth as much as anything else. It afforded me more than normal <u>opportunities</u> to dress in-femme. The negatives of the job were the travel, as it was counterproductive to my marriage relationship and worked to estrange me even more from X2 and my kids. It did, as I stated, make me a great deal less visible to all of them daily. Because I traveled three to four overnights per workweek, my presence and influence within my immediate family unit eroded and was made marginal, even though I was the major provider of family income. Over time, I came to feel like I became just a paycheck to my family ... and very little more. Maybe that was not the case, but it sure seemed like it.

Because of my absence, X2's influence on the kids far outweighed my own. When I returned from my trips and sought affection from my kids, I mainly received in return their teenage indifference. My baby girl was the one <u>primary reason</u> I stayed in the relationship when in truth <u>I should have dissolved the marriage years before</u>.

In retrospect, I realize that I was probably not very pleasant back then, and I could not have been much fun to be around at home. I think this was due to being torn between <u>two worlds</u>, one of <u>reality</u> and the other of <u>imagination</u>, fantasy, and unfulfilled dreams. In the later stages of my marriage to X2, I would declare that I was not a bad person, but I was lacking much as a father and even more so as a mate and husband. Instead, I found myself consumed with the tug-of-war distractions going on inside my mind and wondering what to do about becoming Shannon ... <u>or even if I should do anything</u>.

Poor X2 had her problems too. For years she had been battling the demons of alcohol and the self-deprecation inside her soul. Though I loved her, she was at times unbearable to be around. It took a lot of self-restraints from the kids and me to endure her drunken tirades and fits of anger. Had I not loved her so, I might have thrown her out, or perhaps had her committed to a mental hospital. These sorts of things happened years before I confessed to her about my true feminine desires, so what she did to me and the kids back then can only be blamed on her. The fact that I stayed, and that <u>I was the one</u> that held our family together for so many years became a forgotten achievement to her. During our divorce, she bitterly turned on me the way she sometimes did when she was drunk and disorderly. It disappointed and saddened me. Aha, but the question is ... why did she?

This <u>fem thing</u> within me certainly couldn't have made it any easier on her. In addition to that, she'd had to deal with the untimely murder of her only brother, her grieving mother, and the health problems of our youngest daughter. Her brother's death, and not my pleas, or those of her mother, or her children caused her to quit her over indulgence of alcohol. Whatever the case, we were all glad she did reduce her consumption when she did, for if

Pink Heart

she had continued as she was, I've no doubt she would not be alive today. She was as much of an addict to alcohol as anyone I've ever seen, but to her credit, she was able to save herself from assured destruction had she continued down the road she traveled back then.

All the while, it seemed to me that I was misunderstood by all those who were supposed to love me. As a result, X2 and I drifted apart, steadily becoming less intimately endeared toward each other. She and I were once best friends, but that closeness began to erode, and eventually, we found ourselves going in opposite directions. Our lovemaking became passé and was void of the passion we once instilled in each other. Part of that was due to the effects of the estrogens that I began taking. When I could become aroused, it was never the same for either of us. She would question me about my mental state during sex and I admitted that when we made love, I fantasized that I became the passive receiver ... the woman in the event and she became the man. Thus, in those absurd fantasies inside my mind, there was a complete role reversal. Note*: In my research, I found that this is quite common amongst married MTF trans-women.

During foreplay, I always encouraged her to show my budding breasts and highly sensitive nipples oral or manual stimulation and attention, which she appeared willing to do. She even seemed to enjoy doing so ... at first. However, I believe the physical and emotional changes happening to me served to make her uncomfortable and brought into question her <u>sense of sexuality</u>, which had no doubt become blurred by my increasing onset of femininity. Eventually, I began to experience her disgust and frustration. It was evident that she could not accept my feminine changes and in time she no longer found herself attracted to me. I was not a woman, but I was far less than a man. In short, our intimate life became a complicated compendium of frustrated emotions and unfulfilled desires. It seemed I could not please my marriage partner, nor myself.

However, as fate would have it, the <u>economics</u> of our situation worsened that last year before I moved to Dallas. It helped push me in the direction of an opportunity to move away. My home building business and manufacturing rep position underwent lean times as business slacked up and my income began to falter. I lost money on some business ventures in construction and some key manufacturers were downsizing and pulling their lines and discontinuing business in Texas, forcing me to make a move back to working for someone else as a company employee. For me, at that time, Abilene and West Texas offered no promise for a decent job. I searched the Dallas market and found a job that would suffice until a better one came along. X2 agreed to stay behind with the kids and try to sell the house. She told me she planned to sell it, and then join me in Dallas, but we both knew that wasn't truly what her plans involved. In truth, I also realized this was the opening I needed to sort out what I should do about Shannon.

I managed to alienate X2 and the kids even more by being consumed with my interests ... like taking alone time writing songs, doing karaoke recordings, and chatting on the Internet. As a result, that last year I was in Abilene, I was almost non-existent to the goings-on within my own family. We'd go a few places together, but we were never the loving family unit we once were and should have been. I tried to be there when my kids needed me, but as I stated earlier, I was a road warrior and traveled continuously in my job. When I took the Dallas job, the progestins and estrogens I was ingesting softened and re-shaped my body, which was obvious when I wore a T-shirt or pullover shirt. I stopped doing that in front of the kids, but X2 saw what was happening to me. Although she "pretended" not to care and even posed with me while I was in-femme a few times when the kids were asleep, ultimately, she was fuming inside. I can't recall either of my two teenagers being in tears or gnashing their teeth over my departure to Dallas. To them, X2 was the anchor in their home anyway. My son was almost eighteen and was going off to a technical college, so his plans made our relationship somewhat distant. My step-daughter was involved in a sexual liaison and wound up getting pregnant about a year after I left. She and I were close then and are close now. She's had a rough time with her parents and is estranged from her mom. Her dad wasn't around much either.

I'd confessed to the two older children a few months before leaving about my true femme desires, and my probable intent to transition. Therefore, my moving to Dallas came as no shock to them. Even though they seemed accommodating, I believe they were merely being polite, for after my revelation my son avoided confronting me if possible. From his point of view, I believe he considered me to be an <u>annoyance and embarrassment</u>. To the kids, I lost any marital or parental respect. It seemed to me that only my baby girl and step-daughter cared what happened to me, but I don't think either completely grasped the concept that I might be leaving … for good.

In retrospect, my children deserved better than they got from me. Sure, materially, they had everything any kid could want, but I'd shortchanged them in so many other important issues. They needed more guidance than I provided in their teenage and young lives. When they were younger, I spent more time with them and made them the center of my universe. In those last few years, I was with them, I was absent without leave when they needed me most. Perhaps that was somewhat due to my career and the type of position I had, but using that excuse as an explanation is poor. I pledged to do my all to keep them sheltered and apart from my own selfish needs, but in the end, I could not ignore the battle raging within me. I attempted to provide for them and X2 a home full of laughter and joy, even if there was turmoil inside my mind and body. For the most part, I succeeded at providing a good home; until that last fateful year or so we had together.

As for my partner and marriage companion, X2, with whom I was blessed to have had for a mate, we finally divorced and dissolved our marriage and a love that once was so incredible and beautiful. It was a sad closure and reminder of the real costs involved when one marriage partner is transgender.

After I moved to Dallas, X2 became involved with a man secure in his manhood, and then she quickly absolved herself of me. As I stated earlier, I heard that she'd begun dating him long before our divorce … even before I left for Dallas. If so, that would explain some of her callous treatment of me there in the end. Even with that scenario, I can point no fingers at her, for three of them come back at me. I became like a stranger and just a bad memory from her past. She found solace in the arms of this man who could give her and my youngest what I could not. I did not blame her for seeking her own needs and for attempting to get on with her own life. We both did what we had to do.

Did we have a civil divorce? Are we still good friends today? First of all, there is no such thing as an amicable or good divorce. No one ever really wins in such matters of the heart. People divorce because they feel their relationship has come to end, as was the case for both my ex-wives and me. I instigated the divorce with X1 because I thought it was time I moved on and it would be best for both of us if I did. Even thoughts of reconciliation with her proved of no value in changing my mind to that end. After I made the moves to find myself as Shannon, X2 instigated the motion to divorce me. Even though it deeply wounded me that she had me served near Christmas, I could not nor do I blame her.

As in any divorce, the residuals from the separation leave behind not only an ex-spouse but also the children that were involved. I regret that my kids had to endure this indignity and the mental unsettling it must have caused them, especially my youngest daughter. Fortunately, X2 was able to hold things together and retain the residence I'd built for her and the kids. After she remarried, she and my youngest daughter continued to make it their home. I am thankful for that at least.

Suffice it to say; whatever I lost materially from divorce pales in comparison to the emotional sense of loss I received. Two of my life's biggest disappointments are those two failed marriages and ending loving relationships. I was unable to complete my marriage contracts or live up to being the kind of spouse or parent I intended to be. In retrospect, if I had it to do all over, I probably would not have. For their sake as well as my own, I should have remained single. I ask God's forgiveness each day for my deficiency, and I am sincerely sorry for the pain and hurt I imposed on all of those who lost their husband and father. I was not meant for either of those two roles.

Am I embittered at X2 for what she did or how she handled our divorce? What I do hold her accountable for is her greed and inconsiderate attitude about keeping me informed of my youngest daughter's life and condition of health ... or that of my son. That she made no attempts to have my daughter call or contact me, even twenty years after the fact, annoys and upsets me.

I was initially upset about not receiving some court awarded items, but upon further review, I think I probably got about all I deserved. I think she could have handled some matters better, including those about my parental visitations. I am sad that we could not remain together. I regret that it ended in divorce. That's not a pretty word. In both the cases of X1 and X2, when we were married, they were each my beloved wife, companion, and my best friend.

I regret that my youngest daughter was raised by a man not her father, but then again, he did a far better job than I ever could. I lament that X2 looked not to me for love and affection, but to someone else. I can only file and stow away in memory those many intimate and wonderful moments we each had together and forget those times that weren't so good. Both my ex-wives had good intentions and pure hearts, but life changed all our plans. I was blessed in many ways by both marriages. I would urge each of those two women to <u>remember me</u>, not by how our relationship ended, but rather by all those wonderful moments when we looked into each other's eyes and experienced an exchange of love and hope of the future. We shared much laughter, the joys of bringing some great kids into this world, and the mutual love that we once had for each other. Do I still love them? Absolutely! Bitterness, bad times, and bad memories will fade, but the goodness, the good times, and the love we shared endure forever in my heart and soul.

When I think of that night now, I recall the song by Cher, "If I Could Turn Back Time." If indeed I could, that incident is one I'd erase, as well as two traumatic ones from my childhood.

Question 17: What should a trans-woman expect to be like after GRS?

Having GRS is a great relief and an important step in any trans-woman's life. If she's abided by the Benjamin Standards, by the time it happens, the trans-woman has already had this thing cooking in the oven for years. So, when GRS does roll around it should be the icing and cherry on top of the cake. For the MTF trans-woman that has lived 24 /m7 for a year or more, to society they have already have been a woman, just one with the wrong plumbing.

In truth though, by the time GRS becomes a reality, it is almost anti-climactic. It generally does bring the trans-woman full circle and finally makes her feel less incongruent with her anatomical genitalia. However, genitalia is private bodily items anyway, and once again ... nobody but a chosen few is privy to what anatomy exists between one's thighs. When the trans-woman walks down a street, through a mall, or sits in a movie theater, people judge her as a female by how she appears outwardly, not by what they think her genitals are. If she exhibits the signals of being feminine in gender, then to them she is a woman. Period! Remember what I wrote earlier; perception is reality. To begin with, that is the attitude that created the word transgender.

As Professor Sigmund Freud said, "I am now experiencing all the things that as a third party I have witnessed going on with my patients." In my case, that which has gone on with other tans-sisters. Life will always have its slings and arrows of outrageous fortune. There will be hurt, but finally, after HRT, some cosmetic adjustments, and GRS a trans-woman will experience a feeling of true completeness and wholeness. Past fears of rejection will vanish. There will no longer be the question, "Will I make it as a woman?" She will do so with confidence and aplomb.

Survey Says!

From the above perspective, I now present the comments of a select few of the most prominent GRS / SRS surgeons in this nation and Canada. The following survey consists of their direct answers to five questions that I posed to them concerning their experiences with having performed this type of surgery. The responses are their exact quotes. After I have presented them, I will add my comments to their responses.

Before presenting the questions that were asked, I would point out a situation that happened in Trinidad, Colorado where Dr. Marci Bowers performed GRS. In that small town in southeast Colorado, a fundamentalist minister under the banner of his Christian faith circulated a petition drive to cease having the GRS surgery performed in their community. He cited a John Hopkins study in which a leading psychologist there remarked that their hospital was ceasing to perform GRS and believed it to be <u>an ineffective way</u> of dealing with those that have gender dysphoria. As I was informed, this citizen proclaimed that such surgery is mere mutilation and serves no purpose. Eventually, for whatever reason, Dr. Bowers moved her practice to a larger urban city.

The subsequent questions to follow were posed to five prominent surgeons that perform GRS / SRS surgery:

Questions for: GRS Surgeons

In your professional opinion, does GRS have a negative effect on those that seek it?

Dr. Eugene Schrang: "I do not feel that SRS has any negative effect on an individual -- at least I have never detected any."

Dr. Harold M. Reed: "No, in fact very positive."

Dr. Marci Bowers: "Really, I do not see that. I have been an obstetrician/gynecologist for 19 years and see more positives in this group (transgender) than I have in any group previously treated surgically. What I do see, however, is an occasional patient whose pre-op expectations regarding surgery are unrealistic and that has certainly changed my informed consent procedure. In other words, some see surgery as their personal <u>holy grail</u> (I must be careful at what words I choose as someone invariably takes issue with one or another when they read them). Anyway, the surgery goal becomes all-encompassing and can become, for some, a vision of the end to all problems whereas, what surgery becomes, is the end of yet another journey and life picks up from there. In other words, now what are you going to do with your life? It also can compound patients' lack of libido (sexual interest). If the libido was low before surgery, it is very unlikely that it will be enhanced by surgery. Frankly, even with the best results, A person has to expect that it will be more difficult to orgasm; surgery is simply not a sexually enhancing procedure, even though there are many happy exceptions to that rule. Many, to be sure, find great sexual enjoyment afterward but along the lines of any other women entering sexual maturity."

Dr. Pierre Brassard: No! (Dr. Brassard, whose services are performed from a private clinic in Montreal, Canada, feels that GRS is a viable, legitimate way for the male to female TS to obtain the physical end to her journey. He refers to the operation not as the cure-all, but rather as the "Cherry on top of the cake!")

Have you had any patient or know of any that has had post-op regrets for having their surgery? Do you know of any that claim they made a mistake?

Dr. Eugene Schrang: "I know of one patient I did in the late '80s that apparently had regrets, which surprised me because she and her mother were so in favor of it prior to surgery. I attribute this case to lack of adequate pre-op psychological evaluation."

Dr. Harold M. Reed: "Yes, at least 3, though none of mine thus far."

Dr. Marci Bowers: "Not yet per se … with the caveats mentioned above … I do have one who is very disappointed to not be able to orgasm easily, even with sensation and arousal intact … the precautions mentioned above apply there, I think. Do I know of any that claim they made a mistake? Again, not per se."

Dr. Pierre Brassard: "Any post-op regrets? <u>None</u> of my patients yet to my knowledge."

Do you believe that GRS / SRS is a viable method of treatment for those that have been diagnosed with gender dysphoria? If yes, why do you think that?

Dr. Eugene Schrang: "SRS / GRS is certainly a viable method of management for this condition because the way we feel about our gender is immutable so we can only change the body. There is no other recourse."

Dr. Harold M. Reed: "Yes, if the patient has gone through the necessary steps and is a surgical candidate."

Dr. Marci Bowers: "GRS is absolutely viable and the evidence, in my observation, is overwhelming. Even the landmark study at Johns Hopkins that resulted in the closure of its SRS / GRS program in 1975 showed that patients were overwhelmingly happy with the outcomes. Their validity, however, was thrown out because, as you may hear, Gender Dysphoria is a "mental disorder" and anyone "mentally ill" cannot be a judge of their own results ... that was clearly the attitude back then and those arguments are still in regular use today, as the Marquis statement by the Christian "right." The truth is, gender dysphoria is almost invariably present by the age of 5 or 6. It is not something a person can "catch" and is not something that goes away with marriage, substance abuse, religious guilt, counseling, electric shock therapy, aversion therapy, machismo, or masturbation. It is what it is, like height, or eye color, and compounds most people's lives until they finally ... at some point deal with it. Some are able to displace their feelings or divert their feelings (see drugs, alcohol, and suicide) but these methods, while socially acceptable, are internally less satisfying to one's soul. THAT, in a nutshell, is why satisfaction rates with GRS are so astoundingly high."

Dr. Pierre Brassard: "Yes. It is their only issue to feel complete and normal."

If some local group in your city or area circulated such a petition as the one in Trinidad, Colorado, how would you react?

Dr. Eugene Schrang: "I would ignore such a petition."

Dr. Harold M. Reed: "Unless this gets to the court-injunction stage, I would not let this phase me, as many people are vehemently opposed to male circumcision which I also perform. In the event that the crowd is polite and a forum is requested with proper moderation, then be prepared to appear with consultants and be sure you have supporters in the audience."

Dr. Marci Bowers: "That has supposedly already happened ... recently, from a local minister of a fundamentalist "Christian" church who wrote an article in the local newspaper advocating for such a "coalition of the willing" to stand up against the practice of sex/gender change surgery and its blight upon poor Trinidad. The response from the locals was overwhelmingly opposed to this guy. Many people called me with support, just overwhelming. Many also told me personal information about this guy who, no surprise here, has a remarkably low opinion of women's place in society ... he has now left Trinidad to begin, of all things, a mission in Central America. Perhaps the language barrier will allow him to disguise his message of hate."

Dr. Pierre Brassard: "It would be extremely preoccupied: it means that religion is taking over freedom and acceptance."

Approximately how long have you been performing GRS and how many patients have you dealt with that have had the surgery?

Dr. Eugene Schrang: "I have been doing SRS since 1987 and have done almost 1500 cases."

His Closing Comments: "I do follow the Harry Benjamin Standards. The number of patients I have seen and treated who are relieved and happy is so overwhelming that in my opinion any person or group who tries to persuade the public that this procedure is of no value just does not know what they are talking about. I would suggest that if they are truly interested in the truth about the matter, they should poll the post-op transsexuals and once and for all get the answer. It is about time that the truth becomes known and an end put to all the prejudice and nonsense that we still hear about."

Pink Heart

Note: "I will be ending my surgical career this next year and will do my last SRS at Thanksgiving." (2005) (And he did – Have a great retirement Dr. Schrang)

Dr. Harold M. Reed: "Three plus years, about two hundred or so."

Dr. Marci Bowers: "I moved to Trinidad in January of 2003 and worked with Dr. Biber until he was forced to retire in July of that year. I then began doing the surgery in July and have now performed more than 170 of these primary surgeries plus many of the other ancillary surgeries such as breast augmentation and tracheal shaving. We perform generally between 3 and 5 of these surgeries each week that I practice. We have also seen many, many other patients in consultation and, of course, I still perform gynecological care for all patients in the area in my clinics both in Seattle and Trinidad."

Dr. Pierre Brassard: "Have been doing GRS surgery for eight years. Have completed approximately nine hundred GRS surgeries. (Dr. Brassard's service includes an after-care recovery program at his private care facility known as the "Residence" in Montreal.)

My Comments

I would like to acknowledge and thank each one of these eminent GRS surgeons for taking the time from their demanding schedules to answer my questions and for their candid answers. I wrote down their exact words herein. All of us that are transgender appreciate their professional skills and dedication in assisting us to reach our pinnacle of feminine design ... and the other side. Between them, I have known several trans-sisters that have sought and used their services, including me. In each case, that post-op person experienced and expressed complete satisfaction with the results of their surgery.

Dr. Eugene Schrang performed GRS surgeries from Wisconsin and for many years was one of the leading GRS surgeons in the nation and world. Several girls in my support group used his services and all were extremely pleased with his consideration, methods, and techniques. We all wish him our very best in his retirement.

Dr. Marci Bowers is unique among this distinguished group, as she is a post-op MTF trans-woman. She was trained under the auspices of the renowned Dr. Stanley Biber in Trinidad, Colorado, a pioneer in performing and developing GRS surgical techniques. Dr. Bowers is also an Obstetrician and Gynaecologist and took over Dr. Biber's practice after he retired. She now has become one of the most in-demand and prominent U.S. surgeons performing GRS. Those I know that have had her as a surgeon report they appreciated her empathy and compassion. All had a pleasant experience and were very pleased with the results of the surgery.

Dr. Reed performs his surgeries from Florida and he has rapidly been building a reputation as one of the best in the country. I have known one girl from our group that has used his services and she was well pleased with the results. He is said to be a compassionate man and dedicated to assisting those who seek his services.

Dr. Brassard performs his surgeries in Montreal, Canada. He and Dr. Yvonne Menard work as a team, with Dr. Menard performing more female to male GRS surgeries and Dr. Brassard doing the MTF surgeries. He is a prominent GRS surgeon and many trans-sisters I know had him as their surgeon. All have reported his techniques and facilities with the aftercare received to be second to none. He was Nicole's surgeon and also performed facial cosmetic surgery to her eyes and nose, plus also did a tracheal shave. All of the surgeons mentioned above comply with the Benjamin Standards. All have a waiting list that is constantly growing, so if an MTF transsexual seeks to have GRS, she must first call or write to obtain a place on the upcoming calendar when her surgery can be scheduled. It is not uncommon to have to wait for almost six months to a year or more before being able to obtain surgery from any GRS surgeon.

In most cases, a deposit is required before a date can be set, as is the case for these and most other GRS surgeons. Insurance companies rarely, if ever cover any of the expenses. As a result, the trans-woman is ultimately responsible for coming up with the cash to pay for their surgery. Such a financial obstacle is often a big deterrent for the TS and many that desire GRS does not have the funds to accomplish it.

Health is also a big issue, as most surgeons, including these four, require the patient to be in good physical shape before agreeing to perform the surgery. What's the reason for that? If a patient has hypertension, hepatitis, obesity, a history of heart disease, or some other condition of high risk, she might not become a candidate to receive GRS. Surgery has risks, and GRS is major surgery. There are possibilities that pulmonary edema may occur while performing GRS. If this happens, the trans-woman may not make it through surgery. Nicole and I knew girls that had this happen, and they wound up being tragic losses to the trauma induced from the surgery.

One may conclude that in most cases, GRS is a viable and effective option in the treatment of those that are transgender. It's an efficient means in which the mental image of themselves and that of the physical image come into balance and synchronization.

Question18: What's your relationship these days with your siblings, to God, and how do you answer those who say being transgender is a sin?

Transgender and Christianity

I covered some of this earlier, but please let me go more in-depth with my answering these questions. I am and have been a flawed individual that at times made some bad decisions. However, God is the mirror into my soul. He is the guide of the spiritual labyrinth through which all us humans wander. Through His son, Jesus Christ is the all-pervading conduit to eternity. There is no other explanation or enlightenment needed.

I would emphatically point out that these days faith is not something that comes and goes with me. My faith is a constant, despite my failings and sins. My beliefs in my Savior, Jesus Christ, are stronger today than ever.

You may say, "That's because I'm older and closer to the end of my life." Perhaps so, all I know is all my wandering and exotic days are over.

In this world, there are numerous pleasures, such as chocolate, that almost everyone enjoys. Then too, there are foods like artichokes that very few of us like. As a Christian, I believe it is important that we not only live for the pleasures of the flesh but also those of the spirit. That doesn't mean we can't partake of earthly things that we enjoy; it simply means we must keep these things in <u>perspective</u>, making our decisions carefully and maintaining our focus on God as well as ourselves. I admit I didn't always do that. Still, we must recognize God's supremacy, for He is the Beginning and the End. He is the giver of all existence upon Earth and throughout the universe.

For me, experiencing the pleasures of the spirit hasn't always been an easy task. Yet, not having the distractions of being male, I can devote more energy to praising God for my blessings. I am no longer conflicted and know that life is a lesson and a journey for all humans. No doubt, some consider what I have done in life as being wrong. To them, perhaps I have become an abomination to God. However, to those critics, I would reply that simply <u>is not true</u>.

There is only one unforgivable sin. That is the <u>sin of not believing</u> and not receiving Jesus Christ into your life. The Bible teaches us that if we truly accept Christ as our personal Savior, that nothing can keep us out of heaven. In John 10:28, Christ says of Christians, "I give them eternal life, and they shall never perish; no one can snatch them out of my hand."

I admit to being a sinner, as are we all, but I'm not unworthy, nor have I committed some unpardonable sin by becoming Shannon. A few of the acts that I committed, such as the ones previously stated were indeed sins and I have sought God's forgiveness for them. I partied a lot when younger and wore some rather exotic clothing, as you've noted in the photos within this book. Still, I did not compromise my soul by living an immoral lifestyle. I made mistakes and strayed a few times into dark waters, but I've prayed for absolution. Those that follow the teachings of Jesus know that He said, "Whosoever believes in me, shall not perish, but have everlasting life". Are me, and all those who are transgender ... not a Whosoever? Are we not also children of God? Does not my faith in the Son reserve for me a place in heaven and the Lamb's Book of Life? I certainly believe it does. The way I see it, God must have wanted me to be a trans-woman for that's the way I was made.

I would ask of those that have turned their back on me, am I just some cosmic piece of space junk, merely a glob of biological protoplasm that takes up room and has no value to God or anyone ... merely because I am different?

Never have I been one to blame God, nor have I stood upon a high precipice and shook my fist at Him, cursing Him for my being transgender. He who dwells in the inaccessible light dwells too within each of us. I both fear and admire my creator with a deep sense of awe, but mostly I love and exalt Him with all my heart and soul. That He would send His only Son to die for my sins and those of everyone who believes is a concept that I find truly amazing. His gift of life to me is divine and one I never take for granted. His unconditional love for me is beyond comprehension. By His grace am I saved and, in this matter, truly ... I care not what others think. The blessed assurance is that Jesus lives, and I will one day join with Him in eternity. That is enough to sustain me in this world. It has been said and is true for all of us ... that if we kneel before God, we can stand before anyone. He crafts the sunrises and sunsets. He made the mountains, valleys, and seas; every plant, every tree; all the birds, animals, and humans. He is nature, he is science, and he is indescribable and the all-embracing consummate of goodness. He also reveals Himself to us in the intelligent design of the universe and the amazing wonders of nature. He reveals Himself to us through the complexities of our intellect and ability to reason, allowing Him into our thoughts. He provided us with a conscience and that of free will to make our own choices in life ... and earn from those consequences when we choose wrong over right ... and forgive us when we screw up and sin.

* * *

In the following description of how I feel about being rejected by some siblings: (Again I shall write in the <u>third person</u>)

As God put the question to Cain, "What hast thou done to thy brother?" Applying this scenario to Shannon's situation, how would her siblings answer that question and to whom would God be speaking?

Her ministerial brother's (whom we'll call Alex), life has been dedicated to helping others find salvation through Jesus, and who by profession is a minister in the Baptist faith. To him, it would seem that she, like Shannon, did without a doubt kill off his brother Gordon. Thus, he might say to God, "I have done nothing to or for him, Lord."

From her only sister (whom we'll call Wanda), whose religious beliefs mirror those of her brother, Alex, somewhat answered God in the same way; "I have done nothing to him or for him, Lord."

From her older brother, Vern, his perspective might simply reply to God, "Lord, Gordon is well, but he is now my younger sister, Shannon. I accept her, as should you and others of our family!"

From Shannon's perspective, she might answer God, "Lord, you brought me into the world as Gordon, but as you know, I was meant to be Shannon ... and now I am!"

So then, who is Cain in this scenario? Was Gordon indeed slain by his alter ego, Shannon? I suppose in some ways he was, yet no physical death occurred. There is no dead body within whose soul has been withdrawn. So, must Shannon answer to God for what she did to Gordon? Yes! And that resolution should only be between her and God. Others should not judge or convict her.

Did Alex and Wanda in reality do nothing to their brother? They may have done nothing to him, but neither did she do anything to them. All she asked for was their acceptance of her as Shannon. Yet, she received none of that. From Gordon's perspective, it was more important that they ... <u>did nothing for him</u>. Instead, they wound up ostracizing him from their family and closing their minds and hearts to him/her as Shannon. True friends walk

Pink Heart

in … when all others walk away. Among siblings, these two have not been Shannon's friends. To Alex and Wanda, their younger brother's new coat of many colors was and is Shannon, and when he needed them most, all he received in return was their apathy and backside.

One half-brother that Gordon loved, and to whom he wrote a long, heartfelt letter explaining why he must become Shannon never even acknowledged receiving it. That half-brother, now deceased, avoided any further contact with Gordon as Shannon.

So, how did this sort of treatment make Shannon feel? Her oldest brother, Vern, facetiously refers to her as the <u>pink sheep</u> of the family. In that regard, she can relate to how Joseph must have felt when his brothers threw him down a well. Although they probably didn't know, it was exactly how she felt about her other siblings. They tossed her away like an old shoe and treated Shannon as if she did not exist.

In truth, each of these siblings that turned away from Shannon had good intentions and no doubt were charitable to many others … just not to her. Neither of them fathomed the profound effect that their mother's death had upon Gordon, and neither suspected their brother had within him this deep dark secret that they found so offensive. Alex, now retired, spent countless hours being a pastor to his flock (congregation) and did wondrous things in God's name. Yet, he turned a blind eye to his brother when Gordon needed him most. Gordon beseeched him to accept his / her transition into Shannon, but to Alex, this was akin to Eve partaking of the forbidden fruit in the Garden of Eden.

During hurricanes or other natural disasters or times of need, Alex and Wanda were the kinds that would bend over backward to send money, support, or even open their homes to those evacuee disaster victims. This sort of thing is indicative of the goodness in their hearts. However, when she first transitioned from Gordon to Shannon and wallowed waist-deep in her toxic flood of anxiety, not knowing where her life was headed; neither of those two siblings lifted a finger to comfort her, or whispered to her even <u>one encouraging word</u>. All she wanted was a smile or an assurance that they loved her, but again, all she received was insensibility and unconcern.

She felt hopeless; as if a category four hurricane had just slammed into her coast and destroyed her domicile ... separating her from everyone and everything she loved. She was ostracized and left to wander and worry about what her future held, just as those itinerant souls that inhabited New Orleans after Hurricane Katrina.

She knew where she wanted to go, but the path to get there was blocked by a huge traffic jam and strewn with many obstacles. How much easier would it have been for her if she'd known her <u>entire family</u> loved and supported her need to become Shannon? She was doing nothing illegal, nor was it immoral, though in their eyes it seemed that it was. To them, she was stealing away their brother. In truth, she was only trying to find the person she always felt herself to be. Yet, to them, as Shannon ... she <u>had become Cain</u> ... and slaughtered their brother.

On the other hand, Gordon's brother, Vern, opened his heart, mind, and spirit. He allowed the thought of his brother becoming Shannon to become a reality for him. He too no doubt misses his brother, but his vision is clear enough to realize that Gordon is still alive, inside the heart and mind of the new sister he acquired. Instead of turning his back or sticking his head in the sand, Vern demonstrated true love and tolerance.

He came to an understanding, asking questions of Shannon about why she needed and wanted this change. Then, he saw that for her it was something she felt compelled to do. He realized it would make her much happier. In return, Vern exhibited something the other siblings speak about, but in truth did not exhibit. He showed <u>me</u> ... as Shannon, what it is to bestow true <u>unconditional love</u>.

So, when God poses the question, "What hast thou done to thy brother?" who will answer, and what answer can be given with a clear conscience? Ultimately, I would say to each of those two siblings of mine, and my children, that we are responsible for every one of the souls with which God brings us into contact on our way through life.

I can quote you the Deuteronomy chapter and verse (Deut. 22:5) used by my Baptist minister sibling in which he declares the Bible says what I am doing is immoral. Nonsense! That revered ancient text that I too consider Holy nowhere depicts any mention of those like me who are transgender.

Pink Heart

As I've made clear by virtue of the photos I posted herein, most certainly I am NOT a mere cross-dresser.

Read a chapter back in Deuteronomy and one will see that the text depicts a directive for the stoning of a disobedient son (Deut 21: 18-21), and of approving slavery issues that appear in Ephesians 5:6. Also in Deuteronomy, it speaks of not wearing wool and linen together and of stoning to death a woman who marries but was found to not be a virgin beforehand. Hey, my brother, you better stow that wool suit, and it was a sin when you wore your linen shirt to the pulpit.

Deuteronomy also proclaims that if a man is found lying with a married woman, that both should be put to death. If such a justice system were in place in today's contemporary world, there would be a great outcry of anguish, as many folks would be put to death for going against these ancient, outdated Old World traditions. See my point?

Though I don't presume to declare verbal inexactitude in all scripture, I do say we should apply a common-sense approach and methods of a belief that will awaken our minds, not introduce more prejudice into them. Absolute rigid literal interpretations of the Bible in this manner are a perilous precedent for arriving at every truth in today's current world. However, I have found that usually, it is an exercise in futility to attempt to reason with my minister sibling or those like him ... as to why I had to "do something" about my being transgender. He is a good man, but possesses a great spiritual arrogance that I find annoying. He believes being a minister qualifies him to be my magistrate, to admonish me, and position all trans-women ... and me into God's doghouse.

In some ways, perhaps I did put a question mark on things where God intended me to place a period. Nevertheless, I prefer to think He had in mind to place there a colon or semi-colon. In this sentence of my life, God has allowed a few commas as well, and He even threw in an exclamation point or two!

My minister brother and my sister used various interpretative verses and every form of Biblical rhetoric on me to convince me not to seek to find my true self. They preferred that I was forced into serving a life term inside a mental prison whereby I would live out my remaining days caged in masculinity. Why? It was because they say, that's how God wanted me to be. Too many of us that are trans-women feel we were trapped inside the wrong body and were meant to be women in the first place.

Perhaps I invited a lot of the criticism I took from these siblings or failed to communicate accurately and correct some issues about my desires to transition. I attempted not to become confrontational, but it did become argumentative, even if only through letters and email. For the most part, I believe I was merely dismissed, written off as being a family outcast, and to be excluded from their present or future lives. That became evident years later when I was not included in a family reunion my sister hosted at her home a hundred miles from where I lived.

These siblings have chosen to disconnect themselves from reality and me, considering me to be a selfish, perverted being, unworthy of their company or God's. Perhaps in so doing, they believed that rejecting me kept them in good stead with God. I do not share their same perspective, but as a five-year-old might say, "Whatever!"

According to authors like William Sloane Coffin, too many Christians, even scholarly ones, use the Bible as a drunk does a lamppost; for support, rather than for illumination. These types of people are blinded by their own bias and moralistic nature. If it seems that I'm bitter at my two siblings and others that have leaned against their own lampposts, then you would be right. I suppose I am. To me, the kind of treatment I've received from some in my family is the worst kind of callused hypocrisy.

At this point, my counselor would pull me aside and remind me that those who anger me control me. Okay, I'll temper my temper, and then attempt to forgive them, as I know God would want me to do. Besides, I don't enjoy being bitter, for nobody wins if I am. So, I hope this exasperation within me will pass someday. I also know that I cannot hold them down without staying down there with them.

Mostly, it's mere frustration and disenchantment from how they refuse to even give me a chance and relegate me to exile. It appears, the only hope for some of them, my children especially, and of ever-laying eyes upon me again will be at the funeral parlor when my body is laid out inside my coffin. I suspect that even then they will shake their heads in disgust.

To update one more issue between Alex and me, I would tell you that his wife, my sister-in-law, Jan, developed severe, terminal breast cancer and was fading fast. I received an email from her asking that I come for a visit before she passed. I was touched and phoned to speak with Alex. I offered him my condolences. I then called back a few days later to see when would be a good time to go speak with and visit, Jan. I spoke to my niece, who gave me a message which indicated that my brother preferred I not come at all. She passed away a few weeks later and I was not invited to her funeral. That treatment cut me deep, as I loved Jan and she and I were always friends.

The Baylor Line

I grew up in the Methodist and Baptist religions and graduated from a Southern Baptist university called, Baylor, from my hometown of Waco, Texas. To the dismay of Baylor fundamentalists, the gay, lesbian, and transgender students on campus came out of the closet there for the first time and formed a new union and campus affiliation known as <u>Baylor Freedom</u>. I never dreamed such a thing would happen at Baylor, and although it surprises me, I admire the courage that those students have exhibited.

However, I fear their tactics and this bold step at such a conservative institution, as is Baylor, will not meet with their desired result. Instead, they may have brought down upon themselves the ire of others in the student body and those regents in power within the institution, plus other influential alumni who will attempt to squash such a movement.

It's radical, wishful thinking to imagine they would ever be welcomed openly at Baylor. Although I do respect them and hold in high regard their right to live as they please, I would think they would have been better served to attend another, more liberal university to get an education. To me, Baylor is a sacred institution, and I adhere to the religious principles upon which it was founded. I respect the fact that it deems certain acts and attitudes inappropriate for a Christian school, so I would not be critical of an administration that sought to protect certain ideals of the university and look unfavorably upon those that did not follow regulations. Proclaiming one is gay is one thing, but to deliberately taunt the university principles is counterproductive.

Although there are thousands of folks at Baylor and in the Baptist and Methodist denominational religions that I found to be decent, faithful, honest people, I often wonder how they'd look upon me now. I can only answer that by how they treated me when I sought to get my degree changed to my altered fem name. When I called to do so, everyone I spoke with was sympathetic and did not grill me as to my reasons for desiring the change to become Shannon. On the contrary, they sent me my new degree, with my fem name, and my records and transcripts were all changed to reflect that change. They were very accommodating and professional.

* * *

Some churches that Nicole and I have visited left us feeling rather cold, and as if we were under a microscope. Some churches where our gay or lesbian friends worshiped were open and offered us a hearty welcome. One must always remember that any church is only an institution. Until I became Shannon, for most of my adult life I was a Baptist. Though the Baptist church is not devout of purpose or mission, I do feel their leaders have bickered too much and that their perceived mission has become blurred, diluted, and filled with a bias of less spiritual value. One example of that thinking is their decision of exclusion into the church's ministry by women. Such thinking is narrow-minded, unfair, and antiquated. In a southern Baptist convention in recent years, the Baptist doctrine took up the discussion of those that are transgender. It was decided that the condition is sinful and that if the trans-person will repent, they are welcome to come to join the Baptist faith. No, that doesn't sound discriminatory, does it?

* * *

One cannot believe in heaven without recognizing there is also a hell. Do I believe in demons, or in those who are possessed of evil spirits? The Bible tells us that Jesus cast out demons sending them into a herd of swine, so demons must exist. Many references are made to Satan, the archangel, Michael, cast out of heaven ... the dark lord, and Prince of Darkness.

Pink Heart

Catholics supposedly still perform exorcisms, although the best-known case of such vileness was a Hollywood epic made to scare and horrify the masses. I bring this up because I do not believe that I or any other transperson I know is evil or possessed of demonic spirits.

I would like to dispel any thoughts of such nonsense, as it has <u>been inferred</u> by some that I know ... that because I was born male and later chose to live as and be female, that I am mentally sick, insane, and perhaps ... <u>possessed by an evil spirit</u>. At any rate, they believe me and anyone like me is people who seriously need help. Though I would encourage all to pray for me, I assure everyone I am not possessed by demons. To those that might contend that I have become evil, I would quote Jesus saying, Physician to heal thyself! To me, the essence of everyone is goodness. Those I know that are gay, lesbian, or transgender are good and decent people. Like anyone else, they have issues to contend with in their lives, but they are no better or worse than any other civilized human.

As I see it, those who would oppress and perhaps even cause physical harm to those that are gay, lesbian, bi, or transgender is on a moralistic <u>witch-hunt</u>. Those blessed folk who believes themselves to be <u>normal</u> sometimes convict, condemn, and dish out their brand of justice under the pretense of preserving God, family virtues, and seeking to impose their ideas of right and wrong onto those who are different than them. Never mind that such bias is aimed at groups or individuals whose lives are often wrought with panic, turmoil, confusion, self-loathing, paranoia, anger, fear, guilt, and frustration anyway.

The emotional fallout from gay, lesbian or transgender bashing can even lead to self-destruction. Sadly, because of rejection, or a feeling that they have no other recourse, some gays, lesbians, and transgender are driven to <u>self-mutilation</u> or to commit <u>suicide</u> ... even if it's a slow death by being carelessly intimate with someone that may have AIDS. Today's more open society is still laced with those whose aim is to rid the planet of the blight that they consider deviant and dangerous behavior. Being gay, lesbian, or transgender can paint a huge target on a person and make them susceptible and vulnerable to all manners of allegation, discrimination, and degradation. Love of God or loving another human being, adoring children, and living a respectable life is not a patent owned solely by those that aspire to lead a heterosexual lifestyle or remain true to the sex and gender they were born.

Despite attending church, I truly feel that everyone's pathway to God is found inside themselves when they are <u>alone</u>. The way I see it, no trans-woman, or anyone should rely solely on a pastor, church, or someone else to lead them to righteousness. True faith comes from inside. In one's quest to find the truth, one must search the inner recesses of one's soul, mind, and heart.

Licking Honey from a Thorn

To me, life as a trans-woman is sort of like licking honey off a thorn, yet it is oh so sweet when the nectar of it embraces your senses and at long last, you feel yourself becoming whole. I cannot control everything that happens around me, but I can attempt to control how I deal with it and how I feel about it. To those friends and family who can't or won't accept me as Shannon, I say now, "You are missed. I had to do what I had to do. Should you ever find it within you to accept me as I am, I will welcome you back into my life with a loving embrace and a cheerful heart."

I treasure every one of my friends and family, old or new, and I know that revealing this to some of them has been a traumatic and bitter pill to swallow. I pray that in time they will see that I am much happier now and that Shannon truly is who I am.

Truth cannot be killed with a gun, a sword, nor abolished by law. Thus, the truths of Jesus Christ abound and affect us all. I realize that our life on mother Earth is the childhood of our immortality and that being absent in the body, means being present with the spirit. I want to go to heaven as much as anyone and I'm certain that I shall. In a poem and song, I wrote, I refer to searching for a sense of peace from within, and that's exactly what I've done. I'm doing that now by <u>designing my destiny</u> and finding my true self. No, I do not believe God condemns me for being me. God's delays are not God's denial, and with me, it has been far better happening late than never. In times of trouble, this saying has comforted me: "God sometimes takes us into deep water not to drown us, but to cleanse us." I am bathed in the soft, gentleness of femininity, and may God continue to keep my life and my soul embraced in His goodness and His mercy.

Question 19: Okay, if you love and fear God, why did you wind up living with another trans-woman?

It would seem the question is, am I a Homo-Sapient, or just a Homosexual? I can understand those who ask that question, for although I will always be a part of this human race; most certainly I would now probably be pegged by most as being homosexual. It doesn't matter that they would be wrong. Having another trans-lady as a roommate, mate, domestic partner, spouse, or whatever you choose to call it, I suppose it makes she and I appear so.

I would declare that the lines between which sex to me is the opposite are somewhat blurred anyway. In the past, males were the same sex as me, and I found such a union with a male not to be something for which I yearned. One's sexual orientation doesn't vanish because they have GRS, or take hormones. I repeat: I was a confirmed heterosexual being and other than that one episode that happened mostly out of curiosity, I had no real desire or attraction for men, only towards women.

I found my attraction to Nicole, another trans-woman to be inspiring, enlightening, and delightful; yet, even I cannot completely explain why I feel about her the way I do. As I noted, I do not categorize her as being anything other than a woman. Thus, if I too am the same sex as she, then our affection for each other is certainly a same-sex union, without a doubt. Honestly, though, <u>I do not over-analyze my heart</u>, I simply enjoy the love it has for this fine lady, and I leave it to others to think what they may. It's like Popeye says, "I am … what I am "! We are… what we are!

I admit that it is a bit of a surprise to me we came to fall in love. Not that I have the slightest regrets for meeting her or us becoming mates. I do not. I love Nicole with all my heart and soul. She has been such a blessing to me. I acknowledge though that I was not expecting to ever let my affections plummet for another trans-woman. Having once dated another transgender when between marriages, I knew the pitfalls that such a relationship would entail, for I knew that I'd then be considered a homosexual as well as transgender.

To be honest, I doubt that I'll ever be comfortable with the scenario, but I love Nicole not for what she is, <u>but for who she is</u>. We were friends for almost two years before I asked her to come to share a room in my home. I had other trans-woman roommates, one of whom was a sweet girl, but she was bipolar and her illness caused me much grief and anxiety. She did not administer her meds properly, and as a result, she became violent and abusive.

When I lost her as a renter, I asked Nicole if she'd be interested in sharing my home and the expenses. At the time, I had three bedrooms and three separate baths, one for each renter. That which started as an innocent attempt to have a friend as a roomy ended up growing into a fantastic relationship and that turned into love.

She and I had so much in common, so it was those commonalities of interest that drew us even closer. Nicole admits that she had some attraction to me before moving in, but that she never considered that love would develop either. We are close to the same age, we share the same shoe size, and until she helped with my getting breast implants, we wore the same size blouse. "Okay Nicole, get out of my closet and put back that silk, lace collar pink blouse. I'll wear a minimizing bra the day I wear it, so hands-off"! Sorry, but if I give her a free run, I'll be going bareback by next summer!

We both have the same ideals and respect for life and had parents with high moral values that raised our families and each of us with Christian principles. Nicole claims that one of the things she found most attractive about me is my faith and spiritual beliefs. I invited her to my church and she came a few times but remained loyal to her Catholic faith. I think one other thing that has kept us close. We are of equal intellect. As much as it pains me to admit, for her head will swell three hat sizes, is that she's very bright. Jeesh! There will be no living her with her now!

Pink Heart

As a result, we have some very stimulating conversations about life, love, death, religion, and also our journey into womanhood. To me, she is beautiful, loving, a lovely woman, and my dearest and best friend.

Question 20: You were married previously. Now you are the mate of another trans-woman. Which of these relationships has been the most rewarding and why?

The Other Woman ... Was Me

Slap me with a wet fish! No matter how I answer that question, someone is going to get pissed. Since the other two gals were in my past and Nicole is my present and future, then I'll have to declare her as the conqueror of my heart. She's the one who has provided me most with contentment and feelings of unconditional love. Though each of my previous marriages rewarded me with some great kids and some very intimate and touching moments, in the end, both women found my femininity to be an affront to our relationship. They ultimately rejected that part of me. Since that part of me eventually became Shannon, the dominant force in my identity, they both rejected the real me as well.

Do I blame them and hold them responsible for the dissolving of our marriage? If the roles were reversed and one of them had come to me saying she wanted to cut her hair, have a mastectomy, get a hysterectomy, surgically attach herself with a penile implant, and then go by the name of Butch ... I have to wonder if my reaction wouldn't have been identical to her own.

I'd like to believe I'd have been more compassionate and understanding, but who is to say I could or would have been. Again, one's reality is based upon one's perspective. My only grudge with either of those women was that they both became embittered to the point of becoming vindictive. It seems, especially in the case of X2 that they sought to punish me for what they perceived to be my indiscretion, plus for my sabotaging what they thought were otherwise good marriages.

Again, this is an interpretive attempt of seeing things from their perspective. They might have opposing arguments as to what their reasons were, but I'd wager that my assessment is close to what is being correct and what they were thinking. I believe they simply lashed out at me as a reflex and as a defense mechanism. In a way, me, as <u>Shannon</u>, became the <u>other woman</u> and they felt they'd been scorned. We all know what a woman does when she feels that has occurred.

They were left to fend for themselves, with children that I sired, plus the uncertainty of their futures that made them do things they ordinarily wouldn't have done. Do they still love me? Maybe, but I suspect each one has mellowed in their animosity and disappointment. We all lead separate lives now and life has moved on for all of us.

Do I still love them? If so, it is a love tempered with the reality that it's passed and we each have new lives. Regret is something disabling and should be left to the past and not brought with us into the present or future. Both they and I might have a strong sense of loss, disappointment, and failure, but what happened ... happened. In their hearts, they probably will never forgive me, but they each will realize in time that they ... and I ... are better off now than when we were married.

With Nicole, I know that rejection and lack of acceptance will never happen. Nicole knows me only as Shannon, she's aware that I am transgender, and she accepts me for who and what I am. She will never judge me harshly for being this way. However, Nicole also knows that despite some rough divorce experiences, I shall always have fond memories of those two women facetiously refer to in this book as X1 and X2. Both of

PART 3

Question 21: What is your relationship now with your children and what do you think will happen between you and them in the future?

God's Precious Gifts

None of my children were planned, they just came along and my spouse and I accepted them as God's precious gifts. Some parents never quite get the child to which they thought they were giving birth. The question is, is it only desirable to have them if you've planned or chosen your children? Nobody plans to have a rebellious child, a Down syndrome child, one born with AIDS, or even one that is <u>born transgender</u>. As parents, we must receive and accept what children we are given by God's grace; there are no returns or exchanges. A child is a bequest, not a possession or project ... to be prized or ... given away. As a parent we can't prepare for all the ways a child will challenge us, disappoint us, or come to look and to act just like us ... God forbid!

My children are exceptional in many ways, inheriting a lot of my physical, mental, and emotional traits as well as all their bad traits from their mothers. Okay, are X1 and X2 smiling? No? I was just kidding ladies; the kids got some good traits from you, but all those mean and stubborn ones are from you too.

As I've stated, I care and love all my children and regret that at this time neither my eldest daughter nor son is a part of my life. For varying reasons, they chose instead to separate themselves from me and for the most part no longer want anything to do with me. My son means me no malice, but his apathy does hurt me, as I love him dearly. My eldest daughter is contentious and self-absorbed far more than I'll ever be. I care not to discuss her further. All I can do is pray for her.

In looking at my youngest, I'd say that I hope in the coming years she shall come to understand more about the choices I made, why I made them, and never forget that I shall always love her. Unlike my other two Texas-born kids, she was born in Columbus, Ohio. The day she was born is not one neither her mother nor I shall ever forget. I was present when my son and oldest daughter were born, but mine was an outer waiting room experience back then, I was not allowed into the delivery room to witness the moment of their birth. My oldest daughter was a breech birth, so there were some tough times during X1's delivery. When X2 delivered and my baby girl was born, I was there watching in awe as she burst forth into the world, kicking, screaming, and then took her first breath of life.

From the very <u>instant I saw her; I was in love</u> and I knew she was special. She was also unfortunately different, for she had no scrotum, but had what appeared to be a penis. X2 asked, "What sex is our child?" There was silence in the room and neither she nor I got a definitive answer. None of those present would make that call. For almost three days, we did not know if we had a boy or a girl child. The Children's Hospital where she was born said they'd have to conduct cero typing of chromosomes to determine the exact genetic sex of our baby. This was most disconcerting to me, as I feared perhaps that I had unknowingly passed on something to her from some genetic flaw within my genes.

To this day, I have never been told if that was indeed the case, nor even if something like that is possible. Days later, the physicians told us she was born with XX chromosomes and that she was female. She had a fused vagina, kidney problems, and was born without a bladder. My Lord! While in the hospital, under strict confidentiality, I confronted the doctors about my concerns and they did a cerotype of my chromosomes. I was not all that surprised when the results from my chromosome testing came back pronouncing that I was XXY.

They told me I have Klinefelter's Syndrome, a genetic anomaly, but that it was nothing to worry about. Easy for them to say! Klinefelter causes lower testosterone levels. Thank God for that! In that regard, males and females produce androgens (maculating hormones) and estrogens. With this extra X chromosome, my body produced a bit more estrogens than would a normal male. Nature tends to develop the body as female. It is not the number of androgens or estrogens in a body that affects development one way or the other but is rather the ratio of one to the other. The hormonal imbalance will result in physical characteristics contrary to genital sex. Thus, as a young adult, I began to develop gynecomastia (breast enlargement).

When she was but four years old, my darling baby girl had an eight-hour operation performed at Dallas Children's Hospital in which the surgeons miraculously formed an internal urine pouch using her appendix as a flesh and blood source, and her intestine as the tissue to form the urine receptacle. Afterward, she would come to urinate by inserting a catheter into her navel, which was Mother Nature's old life-giving doorway that they made into a skin valve opening to her urine pouch. As a result, she has to sleep with a medical receptacle urine bag each night to drain the urine. Then, during her active hours of daylight, she must catheterize herself every four to five hours. To her, this procedure is commonplace and it's something she has to live with the rest of her days.

We were told she'd be short in height (she made it to 5'2") and that her kidneys would never perform at a 100% level. She's been in and out of the hospital several times due to kidney infections or becoming dehydrated. She was placed on kidney dialysis and in time required a transplanted kidney. As of this writing, she did have an initial transplant, but her body never accepted the organ and the transplant failed. She could not have another until her body was dispelled of all the built-up enzymes after the surgery. Fortunately, almost ten years later, the hospital found a kidney tissue match and she had a successful transplant.

Specifically, her condition is what was formerly known as Adrenal Genital Deficiency Syndrome. It is an extremely rare condition. Now called Congenital Adrenal Hyperplasia, this condition is one whereby a genetic female with ovaries and vagina develops external genitals that resemble that of a male. This person is sometimes referred to as being a pseudohermaphrodite. I hate the implication of that word for my daughter, as it is a label not befitting her and one that could stigmatize any human being.

As is the case in most that has this condition, my daughter had a fused vaginal opening. When this occurs at birth and the chromosome tests reveal the child is female, treatment is given and the child develops as a female. Such was her case, as she eventually developed at puberty and her vagina separated and the vaginal canal opened. However, if such a condition is discovered after the child establishes a gender identity of a male; a decision must be made whether or not to support the gender identity and to exact GRS.

While in the operating room, the surgeons were stunned to find that she had no <u>right iliac artery</u>. Since she has a right leg, obviously something was supplying the blood to that extremity. Miraculously, they found that near her groin, a vessel had blown up to arterial proportions and served as the iliac for her lower right side. <u>Truly, she is our miracle child</u>. I just know she's a very sweet, darling, young girl. I do so regret that I had to remove her "Dah Dah" from her when she was so young in life. She's struggling with that loss and I hope she one day adjusts to that void in her life. Her stepdad that married X2 is a good man and he did a wonderful job raising her. I am very grateful to him.

After my divorce to X2, it only took me one brief session with her and an Abilene therapist to figure out that it's best that I didn't push Shannon on her. Her mother has no doubt been a big influence in her life and is perhaps one reason she's not comfortable being around me now. I shall respect that and hope that she will let me know if and when she is ready to have me more involved in her life.

A Shannonism: We now live in a dangerous time when the truth is over-edited and facts are deleted for convenience and political purposes.

If you're a trans-woman, be certain to get a yearly mammogram, for breast cancer is a terrible thing that if caught early, can be treated. Don't wait too long!

Question 22: **What was your reaction when you came out to your employers at your work and told them you wished to become female?**

"You Want to Do … What"?

First off, let me inform you that I've had three jobs since I have been Shannon. When I first decided to come out at work and make the transition from Gordon to Shannon, I was working as a sales rep for the largest natural stone and concrete distributor in the Dallas / Ft. Worth market. They were owned by a large Irish company and were well known throughout the Metroplex. What was their reaction? The company president gave me but forty-five days to exit the company and find new work elsewhere.

He hinted at a severance package, but the one that was originally offered was an insult to my intelligence. My immediate supervisor, the sales manager, and vice-president were all very compassionate toward me, and yet my ultimate fate therein was left to the company president. When he was told of my coming out, he couldn't deal with having a trans-woman selling and representing his company, so he only wanted me gone.

Nicole and others encouraged me to stand up for my rights and so I did that … sort of. I got an attorney, who is also transgender to represent me. I came away with a moderate severance package that would pay me for six months after I was dismissed. If I had pursued litigation, no doubt I could have gotten a hundred times that, but I just wanted to get on with my life.

In the new job and position, I took as a woman, the pay was considerably less per year than what I was earning as a male. That is another factor that any trans sister should keep in mind. Most women, no matter what their expertise or experience earn less income than a guy does. It's just a fact of business life.

Corporate America has made many strides to create better equality between the salaries paid to women versus men, but realistically, there is still a wide gap between the pay men get compared to that of a female employee.

Another mention I would give to anyone thinking of changing his or her gender and identity: If possible, the individual should plan far ahead. By that, I mean the individual should establish savings that can be used for the various expenses needed to transition. This trans-journey is not a cheap one. Decades ago, GRS surgery cost upward of $15,000 to $25,000, depending on where and who performs it. There are those surgeons in Thailand that will do the surgery for under $8,000, but then one has a long flight and I sincerely question the quality of the work done there.

Then, there may exist desired cosmetic surgeries, expensive electrolysis, or perhaps breast augmentation expenses. Just the routine maintenance items are far more for a woman than a man. Collecting a completely new female's wardrobe is expensive, make-up, accessories, wigs, costs for doing and maintaining one's nails, hair styling, hair care, and hormones; all these sorts of things add up and become very cost consuming.

I would suggest that the economic issues be well thought out before anyone takes the plunge into the deep end of the gender pool by going 24 / 7. I'd strongly recommend that the prospective full-time trans-woman make every attempt to become better trained to do her work of choice as a woman in whatever field of endeavor she may attempt. It's always a wise idea to become educated and to upgrade one's secretarial, administrative, computer skills, communication skills, and to develop a believable and realistic, plausible everyday feminine appearance. When one is working in femme, one must be that way day after day and must, in most cases, pass easily enough to interact with their bosses, other coworkers, and customers. This will make it essential that one practice and perfect their look before going on interviews and job searching. Re-inventing the wheel might sometimes seem easier than re-inventing one's gender identity.

Pink Heart

Bi, Gays, and Lesbians can at least remain stealthy and still maintain their same economic lifestyle and employment if they so choose. An MTF trans-woman should be passable in her new gender role, for she <u>has no option but to become exposed</u> to scrutiny by all who meet her. To some, she will be forced to be open with her new gender identity and hope that nobody she doesn't wish to know will question her gender.

When one's transition is within the same organization, as Nicole did, going from male to female presents many challenges, and the acceptance factor is much tougher to accomplish than if someone begins anew with a different organization. Nicole worked on her job for over thirty years when she decided to go full-time, she faced extreme pressures, prejudice, and scrutiny from peers…as well as her supervisors.

Fortunately for her, she was a Federal Government employee of high enough tenure and seniority that even with such scrutiny, she is immune to being laid off, reassigned, or demoted. She is also a disabled veteran and a Teamster's Union member. Thus, she was insulated from dismissal and the consequence of reprisal from a lot of the harsh or cruel treatments others in transition often receive from management or co-workers. Still, Nicole has not been impervious to innuendo or rumor and has had to endure more than her fair share of cruelty and harassment. Some of her co-workers campaigned to get her bathroom privileges denied, but she eventually won that battle. I greatly admire the courage it took for her to take that step in her career when she came out at work … as Nicole. Being known as a male for thirty-plus years on the job, and then to step off and all of the sudden become a female has to have been a difficult object to overcome. She's had to make a lot of adjustments, but then so did her supervisors and co-workers.

Starting over in a new job with a fresh employer has many advantages, as I well know. At work, I am generally not known as a trans-woman, but I did confess my status to management and some co-workers I trust. I did so long after I was hired and on the job. To most people there, I was simply one of the girls!

I had several genetic girlfriends there. They and I became a good work team. My manager was a young woman with an open mind and a good heart. She and my sales manager treated me with respect and fairness. As do all women, at work we exchanged views, discussed our family, careers, gossip, and talked as women do of feminine things. We chatted about our relationships and the world in general. I can never explain adequately enough the joy and satisfaction that afforded me.

Question 23: What's different about being a transvestite, versus being transgender?

Looking Fab ... Not Being Drab

If you're going to play on a football, baseball, or any sports team, you must practice getting better at the game. The same logic applies to becoming female ... especially if you were born with male equipment and lived for many years as a male. You must practice being a female.

Therefore, to answer that question, I would have to compare chocolate and vanilla ice cream. They both are ice cream, but at the same time, both are separate and distinctive flavors. The same reasoning may be applied to describing what differences there are between someone who is a transvestite (fetishist) versus someone that is transgender (gender identity disorder).

A transvestite uses make-up, female garments, wigs, high heels, and accessories as a means to satisfy a fetish, a sexual urge, or fantasy; to perhaps express a repressed feminine side. Some cross-dressers are without a doubt a campy version of a homosexual. Most transvestites that I knew long ago were males dressing to appear as women. Yet, often that person is otherwise heterosexual and only cross-dresses part of the time.

I knew some transvestites who are married but usually dress only in private when they are absent from anyone, including their mate. Their "secret" is hidden in the closet of their minds, which in itself is not unlike that of the trans-woman that guards her secrets and remains stealth to others and the world.

Though some are more outgoing and open with their fetish, most transvestites I've encountered cross-dress in solitary and confine their dressing to the private sanctities of hotel and motel rooms, or if they are married dress when their mate is away from home. They may assemble their wardrobes, or if sizes permit, dress in their mate's, or some other convenient and available female clothing.

Experience also revealed to me that these cross-dressing folks are not all adults, and in fact, some are teens or children. I've personally known males that when they were little boys told me tales of dressing in their sister's or their mother's clothes. This sort of behavior is similar to my past and can be precarious. Such action can result in producing their greatest fear … that is <u>discovery</u>. Are such children then transvestites, or do they too perhaps have transgender tendencies? One cannot assume just because they enjoy cross-dressing that they "are" indeed transgender. Only the child knows his or her motivation and more often than not the exact reasons for this action does not come forth until much later in life.

If they do cross-dress just for the fun of it, or they just enjoy doing it and yet do not aspire to become female or the opposite of what is their anatomical birth sex, then they are likely just young boys at play. These types of males cross-dress to merely use feminine vestments as a means of fantasy and escapism from masculinity, or else for assuming momentarily the guise and role of a female. To those more physically mature males, it becomes a sexual turn-on and one that excites and arouses them. Some children who cross-dress in childhood may come to realize later in their adult years that they have transgender tendencies. Some transvestites are called; "drag queens," some do female impersonation shows, and some fall into that all-encompassing word of being transgender.

When I first met Nicole, she had many friends that were gay and put on regular "drag" shows as a means to raise money for their organizations and charities. Most of these men were effeminate to a degree, but all claimed that cross-dressing was just for amusement and they had no desire to alter their bodies via hormones or surgery.

A trans-woman usually does not dress just for the thrill of it, or to satisfy some sexual urge. Female clothing, cosmetics, or any other feminine accessory <u>are how</u> a male-to-female trans-woman attempts to define herself. For a trans-woman, this whole feminine thing is about gender identity.

The MTF trans-woman dresses in feminine attire as a means to assume the chosen female gender role. As previously pointed out, the MTF trans-woman seeks to correct what she sees as nature's mistake. It becomes her obsessive desire to have her body feminized as much as possible to live, work, and pass as a female full-time. As noted, this requires total commitment and the assistance of chemical, surgical (for most), and psychological regimens. Trans-women are <u>always driven</u> by an urge to modify themselves from the gender role and the anatomical assigned sex gave them at birth.

Were there times when I became aroused merely from dressing as a female? To be honest, yes there were. For the most part though, it was not a sexual obsession, but it did bring me great pleasure mentally. At times there was a physical exhilaration from seeing myself going from being male to appearing female. However, I would point out that arousal was never my motivation for cross-dressing. With all my heart, I wanted to <u>become a female</u> and not just to dress like one. I wanted breasts, a vagina, smooth skin, long hair, and to languish in the very essence and softness of femininity. As I see it, the differences between those considered being transvestites and even the all-encompassing transgender status versus those who arc trans-women are <u>in the depth of their conviction</u> and their desire to change genders.

I've heard it told that in sheer numbers, there are almost 50 to 1 more transvestites than there are trans-women and that the gay male out numbers trans-women 900 to 1. From experience, I can tell you that much more than half of all tran-people are MTF (male to female). To a true trans-woman, the gender incongruity is so strong that the only relief possible is to change genders. An MTF trans-woman is obsessed and driven to do whatever it takes to alter her mind, body, and spirit to assume the identity of the woman she seeks to become. As I stated, if I dressed now as a male … <u>that</u> would be cross-dressing!

I've heard TS sisters tell me, and accurately so, that they were born female, only with the wrong genitals. When one goes full-time, she must prove that to others as well as themselves. I encourage every TS "newbie" to seek and locate the help of other Ts sisters in her transition.

Pink Heart

One cannot live in a cave, segregate, or eliminate oneself from public scrutiny or other humans. Unless we are lucky enough to be independently wealthy, we all have basic human needs that require us to all either work amongst others, shop, and socialize amongst the populace.

I have known cross-dressers and some transgender whom I describe as having <u>Vampire Syndrome</u>. By that, I mean they are so uncomfortable with their feminine appearance and lack of confidence about passing that they <u>come out</u> only <u>after dark</u>. Even then, most will only go where they feel it is safe or comfortable for them to be around other sisters. This would include going to movies, to a support group meeting, gay or lesbian clubs, or other establishments that they deem are friendly, and will not harass them.

Shannon and Nicole – Still Happy After 11 Years

Many transvestites and some trans-women that don't have a lot of confidence in their femme appearance only venture out in public after dark. Some find that gay clubs, fem impersonator clubs, social clubs, and such places offer a more tolerant and less threatening environment where they hope that they won't be hassled by others.

At a Texas Rangers Baseball Game – 2013

Pink Heart

With practice, a trans-woman can use a little polish to cover up a lot of her former male physical traits and characteristics.

Feeling a Little Behind

As a trans-woman in public, find out where the ice is dangerously thin ... and try to avoid it.

Huh # 6:
Who's the Fool?

There's no fool like an <u>April fool</u>. Those who know me know that as much as anything I enjoy pulling a good practical joke now and then. One of my best gags was against my family on April Fool's Day.

We lived in a suburban area near Abilene, Texas, and my spouse (X2) worked five miles away in town for a technical college. She was the dean's assistant, and prided herself in being on time each day, and being his "Girl Friday."

We went to bed that evening on March 31st with her and my kids oblivious to the fact that the next morning was to be April 1st, a day I hold in high esteem, as I always manage to come up with some sort of Tom-foolery on that day.

Thus, before we went to bed, I stealthily went around and set all our clocks <u>forward</u> two hours. Neither she nor the kids noticed this, and we all went to bed as usual after the ten o'clock news.

The alarm went off at its customary time of 5:00 a.m., only it was 3:00 a.m. My still sleepy kids and spouse rolled out of bed, showered, got dressed, and while my wife sipped her second cup of coffee, my kids went out to feed the horses. A few minutes later I bid them all farewell, as she sped off to town and work. My kids dressed and went out to wait for the school bus. This was back when I was a manufacturer's rep and had been out of town all week. This Friday I was able to sleep in. I again went around and moved back all the clocks to the proper time, and then waited in bed for the outcome.

An hour later, my spouse called from a payphone, she was madder than ... well she was upset ... and saying she couldn't get in at the school office. The security guards told her it was only 4:00 a.m., not 6:00 a.m. I expressed my regrets, not telling her what I'd done. She said she was going to breakfast someplace in town and would speak to me that night.

My kids came in a few minutes later saying, "Can you take us to school? The bus must not be running today." I said, "Sure" and I slipped on some clothes, drove them to school, and we sat there for another hour in the parking lot till the janitors opened the school.

I got a stern lecture that night from all of them after they figured out what I did. My saying, "April Fool," did little to ease their annoyance. The next year, I got paid back by all of them when they plotted against me to pull a practical joke on me. I'll skip what they did to me, but it was pretty cool ... and I deserved it.

Question 24: What was the length of time involved in the process of your going 24 / 7?

Time is something of which everyone wishes they had more. For me, the days and times of my young adulthood raced by with a velocity that almost gave me whiplash. It was a time when I felt like I was flying against the wind as I struggled in the gender role of being a male. To answer as to what length of time it took me to reach my heart's desire and become a female, I'd have to say ... up until this exact minute ... it's was something that took me a lifetime to achieve!

Realistically, I suppose the timeline for actually doing something about my gender incongruity came when I began taking estrogenic hormones all those years ago. Up until then, I'd only been wading in the water and not immersing myself in womanhood. Still, I would affirm that getting one's feet wet will only result in wet feet.

When I took the job in Dallas in '97 and began living alone that was the start of my journey into womanhood. Though it took me another year to garnish the courage to go full-time, for the most part, I had been en femme since 1997 anyway. Once I made the plunge and faced my fears, the dye was cast and there was no looking back and no worry of it not working out. Being Shannon took all of my concentration and effort. I'd done things like having my ears pierced, growing my hair out, and preparing myself for over a year before going 24 / 7. Hiding my long hair beneath a baseball cap at the stone yard was the one clue that gave me away ... that and the fact that my shirt bulged a bit too much in front ... despite my binding my blooming breasts down.

The nice thing about not having to live part-time as a female was that I could then have my breast augmentation and do those many little things that women enjoy.

Before going full-time, I had been living a part-time existence as a woman and that took its toll on me physically and mentally. I think that the awkward pre-transition stage is a commonality amongst all trans-women and causes the struggling transgender lady more consternation and frustration than at any time in her life. Poor Nicole had to endure the emotional roller coaster ride I was on during that period in my life. I had to work as a guy, but in the afternoon, as soon as I hit the door at home, I removed any semblance of my male existence and got into my femme attire and role.

Other than work, if I went anywhere in public during that time, I went en femme. Because of that, my fingernails took a beating. I'd been using glue on nails for years and had been putting on and taking them off so regularly that I wound up almost losing three of my nails. All of them were severely damaged from the constant abuse.

During this time in the "Yo-Yo" life I lead, I was fraught with self-doubt. I wore wigs and though they gave me a lot of variable looks, I preferred my hairstyles. I always was self-conscious wondering if my wearing wigs gave off negative signals to anyone evaluating me as a woman. The thing I noticed about this period was I always wanted and needed to go someplace, on weekends and even during the weeknights. The main reason for that was because <u>going out</u> was my only opportunity to dress and become Shannon. Nicole was wonderful to me and sympathetic, for I whined and whimpered each Sunday night when we'd drive back into our driveway. I'd then realize I had to take off my dress, cosmetics, jewelry, lingerie, and all my femme attire so that tomorrow morning I could go back to my job and become ... a guy again. All this up (exhilaration) and down (depression) made me an absolute basket case. When the day did come when I decided to come clean at work, even though the response from my employer was "bad" and they decided to let me go, I was relieved and glad that I'd leaped.

I recall announcing to my counselor and our gender support group about my getting hired on at a new job as a woman. It was a giant forward bound for me. All congratulated me, then reminded me of how I used to whine and pity pout about how I never thought anyone would ever hire me as a woman. The counselor and the other sisters had more faith in me than I did in myself. As it turned out, I found, like so many other trans-women do when they are challenged that the courage and the strength necessary to clear the hurdle and to recognize my skills and the worth was there inside me all along. I just had to discover it.

Although I changed jobs from that first one (due to a long drive each day in heavy traffic), I still carried with me to my other position all those previous male years of experience; simply transferring my intelligence, ambitions, dedication, and hard work and applying it into my female role. I found myself being much more productive, less distracted, and with a better ability to focus on the task of being self-supportive and successful. In that regard, I believe I accomplished my goals.

It's true that I lived a life in "Blue", but inside I have a "Pink Heart." When I became a woman, all of me came forth from out of the blue.

Question 25: What legal documents are required to be changed for you or other trans-women to live and work in your new gender role?

Changing Names and Legal Documents

Shannon – My First Fem Driver's License - 1998

I began the legalities of becoming Shannon when going full-time in late '97. I'd suggest that any trans-woman wanting to change their identity do so before they attempt to commit going 24 / 7. If they are going to transition within their current job, they can still prepare for the transition by getting some of the legal changes made before introducing their company and workers to their femme self. The most obvious document to change, in the U.S., is the driver's license. It, more than any other document, is used to verify proof of identity when one is in public. If one does not drive, then they'd best obtain or change whatever is their choice of an acceptable form of identification. The license above is void now, and I had my renewed license number changed, so don't go copying it, or writing to me, for I don't live there any longer either. Plus, it is NOT my true birthdate on the license. I fudged, and am a bit older that the license denotes.

For an MTF trans-woman, to effect a change to a document, one must first derive a new applicable feminine name. Tom may desire to become Tommie, or perhaps Paul becomes Paula. Whatever the choice of femme name, if it entails a name change, then one must apply through their district court to get that done. Many of my friends used the services of an attorney and paid upwards of $1,200 to have this done. I researched this requirement and found that paying expensive fees to an attorney isn't necessary. Neither does it always ensure that the desired results will be accomplished.

For me, I found that by going to my local county courthouse, I could copy the standard documents they have on file, and then follow the instructions they post therein. The process required to have this done for me was simple and I was charged the county fee of $167.00. Friends of mine that used the services of an attorney to do this paid wat too much for their name change.

I customized the forms to fit my needs, filled them out, paid my fee, and then went before a judge all within about two hours. Without much effort, I was able to get my legal court-ordered name changed. By tactful wording of the document, in my favor (hint), the judge also signed off on allowing a change of my gender to female. It is my understanding that more judges in Texas now frown on granting this gender change before one gets GRS, so I was fortunate to avoid that problem.

Depending on the judge and county, the fledgling trans-woman may find the court requiring the documents and physician affidavits for GRS before agreeing to a change of gender being recognized by the court. For me, once I had the certified copies of my name change done, going for the new driver's license was my next stop.

In retrospect, my heart raced almost as fast as my car did, as I sped off to the driver's license bureau with my needed name change documents in hand. I was extremely nervous and apprehensive about that change, for I was afraid they might give me grief about wanting to change the gender designation on the license. I expected some embarrassment or having them possibly hassle me about taking a photo of me in femme. I also worried they might take my femme photo, but still leave the space on the license that noted sex as being male ... and still marked by the letter **M**, even though I looked nothing like a male by then. To my great relief, the very kind woman who helped me at the Texas Driver's License Bureau was very sweet, sympathetic, and compassionate. She looked at my old license, the form I gave her about my name change, and then without hesitation marked down an **F** next to the designation for sex. I think it helped that she'd overheard my conversation with another female standing in line behind me. That woman remarked how nice it was to have another woman over 5'8" present. Such confirmation of my femme gender presentation must have impressed the lady clerk. I made every attempt to wear nice feminine clothing, did my medium-length hair as well as I could, put on street make-up (not too exaggerated), and did all I could to look the part of a woman. It must have worked.

I walked out of that place and felt about ten feet tall and almost floating with sheer glee. Up until that time, getting a new female driver's license was the single biggest step I'd made since going on hormones. I now had a legitimate document, legal proof of who I was, and I'd never again worry about driving my car and being pulled over or stopped when in femme. I was full-time and a woman. Other than one legal matter I had to attend to a month later, I've stored that Gordon I.D. away. When Nicole and I moved into our new home, I burned it.

It was surprising just how many documents needed changing after I Shannon Leigh O'Shea. Besides the driver's license, I had to get a new Social Security Card. I went to the Internet, and online downloaded the form and info the government website supplied for just such a purpose. I sent a $10.00 check and mailed them my new info. A few weeks later I got my new Social Security Card. My new name was now legally registered with the federal government. Not until after GRS are they also allowed to legally switch gender designation.

I had to write Baylor to get my name changed on my BBA degree and transcripts. There was a minimal charge for doing that. Immediately, I had to open a new bank account, and yet I retained my male one for months afterward just in case. It turns out I did need to get a document notarized, and although it was a bit confusing to the clerk when Shannon showed up to sign for Gordon, it all worked out because I'd kept accurate records. I advise all to do the same.

I wrote my credit card holders and sent them proof of my name change. I changed my life insurance, health insurance, and auto insurance. I notified the attorney general's office and the only thing I did not change was my U.S. Army DD-214 discharged papers. I did not get the sex on my birth certificate altered in Texas, even with proof of my GRS. I amended the name on copyrights to some manuscripts, poems, and music I wrote.

Finally, one should not forget to make allowances for inheritance and catastrophe. For a trans-woman, especially one with another post-op trans-woman as a domestic partner, it is of paramount importance that legal documents be completed that establish the wishes of the trans-woman regarding health care issues and in the event of death.

The trans-woman should arrange to have in place a Living Trust with clear directions about the responsibilities and authority of the named trustee. Also, I believe there should also be a Testament made. This should avoid probate and assist in the passing of estate property, and express the person's wishes for funeral arrangements, organ donation, and the hierarchy of passing on heirlooms, possessions, or other notable items of value. It is important to designate with a document, in the event they become incapacitated and are unable to decide their medical treatment, which person they want to decide about the extent of care to keep them alive.

If the trans-woman has life insurance, a name and gender change might affect premiums and benefits. I would not suggest the trans-woman ignore any paid-up policy, for if they were to die and it was discovered she'd not informed the insurance company of her change that might tie up the funds or else create an out for the company not to make a payout.

PART 4

Question 26: How would you better describe your childhood and adolescence?

The Wonder Years

Of one thing I am certain; some things that happen to us in our childhood <u>remain with us forever.</u> As I stated, because of my adoption, I always felt loved and appreciated by my adoptive parents. I was the center of their world and the pride and joy of their lives. Though I loved them deeply in return, there was this void and scar left upon my heart by what had happened to me and for not being part of my biological parent's family, or sharing a home with my siblings. This was a unique kind of separation anxiety, more a feeling of abandonment than simple disconnection.

A casual observer of my early life might surmise that as a child I was happy ... for the most part. Yet, even though I had my adoptive family, in many ways I felt alone and as though I was the world's biggest freak. In my young heart, I always carried this guilt and the despair of my gender discomfort; feeling that <u>I was the only one of my</u> kind and that I among all humans was unique in desiring to alter my gender and become a female.

_{As you know,} I kept that secret locked deep within me and feared anyone discovering that about me, much less my parents ever finding out how I truly felt. It wasn't so much that I dreaded some cruel reprisal by my parents, or that they would reject me if I confessed to them. Rather, I was apprehensive about losing their love and respect, or worse yet risking them changing their minds about me ... somehow having them consider me <u>damaged goods.</u> In my young mind's ramblings, I used to envision that after my confession about desiring to be a girl that they had psychiatrists and medical doctors' probe and poke me. I envisioned being medically sedated, and then reasoned they'd have me institutionalized and placed into a mental asylum; thus, I'd be relegated to being placed on psychotic drugs, receive shock treatments, put into straitjackets, or even possibly be lobotomized.

Pink Heart

Yes, I knew what that was, even back then, for I'd visited the school library and read up on mental abnormalities by the fourth grade.

Now, I know that sort of thinking was absurd paranoia, but back then as a youngster, it was a real fear that I could not seem to overcome. However, despite these terrors, the feminine compulsion within me did not wane, even with the constant lingering threat of discovery.

There were good times and there were bad, but looking back on it, I am nostalgic and miss that time in history when things moved slower; and when my extended family was so happy. My adopted parents each had several relatives. My Dad's family was extensive. He came from a family of thirteen, so there were aunts and uncles all over the place for us to visit, which we did regularly. I had dozens of cousins and each weekend we'd visit a different set of them. It was an exciting time to be a kid, and the holidays were magical. Roy Rogers, Gene Autry, Hop-a-long Cassidy, and my favorite, Annie Oakley were my cinema cowboy/girl heroes. I also secretly had a crush on Marilyn Monroe, Elizabeth Taylor, and of course, Vivian Leigh.

Things seemed simpler, slower, and much more family-oriented back then. I recall the many Christmases and New Year's parties we'd go to, both with family and with Dad's company, Texas Power & Light. They had the best parties, and although as a kid I was not privy to adult ballrooms and dancing, I could watch. Christmas parties were held each year in the huge second-floor ballroom in a posh Waco hotel.

The other kids and I always took pleasure in getting a visit from Santa, as he came down the fire escape and passed out basket-weave red stockings filled with fruit and small toys. The adults played Bingo after dinner. Back then, the company used kernels of corn to cover their bingo card numbers, not with marker daubers as they do now. My ministerial brother, Alex, and I unwittingly each put two of these corn kernels in one of our ears. True story … a week later, the kernels germinated inside our ears… and mine had to be meticulously cut out by an ear specialist. To this day, I am a bit hard of hearing in my right ear. That's yet another … Huh? What'd you say?

I also enjoyed the big band music and sound of the large orchestras that played there. I especially liked seeing my <u>parents dance together</u>. Their love was never more evident than when they were dancing. Before I came along, they were regular honky-tonkers. Red would drink after lodge meetings, and then Hattie and he would go out on weekends and party. To my biological father's credit, he insisted they stop that scene and never drink again in front of me. Sure, it was hypocritical of him, but my adoptive parents took his threat to heart. He swore he'd take me back if he caught them drinking again, so they ceased that lifestyle and raised me in a chaste, Christian home.

At those Christmas dances, I also got to admire all the ladies in their wonderfully feminine ball gowns. Hattie and Red's families were all very close and loving and I grew up hoping that I could someday have a family like that. I so wanted my brothers and sister to become as close to me as Hattie and Red's were to their siblings. That dream faded too and then became part of the past.

In many ways, as a kid, I was lonely and longed for that companionship that came from knowing I had two brothers and a sister, but that I could never actually experience living in a household in which I was their little brother. Anyone who knows me is aware of the great difficulty in adjusting to the fact that my biological parents abandoned me. Of course, abandonment is an improper word, but that is how I looked at it back then.

My siblings say that the notion is absurd, but I am convinced that it is so. I have always felt that if I'd been <u>born a girl</u>, my mother would have insisted I be kept on in the family. The arrangement made between my adoptive parents and biological parents had the former ones raise me as an only child, but the notion of being abandoned and unwanted <u>never left me.</u>

Working-class families inhabited the neighborhoods where I grew up and most were economically in the low to the middle-income group. The one thing that made it easier on me was the stability that my adoptive parents afforded me. Though I had the issues of wanting to be a girl, we lived in the same house from my first day of grade school until I later graduated junior college. The house I grew up in had two bedrooms and one bath with around 850 square feet. Certainly, we had meager material things,

Pink Heart

but we were not destitute. I never wanted much, so long as I had a few toys to play with. Back then, I made do with so little and was happy with what we had. I had friends, received a good education, and had a roof over my head, clean clothes, plenty to eat, a bed to sleep in, indoor plumbing, and adopted parents who loved and cared for me. Thus, I considered myself lucky in so many ways.

The kids in the neighborhood attended the same schools as I did, so we all became close friends on into adulthood. One boy on my block was on my city champ junior high and high school basketball teams. He and I were co-captains on our senior team. He and his brother, plus another guy in the neighborhood all became four very dear friends.

Years ago, this friend and co-captain called to invite me to a planned reunion to celebrate our winning season. Team members were coming in from all over the country, and it was to be a very special time to spend with old friends. Both our junior high and high school coaches would be there.

I winced when I told him I could not attend the reunion and had to decline his invitation. I could not come as the guy they had all known, for that part of my life was over. I mustered the courage and confessed everything to him. Then, I asked him to relay that info to those old teammates, friends, and coaches, plus his brother and my other dear friend.

To say the least, he was stunned but did not condemn me. He was the salutatorian of our high school class, so his intellect could grasp what I tried to explain, but he did admit he would have a tough time calling me Shannon. Still, he respected my wishes. He later told me how he tearfully explained to the other two men how their old <u>buddy</u> had decided to become a female. Somewhat stoic and reserved, when informing them he became uncharacteristically emotional when he did so. The others took the news, were completely surprised, but he said they all wished me well.

One thing I have not mentioned is that as a male, I was an exceptional athlete. In basketball, I was 6A-All-District and the second leading scorer in our district. In baseball, I had over a .340 batting average all three years I played in high school. In college, my freshman year I had a .360 batting average, and my sophomore year I hit several home runs and had a .480 batting average. This got me invited to a try-out camp for the New York

Mets pro baseball team. At the camp, there were over fifty young men the Met scouts invited to test our skills. Out of the entire assemblage, I tested the best in throwing distance and accuracy (I was an outfielder). My defense was above average. The scouts knew my hitting history and when the time came to select the All-Stars for that second night's game against some minor league players ... I was the head scouts first choice. He was the same scout that signed Nolan Ryan for the Mets, who went on to have a hall of fame career. My parents were there and I'm sure my dad's chest must have swelled when he heard my name called.

During the game that night, I went 3 for 4 batting, with a single, double, and a home run to help my team win. My home run came against a guy that later played for the Mets major league team.

So, I dropped out of college, played a few minor league games, did well, and then ... I got a greetings letter from our Uncle Sam. I won't go into what happened after that. Suffice it to say, my baseball career ended when I hurt my arm and knees in our Uncle's Army. I always wondered how good I could have been. Still, being transgender may have been such a distraction that I might never have been as good as I thought I could be. What happened was for the best I suppose, or else I may have been another Bruce ... you know who.

"Lions and Tigers and Bears ... Oh My!"

As a youngster, I was made aware; by my parents and by friends, that there were men in the world that were aggressive sexual pedophiles who preyed upon little "boys" like me. I never paid that much attention to the warning, but an incident happened when I was around nine years old that made me acutely aware of what they spoke. It was on a Saturday, and like I'd done often before, I went with my parents to downtown Waco and they dropped me off at a movie while they paid bills and shopped. I don't recall what was showing, but I do know it was a western and I was at the old Waco Movie Theater. I was enthralled in watching the show, sipping on coke, and eating my popcorn. I paid little attention to the somber figure of the man who drew closer and sat two seats away from me there in the dark.

Pink Heart

I am not sure when he did so, but before I realized any misgivings, he was sitting directly next to me. I can still smell his acrid alcoholic breath. In the dark, I could just make out that he was a Caucasian, middle-aged man, and one of impending size compared to my small child's body. I can still smell his cheap cologne and body odor.

At some point I became uncomfortable and during a loud shoot-em-up chase scene in the movie, I felt a strong hand sternly placed upon my crotch. I then heard the sound of my own blue jean pants zipper being undone. Without going into more detail, suffice it to say I sat like a deer in the headlights ... paralyzed with fear, totally immobilized and aghast at what was happening to me. I thought of screaming out, but my mind was so confused by what was happening, I could not get my vocal cords to work.

When I finally did muster the fortitude to get my limbs to move, I tried to remove his hand from my crotch. I thought again of crying out, but he motioned with his finger to his mouth, with his glistening eyes warning me to remain silent. Not knowing what he was capable of doing, I sat like a mannequin while he fondled me throughout that movie. Of course, being pre-pubescent, I had no erection and the event was completely devoid of any pleasure. I was wringing wet with sweat, and I could hear my increasing heart rhythm pounding in my ears. Just before the movie ended, he slowly removed his hand and whispered into my ear, "Thanks for the fun." Those words still echo in my mind to this day. May God forgive that man for traumatizing me the way he did, for I cannot find it within me to be so generous.

Like a wisp of smoke, he disappeared into the darkness. I just sat there like a frozen statue. Looking back on it, I suppose I was in shock, for when the lights came on after the movie's end, my legs were shaking and I could not stand. Though my hands were trembling, I somehow managed to re-zip my fly. My eyes filled with tears.

In a daze, I glanced around and saw that I was the last one remaining in the theater. I got up slowly, and then went outside to where my mom waited in her parked car across the street. She expected me to be smiling, but when I saw her, I again burst into tears. I was so ashamed that I hadn't gotten up, but my parents later told me that it was probably best that I reacted the way

I did. They contacted the police and theater management to warn them of such predators, but never mentioned the incident again. Until I was in junior high school, they never let me go back to that or any theater alone … and I never did. Now when I go to a movie, I do so with Nicole or with a friend. I give myself space, and if possible, choose seats away from anyone else.

A Darker Day

I wish that were the only traumatic sexual encounter I'd had when I was a young boy, but alas it was not. About a year after that fondling incident in the movie, I had something happen that even today angers me and sends chills down my spine. An older neighborhood boy I knew had a midnight-black Chevy car of which he was immensely proud. His parents owned a nearby lumberyard and were affluent. In our modest income neighborhood, he was considered a rich, spoiled, juvenile delinquent. He had few friends and most of my best friends all avoided him. At the time, I wasn't sure why that was. One day, while I was sitting at our curb, I innocently picked up some pea gravel and flipped it into the air with my thumb. As fate would have it, his car came buzzing by … and he saw me flip the small stone. The small stone dinged off his windshield but didn't harm it. In a rage, he came to a screeching halt right in front of my house. I apologized and explained to him the tiny pebble hitting his windshield was unintentional.

He checked and his window was fine and showed no evidence of any damage. He got this glazed-over look that I now believe was pure evil. He opened his passenger door and said to come on; he'd take me for a ride. I had always wanted to ride in his nice auto. I was apprehensive, yet curious where we would go. "Just around the block", he said. So, I got in with him. He drove me to a secluded spot nearby where we parked. There was a creek and a bridge overpass where the area was remote and thick with brush and trees. We were totally out of sight from others, and he instructed me to follow him. He claimed he wanted to show me a spot where some crawdads were lurking.

When he'd gotten me under the bridge and out of sight of anyone, he turned, grabbed me, and then demanded I pull down my pants. He wasn't a big guy, just older and far stronger than I was at that point in my life. He

Pink Heart

warned me not to scream. There, under the cover of the thick vegetation and away from anyone else ... in broad daylight ... he proceeded ... <u>to sodomize and rape me</u>! He muffled my cries with his hands and after he'd finished pleasuring himself, he warned me against telling anyone about what had happened. If I did, he claimed that he'd come after my parents or me. I was a frightened, traumatized kid, and I never told either of my parents about what he'd done to me. They knew something was wrong, as I cried that evening and my arms and face were scraped and bleeding. I hid from them the source from whence came other spots of blood. If I had told them, my dad would've tracked that young man down and beat all hell out of him. Instead, I bore the indignity of that incident, and it too became another dark secret to be hidden from those I loved.

The resulting mental scars of those two incidents remain with me and are no doubt the reason I've had problems relating sexually to most males thereafter. In general, because of those two incidents, I grew up somewhat <u>homophobic</u>. That may sound contradictory based on what I am. I admit my opinions and acceptance of homosexuals changed when I met those gay and lesbian friends in Dallas. They were all decent people in monogamous relationships. My bond with Nicole is unquestionably one involving a person of the same sex and is <u>based on love</u> and <u>more than the physical aspects</u> of our relationship, so it doesn't feel wrong to love someone.

Desperation

Those two incidents came at a point in my young life when I felt completely vulnerable, frustrated, and in agony at my assigned plight in life. The sense of desperation and sheer exasperation frustrated me to the point of breakdown and caused me to attempt a feeble suicidal event in my life. Even now, this brings back painful memories.

Not long after that incident in which I was raped, because I felt so frustrated with being a male instead of a female, I did something foolish and dangerous. In our home's medicine cabinet, my mother kept a full bottle of orange-flavored baby aspirin. One hot summer day when I had a headache, I withdrew the aspirin bottle from the medicine cabinet. While holding that bottle of aspirin, I suddenly became guided by an impulse, or some subconscious command to gulp down all the pills and empty the entire contents of that bottle into my stomach. A sense of hopelessness swept over me. The realities of what I was doing did not sink in, for I was not coherent. All I could think of was that young man … raping me, and how in that one desperate moment, I wanted to die.

My hands trembled and I went to lie down on my bed. I had no clue what the aspirin would do to me, but I reasoned such an overdose would at least dull my mental pain. As luck would have it, the neighborhood boys were playing baseball and came by to invite me out. I didn't feel well, but they needed me so I relented, momentarily letting myself get sidetracked and putting the fact that I'd swallowed those pills out of my mind. I was nervous and frightened, but I went with them and ran around for about ten minutes before getting too hot nauseated. I told them I was hot and was going home to cool down.

I became filled with regret, seriously frightened and sorry that I'd done what I did. I didn't know the thing to do was to induce vomiting. The aspirin I'd ingested combined with my cooling off too quickly while lying under a fan caused me to suffer the onset of almost complete paralysis. In a few minutes, I was barely conscious but aware of what was going on around me. My nearly invalid old grandmother was staying with us … and she found me gasping for air and unable to move. In a panic, she called my mom and dad who told her they'd come home immediately.

My Uncle Leslie, a Waco policeman was patrolling close by, so he was called to come check on me instead of an ambulance. I still remember him finding me there on the bed. I was wringing wet with sweat and shaking, but unable to move. I recall his somber face as he lifted me into his strong arms. He carried my limp little body to his patrol car, switched on his siren, and drove me quickly to the Children's hospital a few miles away. He was in tears, as he carried my frail limp body into the emergency room.

I did not tell anyone there what I'd done and the doctors were at an immediate loss as to what caused the onset of this bizarre paralysis. They initially thought I might have contracted polio. It turns out, that by getting up, running, and playing, my blood circulated and flushed enough of the drugs out of my system … so I survived. I regained movement of my limbs

Pink Heart

about two days later, and then the doctors let me go home to my relieved and concerned parents and friends. Years later, I fabricated a story about taking the aspirin by mistake, thinking they were candies. Only a few years ago did I admit the truth to my spouses and a few select friends about why I'd done that.

Roadblocks

I mentioned that many trans-women put up their roadblocks in life and make for themselves many obstacles to leap over or climb. I was no different. All my early years I lived in denial and in fear that I would be caught dressing in my mother's clothing or else become embarrassed if someone discovered my dark secret. I played dress-up with the <u>girl next door</u> as a child, played with her dolls and I loved that fantasy. My <u>sister would dress me up</u> at times when she would babysit me and I even did a few nightly feminine forays as a young teen in our neighborhood when my parents were late coming home from a night out at friends.

Know anyone claiming to be transgender? The best way to learn more about him or her, and the transgender condition is by reading, the Internet, and educating yourself.

Nicole and Me in Vermont - 2001

I did everything I could, even as a child, to make my adoptive parents proud of me. I sang solo in our church when I was but ten years old. I excelled at sports and became quite an athlete. Sadly, at puberty, my male body shot up and I grew to just over six feet tall. I was coordinated, but gangly, thin, and I felt homely and ugly as a mule! By the age of sixteen, I had twice broken my nose and it was bent, thick, and unsightly like a boxer's nose. Years ago, I got my nasal abnormality corrected and my nose was made thinner and more aesthetically pleasing.

Girls and Adolescence

For the most part, although my life was uncomplicated when I was growing up after I graduated junior college, I managed to change all that. I'd never had an attraction to men and I was mostly estranged from girls and women. I felt uncomfortable around girls, thinking they might see through me and discover my desire to become feminine. Mostly, I was in awe of any beautiful woman, yet I wanted to be one of them more than I desired their affections. Sports served me as a means to divert my attention

Pink Heart

away from this obsession that haunted my every minute as a child and as a teen. As I watched the young girls in my neighborhood metamorphose into young women, my soul cried out in envy.

What an injustice I thought for them to flourish in the onset of their feminine puberty, while for me I was to suffer through the rigors of my body being out of control and under the obvious maddening influence of testosterone. My first puberty came late in my teens, and I was often chastised and teased by the other boys, who called me "Baldy" or "Shorty" because they all had hair on their legs, chests, and around their genitals.

My pee-pee was such a peewee. I had not gone through puberty yet at fifteen, so I was bald down there and had no pubic hair. I became so self-conscious of this fact that I avoided taking showers after sports and basketball practices. Then some guys started calling me "Shoe" because after practice I smelled like an old sweaty gym shoe.

It was a very tough and awkward time for me. I found the male athletic world to be very violent. I had the competitive drive needed to be a success in sports, but I could never establish that violent streak that so many other man-boys had. I suspect that although my physical body finally gave up and kicked in with testosterone, there were also still some estrogens being produced someplace inside me that kept me from going Neanderthal-like some other of my male classmates seemed to be doing. High School was a time that I felt the most awkward and uncomfortable. I felt pressured into <u>becoming the man</u> my parents wanted me to become. At the same time, I was trying to be the one that my teachers, coaches, and classmates thought that I should be.

I tried dating girls, but everyone I went out with left me feeling sexually inadequate, ugly, and frustrated. From the end of a school year in May and just over three months before the onset of the fall school semester my sophomore year in high school I shot up almost 5" to my present height. I didn't gain a pound, but puberty kicked in at near age sixteen and I found myself relegated to becoming a "pecto-patty face" of pimples and feeling rather like a repulsive toad for the next four years.

Couples pairing off had begun my junior year and I was one of the most popular athletes in school that didn't have a girlfriend. As a senior, I dropped out of football, as I thought it too violent and frustrating. Instead, I concentrated on basketball my senior year. I wound up getting scholarship offers from several Southwest Conference schools. I decided to go the junior college route because the coach there had been a star player for Baylor. After all, back then freshmen couldn't play on the varsity teams. The head Baylor coach was ambivalent about any interest in my skills, so I went the junior college route and turned down four-year offers to other schools.

In college, I grew up a lot. It was my first time away from home, and I learned to think on my feet and to "be my own man", as my mom called it. Yipes! I dated some girls there, and yet I still managed to remain a virgin.

In Waco one weekend, I wound up getting a fill-in date to a movie. This girl was from my high school and was a sophomore. I dated her and we hit it off. One summer night at the lake as we were embracing, I copped my first feel of a vagina and breasts. It was a mutually agreeable incident, but I felt it cheapened both her and me for having done it. I apologized to her and we went about our courtship.

I wound up steadily dating her, falling in love, and becoming engaged to this girl right after my sophomore year in college. Later that summer, we got married far too young. As I mentioned, then my Uncle Sam came calling. What happened after that is another sad story. At any rate, I would come to have by her (X1) two children, my son, and my oldest daughter. As a wife, she was loyal, loving, and a good friend … but she was not capable of accepting that part of me that was feminine.

Do I still love her? Absolutely! Even on the day she became another's bride, my heart still yearned for her affections. I left, as I stated, because I knew she'd be better off without me in her life. WE met after 30 years apart at a funeral in Waco for a dear old friend of ours. There, we found a quiet place and spoke for quite awhile about how life was treating us, our kids, and I explained more to her about why I could not stay Gordon.

Question 28: If you had a return button and could go back in time with the power to change <u>one thing</u> in your life, what would it be?

<u>Only one thing?</u> Pooh! There are so many things I'd like to change that it's extremely tough to choose only one. First and foremost, if I had the power to change it, I'd have made certain my youngest daughter was born without any birth defects. If I could have spared her and her mother that pain and suffering ... I would have, even at the expense of giving up my dream of becoming Shannon.

If I could have, I'd arrange for my mother to meet another man, other than my father. That way, her life would have been much happier and maybe I'd not have been given away at birth. If I could expand on this fantasy, my father of choice would be a thin, Italian man, (my mom would have liked that) with a dark complexion, brown eyes, dark hair, and someone not over 5'8" tall. Then, I'd make sure he could only deliver sperm that would make <u>girl babies</u> (I'm sorry brothers!). Thus, I'd have been born a girl and this transgender condition would have never happened to me. My entire life would have been less traumatic, and I'd have grown up like 99.9% of society and been congruent to the sex and gender into which I was born.

With such a parent, perhaps his genes would have passed on to me a darker complexion of skin (which I have always envied). Maybe I'd have had brown eyes (which I always wanted). Yeppers! Now that I think about it, 'that' would be the things I'd like to go back in time and change.

However, because of who I am and what I was ... I never got to experience the joys of a deep suntan, being a little girl, the mystery of having a menses, the miracle of conception, giving birth to a child, or being a wife and mother. Still, life as Shannon or Gordon hasn't been all that bad.

I was the final child of two people; I was privileged to be the son of two loving adoptive parents, a brother to three siblings, a husband to two lovely ladies, and the father of three marvelous kids. For that I am thankful. Yet now, the page was turned and I left that life behind. The final chapter in the life of that person named Gordon was written.

Question 29: What part does <u>fear</u> play in the lives of those who are transgender when they attempt to pass in public?

Fear ... Less

Do you know what subject and words appear most often in the Holy Bible? That most used phrase is: "Do not be afraid!" So, quit worrying about this life ... none of us are going to get out alive anyway, so enjoy each breath you take and be not afraid.

When fair-skinned people go outdoors and expose themselves to intense sunlight, it's a good idea that they first treat their skin with an SPF 30 or higher sunscreen. Only then will they reduce the risk of their skin being overexposed to the UV rays of the sun that if left unprotected would blister and burn. Having grown up as a "carrot top" redhead in an era before the onset of SPF protection, I know all too well what effects the intense Texas summer sun can have on fair skin.

Would that there was something like an SPF 100 sunlight screen that could be spread upon the skin of a trans-woman before they go outdoors and expose themselves to the rigors and intense rays of scrutiny among the general public. Instead, each individual trans-woman must become aware of what makes them afraid to expose their faces and bodies to the glaring rays of a sometimes cruel and indifferent well-illuminated world.

Besides preparing and practicing for the moment, the only true protection one gets during such exposure is from having previously primed themselves for the moment by slathering on a huge dose of ... courage. Whether they are pre-op or post-op, they must exhibit a confident attitude when they present themselves openly to the public. They may be on estrogen therapy or have become able to present a head-to-toe feminine appearance.

One must learn to become <u>fearless</u> if one is to truly find peace when one attempts to change genders. I would suggest that trans-woman groom her image to the point that when she does go out, she becomes somewhat callous and not oversensitive to the goings-on of others around them. Don't be rude and meet a smile with a smile, but don't let others direct your actions. Slip into the role you are presenting 100% and go for it. Go and do what you set out to do and do not allow others to interfere with your plans. I know this isn't always easy to do at the beginning of the transition, but it is part of Transition 101 and a requirement if you are ever to make it in society as a woman. Learn from your mistakes and correct them. Use common sense in the way you dress and in where you go. Avoid places that might put you at risk of physical harm.

Question 30: **What can a family member or friend do to help someone that confesses to being transgender? Unconditional Love**

To begin with, asking this question would indicate a willingness to help your relative or friend cope with the challenges ahead of her or him. Just knowing that someone does care is incredibly affirming and a major relief to the trans-woman. If someone is concerned enough to ask, to me, such a question would be a good indicator that the person asking has a great deal of love and respect for the trans-woman and is exhibiting an open mind and heart.

You cannot imagine the amount of stress and worry that builds up in a trans-woman that is confessing her gender dysphoria to someone like a parent, sibling, child, employer, or friend. After such a revelation, if those folks are still talking to the trans-woman and asking questions about how they can help, then the trans-woman should feel very blessed indeed. Unfortunately, more often than not the reaction is much less positive and when the trans-woman confesses, the person or persons listening are confused, possibly angry, and do not accept, understand, or want to deal with what they are hearing.

As much as anything, one of the best ways a relative or friend can help is <u>to be there</u> when the trans-woman <u>needs a friend</u>. I don't know what I'd have done if hadn't been for friends like Nicole and my oldest brother, Vern. If Vern hadn't openly embraced me with all his heart, then there wouldn't be anybody from Gordon's immediate family that carried over into my life as Shannon. He and Nicole became my dearest friends and provided me with an outlet to express my grief, my anxiety, my uncertainties, my dreams, and my hopes for the future. Vern is always willing to listen to what I am going through and experiencing. He exhibits what true love is all about. To me, one of the dearest things he's done for me is he kept me apprised of my two other siblings and what was going on in their lives.

Although they did not have anything to do with me, I never quit caring for my other siblings. I would strongly urge every parent, family member, or friend to guard against a knee-jerk reaction and not close themselves off to the trans-woman. They should ask the tough questions and allow the trans-woman to explain themselves before passing judgment. Better yet, don't judge them ... just love, accept them, and seek understanding. Read books on the subject, watch YouTube videos of those in transition, and educate yourself about what is going on inside the heart and mind of your loved one.

Keep the lines of communication open between you and the trans-woman and expound on key areas of concern. Please remember that when a trans-person reveals to you their desire to transition, it is not an act of betrayal. To grow and become the person they wish to be, means divorcing themselves from who they were, thus perhaps leaving you to grieve over the loss of your brother, son, husband, or father. This necessary step in the process is tough on a friend and relative, as well as the trans-woman. If you truly love this trans-woman and want for her what is best, then it ultimately comes down to your attitude and whether or not you can live with her decision.

As a friend or loved one, you can either make lighter their burden, or you can cause it to become intense, weighty, and much lonelier. The trans-woman knows that you too have a heart, and knows that her choices can lead to yours and her heart being broken. I'm well aware that my revelations broke a lot of hearts, but let me make it clear that I never meant to sadden or hurt anyone.

I applaud all those who hear from the lips of those who confess they are trans-woman, and when that loved one stays the course and does all she or he can do to assist that trans-woman in their transition.

PART 5

Question 31: Do you ever fall back into old male habits of the past? Is there anything you "miss" about having once been a male?

Spring Forward ... Fall Back

What's the sound that Homer Simpson utters when he's suddenly been stunned? Doooooooh! You had to ask me that? Okay, I admit it. I suppose there are several things I miss about the maladies of being male. The first and foremost thing I miss is male privilege.

Guys get away with so much more breaking of social etiquette and malingering. By that I mean, if a guy feels like voiding his bladder behind a tree on the golf course, belching after downing a beer, or cutting loose with gas after a meal, he does so and his buddies all laugh, and nobody seems to take special notice or care. It may be rude and crude, but in guy circles, it's a guy thing to do. However, now that I'm a lady, doing such things, or acting so vulgar would be taboo and unthinkable.

Guys must have their space. They require their territory in which they garnish and demand the respect of other males and females to grant them their dominion. As a woman, sometimes at work, I found myself trying to get a guy's attention, but even if he did, it usually wasn't the same as they would have done if I were another guy. I don't mean they were impolite; for most of them were courteous, they just didn't treat me with the respect they did their fellow men. I did not want them to become aroused or anything, just that they pay attention and give more credence to my ideas and respect what I had to say.

Being aggressive is a male trait, so I started my RLT by being passive and giving in to this sort of behavior. However, in life and business, I found that a lady should probably stow those passive traits and exert her assertive self, exhibiting a competitive drive and ambition if she's to get ahead in the world of corporate America. I'm not saying a woman must become a pit bull, but showing your teeth every once in a while, is not a bad thing either. Keeping one's emotions in check isn't always easy for someone on estrogen, but if we react to stress with tears, then it's likely some guy that is in a higher-ranking position will note that and see it as a weakness.

One of the lessons I learned from being male was that you must toot your own horn; for it's rare that anyone else will do it for you. If needed you may have to lay down on the horn, so an occasional toot is constructive, I think. I could still be feminine, but I must manage to hold my own (as well as grabbing his own now and then…and squeezing) in a man's world. Also as a male, I commanded more pay for the work I did. I have the same intellect, qualities, the same education, and same values as I had as a man, but as a female, I make around 40% less than I did as a male. I eventually closed the gap, but I took a big financial hit when I first went 24 / 7 and worked en femme when compared to my previous salary as a male.

Catching Life

You might have gathered by now that I enjoyed playing baseball. The one thing I think I miss most about my youth and being a male is that wonderful game I know girls now play softball, but they didn't back when I was young. God, I loved to throw, run, and hit a baseball. I was danged good at it too. I miss being on a baseball field, the smells of the ballpark, the action, and the excitement of playing a game that I still adore to this day. I may be a woman, but I still have those very fond memories of when I roamed the baseball diamonds of central Texas and participated in our national pastime.

I cannot watch the movie "Field of Dreams" without breaking down in tears as I see Ray playing catch with his dad on that baseball field Ray carved out his Iowa cornfield. Thinking about once more playing catch with my dad … well, that's a moment I'd relish as much as life itself. Of all those I miss; my terrific dad is right at the top of my list.

Then, there's the issue of <u>vulnerability</u>. I refer to a very valid concern in several instances in my story. The bottom line is, as a woman one is much

Pink Heart

more prone to be subjected to the uncertainties of rape or brutality that come from being female in such a violent society. As an adult male, I rarely worried about confrontation, but as a woman, I must always be aware of my surroundings and my situation. It wasn't that I was any more daring or had more courage as a male. I simply was a guy. I wasn't reckless, nor did I do stupid things, I was just confident that I could handle any challenging situation that arose. Now, I've become a close observer of people, especially men. I always keep up my guard. I am taller and likely stronger than most women, so it's a foolish man that would mess with me, but still, I am made of flesh and bone and can be cut or broken.

A woman, even one that is of my stature, is like fine wine … with age, we only get better. Yeah right! Yet, with the years of living comes some semblance of accumulated wisdom, so I would like to think I am a bit wiser today than I was yesterday. However, since I am also human it means that I too am subject to sometimes finding myself the victim of my past and to some conditioned response that came from living life for all those years as a male. Nicole would tell you that <u>I am a sports fanatic</u>. I watch a baseball game while she watches a cooking show. I watch a football game while she watches the Iron Chef. Does that make her more feminine than me? Nope! It just means she likes to cook more than I do and we all tend to watch what interests us.

Old habits are tough to break for all of us, and I am no exception to that rule. Unless I do something out of unconscious habit, I try to avoid making any social slip up that would call undue attention to me as a woman. That is to say, I make a concerted conscious effort to <u>act</u> and <u>be feminine</u>. I learned to control my gestures, voice, posture, and attitude when in public, but I am sure there are times when I do something that isn't quite as femme as it should be. If I do, I'd wager that it comes from all that time of conditioning as a male. It doesn't hurt that I'm pretty darn feminine and made an attractive lady.

For most of my life, I've been principally religious, family-oriented, and devoted to raising my children and being the friend, spouse, son, and brother that my family wanted me to be. It turned out that I had my failings at being a mate. Although I am today living full-time in the gender role of a woman, no doubt I likely retained elements of my male personality and those traits that were so ingrained in my psyche, including my spirituality. Despite my past gender dualistic nature, I contend that I am in no way androgynous. Yet, I and any male to female trans-woman whose childhood, puberty, or adulthood experiences were lived as a male will likely retain some aspects of that masculinity, be it merely some mental characteristic, gesture, family values, sexual attractions, or emotional restraint.

Comment:

Many (transwomen) and men have nightmares after serving in the military or combat, as they find themselves reliving the hell they endured in the service or a horrid war. Like them, I had my nightmarish moments when I fought the warriors in my mind and those of my past. I lost friends in Vietnam and wondered why I was born a male to be one declared to serve.

People have told me how brave they think I am for having done what it took to become a female, and how much courage I've exhibited in my life. Pooh! I tell them it took no courage to do the right things for me or for my country. After college, I did what was expected and chose to serve my nation (after getting a call from my Uncle Sam). At points in my service, I almost wished for death, for unfulfilled dreams of womanhood seemed as remotely possible as me growing wings and being able to fly off some of the Army bases on which I served.

I made some bad decisions, wrong turns, and became lost several times in my journey. Still, I simply followed my life's dream of becoming female … and somehow it happened. Others abandoned me, but I knew that Jesus and momma always loved me. I wish my birth Mom would have lived to see and know me as Shannon. My brother, Vern, told me she'd known other transwomen through her nursing experiences and respected and accepted them. So, I sought my destiny and found it. God allowed me the distinct honor and privilege to witness life from the vantage point of two genders. Very few humans can ever say they've done that. To my gender counselor and all those pioneering sisters whose lives influenced, guided, and inspired me, I give you my most heartfelt appreciation.

Pink Heart

Question 32: Do you believe the world is more or less tolerant now towards those that are transgender?

That's a good question. Any attempt by me to answer such it can only be based upon my subjective opinion, personal experience, observation, and mere speculation. I do not believe there is any sure way to accurately predict how people will react to a trans-woman or someone that is transgender in every given situation. I suppose there may be a trend towards more tolerance being shown to some trans-women, but certainly not to all that are so inclined.

Has there been a significant positive change in the public's conception and attitude toward those that are transgender, and do more people now accept the trans-woman into society and the workplace? Without a doubt, there seems to be a greater degree of acceptance among the public of today than there was in my teens or during my young adulthood. Why do I think that has occurred?

Years ago, ignorance was one of the chief reasons that people used to lump all transgender into the same category as those that are transvestites, lesbian, bi, or gay. Before the Internet became so popular, before the late '80s, for many people an MTF trans-woman was looked upon as simply being some <u>campy gay guy</u> of low moral quality. Some people considered trans-women dregs of society, someone that scuttled off to some foreign European country to get a "whack job" and lopped off his penis to have what the public called "a sex change"!

As the '90s ushered in the age of the personal computer, those that are transgender began to connect over the Internet. This online connection now made it possible to access more and more information about gender identity and allowed any curious trans-woman to not feel so isolated and segregated from society. Many transgenders, both MTF and FTM, developed personal websites and began to share their own experiences about their transgender journey. Thus, others began to become better aware of ways to seek out help for therapy, cosmetic procedures, hormone regimens, GRS surgeons, electrolysis, and dealing with family relationships, friends, plus employers, and all manner of assistance to someone that is transgender.

The Net became a flurry of information in the early '90s, as webrings and interest groups formed. Chat rooms became in vogue and the trans-woman could instantly access other "sisters" to just chat or perhaps to seek their help and advice about the transition or other personal matters concerning the challenge of switching genders. Websites began to spring up hosting all manner of trans-women subject matters. I can attest that many such websites became like a Bible to others and me that sought responses to questions that before we had found no definitive answer.

As a trans-woman, I witnessed hundreds of trans-women transition success stories on the Internet. Dozens of ladies I admired exhibited online how to go about the process of the changeover from male to female. What this accomplished was educating me about what to expect from my adventure and foray into becoming a woman. At the same time, the educational websites that sprang up began to teach and inform the general public more about this rare human condition. There were also some very good books published on the subject of gender dysphoria. Many of these became best sellers. As more and more trans-women began to transition into society in the '90s, and then television got into the act, the public began to become exposed to transgender folk on the talk show circuit.

Some of what was seen on those types of programs were detrimental and counterproductive, as some of those types of people chosen to appear were from the seedier elements of society and gave the public the wrong impression about the true nature of the majority of those that are transgender. On some of those tacky shows, a trans-woman was either a prostitute or someone with little to no morality or ethics. This type of novelty, exhibitionist television did little to endear or educate the public as to the true transgender condition.

In time, legitimate programs began to appear on networks and private cable channels (like the Discovery Health Channel) that did address the real issues that confront those with gender identity disorders. For the first time, thousands of the public were privy to seeing firsthand these human beings struggle to find their true selves. In personal on-camera interviews with a trans-woman and those who assess the mental health of trans-people, the public could witness personal testimony as to how a person becomes transgender, as well as what they each must deal with in their journey.

Such programs do features about GRS surgeons, cosmetic surgeons, and many others who by profession deal with this condition. The programs tell how family, friends, and employers cope with the transition and what the expected potential outcome can be for someone that is transgender. Shows on major networks have even covered the life-changing events of a young pre-teen male that is going through the transition at a young enough age that puberty will be delayed and "her" true gender of choice will be more easily be adaptable to her young body.

Thus, I would have to declare the element of change that has made the general public, employers, family, and friends more tolerant of a trans-woman in today's world has to do with edification as much as anything else. As the public becomes more aware of <u>what a trans-woman is and isn't</u>, then they become more accepting and perhaps sympathetic to this small segment of the population that as early as ten years ago was still an enigma and misunderstood.

Does this mean there is less violence or bias aimed at all those who are transgender? Not at all! Unfortunately, for many trans-women whose gender has been changed and who live their lives in a stealth mode, they are still susceptible and sometimes become targets for both violence and bias. Frequently, I hear about some MTF trans-woman somewhere in the world that became a tragic statistic of violence. There are several reports about trans-women that became intimately involved with a male that goes berserk when he learns that the woman he is with didn't start life as a female. Some trans-women in that situation wind up being raped, beaten, or worse were … getting killed.

We no longer dress in animal skins, as did our early ancestors, but for a trans-woman, this world can be just as much a jungle today as it was before civilization evolved. Consequently, through this inquisitive and profoundly disturbing dichotomy, some trans-women arrive at the muddled stream of humanity and attempt to quench their thirst. When they do, often they find themselves becoming prey to those who would deny their right to subsist.

That surreptitious undergrowth consists of those types of predators, as mentioned above who would rather eliminate the trans-woman from the jungle entirely. Thus, resisting extinction and fighting for our right to exist is something every trans-woman must face at some point in her life.

The question again is, do I believe today's world is a more tolerant one toward those who are transgender? Based on what I stated above, there are still bloodthirsty resentments that abound among groups that despise homosexuality, or trans-people. Some of these types are of a similar breed to those prejudiced against people of different skin color, or ethnic backgrounds. Discrimination is a plague that, like it or not, will probably always exist in our "real" world.

As all Americans can attest, some are extreme zealots, who possess a suspicious political overtone, that claim their religion extols ferocity. These "terrorists" encourage those in their cult, sect, or whoever shares the same radical beliefs as they do. They gorge themselves by taking the human lives of the infidels who dare to believe in freedom, a loving God, or in Christ.

Their disdain for our way of life inspires them to commit acts of unimaginable violence to our civilization here in this nation. Other Zealots such as Antifa and Mexican gangs methodically cause chaos and loss of property or lives. Some of these types of people become suicide bombers and/or hijackers that use jet aircraft as missiles to destroy as many innocent lives as possible for their cause. The naked face of brutality is still ... brutal.

Though this murderous mania belies the existence of a more tolerant world, for most people in the U.S., including most trans-women, we are spared the inhumanity and atrocities that befall many others in war-torn terrorist regions like Iraq and Israel. That does not mean discrimination does not exist in our nation, for, unfortunately, it is alive and kicking with few signs of letting up anytime soon.

Too often I hear of some trans-woman that was discriminated against by their family, friends, or employers. More tolerance, you ask? Yes, in many ways there is, but in some ways, there is less. What bothers me most is the rising tide of prejudice that may be aimed at trans-people per se, and have a negative, trickle-down fallout to all of us that are.

Pink Heart

Legislating amendments into the state and U.S. constitution defining marriages made it better for any future trans-woman to have included in the world of a binary society whereby marriage is considered only between one man and one woman. If Congress and the Justice system will recognize a post-op trans-woman as being the sex and gender to which she aspires, then there is no problem. However, in some states, automatic discrimination is built into written laws that, in reality, <u>deny</u> trans-women the recognition of their chosen gender.

It was Darwin that made a point about how intelligence is measured by the speed and ability to adapt. If the world is to become more intelligent about and more tolerant of trans-women, <u>it must adapt</u>, become more open-minded, and be better able to accept that such a condition and such people do exist. The public must learn to move forward with more sensitivity and greater perception towards new frontiers of human experience.

However, I would also point out that we who are trans-women ... though we speak of the multiple shattered lives and interminable sufferings and danger, there are yet many in the public domain that does assist us in carrying our torches. Some fervently support our causes and are gentle souls who exhibit kindness and understanding, plus are filled with joy, sympathy, and love.

To those brave and gallant souls, I offer my salute and my sincerest thanks for your efforts.

A Favorite Quote: By Georgia O'Keefe

"I have been absolutely terrified every moment of my life, and I've never let it keep me from doing a single thing that I wanted to do." That's good advice, so even if you do have trepidation about transitioning into a female, don't let fear stop you from doing what you want to do.

Question 33: You lament not having been able to be a "mother." What sort of mother do you think you would have made?

Mommy Shannon

Now that's an excellent and fascinating question. I'm afraid that I can never accurately answer such an imponderable situation. To speculate on what sort of mother I would have made would again depend on some point of reference. Alas, I have none. The allowance of having had a vagina with ovaries proficient in producing an "egg" that could, in turn, be fertilized is … well, for me the ultimate of humanity and femininity. The very thought of procreating the species by having a living soul/person cultivated inside me gives me Goosebumps.

Sadly, crossing that biological boundary is one that no trans-woman has or likely will ever be able to experience … at least not by today's medical capabilities. However, in the future, who knows what new miracles might be discovered? Perhaps such things will be possible for some future transwoman. Yet, for the point of sheer imagining, let's assume for a moment that such a thing was possible right now … today.

Let's pretend I am younger and that I have ovaries, a uterus, and that … I am pregnant. Hey, I like this fantasy! After I've notified Guinness, what then? Could I handle the toil of carrying a child to full term, of dealing with the excruciating pain of childbirth, or the responsibility that comes from bearing a child? Again, this is pure fantasy and subjective speculation, but I believe, like any mother, I would be apprehensive, but in the end, relish my pregnancy. Somehow, I'd find the courage to tolerate carrying the child to full term, and then endure delivery and giving birth when the time came. There is no doubt I would cherish my precious child, nurture and protect it, as would any human female.

Mothering is instinctual and I'd be no different in that regard. Likely as not, I would breastfeed the child, hope and pray that it would be healthy, and that "she'd" have all the same opportunities for the future that I'd wish for any child. Yes, I dearly fancy the idea of being a mother.

Pink Heart

Hot Summer Day Cool Off

Shannonism: If you were to survey a hundred thousand older Americans, I'll wager ten percent of them could not tell you their blood type, but over seventy-five percent of them could sing you the tune from "The Flintstones," or whistle you the theme song from "The Andy Griffith Show."

Shannon - A favorite saying: Life is like having to play the violin before a crowd of people and trying to learn the instrument as you walk on stage.

Shannonism: I once got a call from a guy that thought he was calling a 1-800 phone sex line. To humor him, I allowed him to vent his boiling passions for a half-hour. Two days after that I got an insufficient check in the mail, an ear infection, developed strange maternal feelings, and despite using my breathable panty shield … I got an allergic rash between my thighs. ;o

In a Warm Pink Robe and My Favorite Wig

A trans-woman that keeps on her toes will keep away from the heels.

Okay, remember the pool balls? Here's another example of blunt, but truthful advice for any pre-op trans-woman. If some man wants to play house with your "Joystick," reboot, pull the plug, and end the game

Question 34: What do you believe are the biggest problems and challenges facing someone who is a male to female Trans?

Transition Challenges

I've presented quite a few already, but since you ask here's a few more: Since every transsexual is a person and every person is unique, the problems and challenges they would face would also be unique and different for each of him or her.

The main challenge for the trans-woman as I've stated is to be able to "Pass" and maintain the physical image of the woman one is attempting to become.

Unless we are lucky enough to be independently wealthy, we all have basic human needs that require us all to either work amongst others and shop or socialize amongst the populace.

Shoes and Old Souls

Deciding to go 24 / 7 is <u>the</u> most challenging time for any trans-woman. To describe what it is like, I would refer to an old Patsy Cline song called, "Shoes". Being transgender is sort of like walking around in a pair of shoes that just don't fit, ones that seem to have holes or even pebbles in them. Over time, the pebbles begin to rub and cause blisters or sores. Thus, she is never quite comfortable in those old shoes and becomes in dire need of a new pair.

When a trans-woman first tries on her new gender identity, it's like trying on and walking around in a <u>new pair of shoes</u>. At first, they might fit, but they are still too tight and may even hurt her feet for a while. As time passes and one breaks in the new shoes, they begin to loosen up and one develops <u>a more comfortable fit</u>, and then she can walk around without worry that her shoes will cause them blisters.

To apply this analogy to their new gender identity at first it doesn't fit them as well, but over time, it's like breaking in that pair of new shoes, and eventually, the new trans-woman begins to feel more comfortable. The real test is to make this pair of shoes last and not to wear holes in them too quickly, for in this race, being transgender is a marathon, not a sprint.

Along those same lines, I would say to X1 and X2 that the shoes I wore when I was their husband became old, worn, ragged, and no longer fit me. It wasn't their fault that the shoes became that way. It was just that the shoes I tried to wear were wrong for me and never fit me properly. I stepped out of them and now someone else is wearing those old shoes of mine and walking around in the life that I used to share with them.

Economic Needs

Okay, this is for all of you reading this that considers yourselves to be transgender and in transition. If you take nothing else from this book, I hope you heed this one caution and piece of advice. The one reality that everyone must face up to, whether they are transgender or not is that they must have some means of self-support. As I said, some are gifted by inheritance, by possessing a special skill and career, earning their riches, or merely by some windfall that will provide them the monetary means to achieve their goals for surgery, transition, and life after they've switched genders.

For most of us though, we had to face economic challenges and either transition within the company and job we had, or else find a new job that we could perform as a woman. Career training is a big plus for some and upgrading computer skills and proficiency in some specialized fields will serve you well in your quest to become employed as a woman. Unfortunately, all too often unemployment becomes a major obstacle and problem for the trans-woman.

If seeking to transition on a job, if an employer would only give the employee who desires to transition the opportunity to do so, they will not only avoid being charged with discrimination and dislodging someone's life and career but more often than not they will find a <u>newly motivated, dedicated employee</u>. They'll also find an employee that no longer has to deal with the distractions of hiding their true nature and gender.

Pink Heart

Thus, a basic economic need has been the one thing I have found that <u>most negatively affects</u> almost all trans-women. Too many girls I've known have been ill-prepared when they came out or attempted to transition. I cannot state this enough: I implore those who consider changing genders to plan and organize themselves for the challenges before them in the harsh world of reality.

I still feel it is better if a trans-woman up relocates to a friendlier environment; one where she can begin fresh and her chances of securing meaningful employment is improved. Some trans-women, like Nicole, are fortunate enough that they have a long tenure in their positions and are in a civic or governmental career whereby discrimination and lay-offs are not an option when one decides to transition.

* * *

I also find that some females, especially some that are immature primps and teens can often be brutal, like a shark that smells blood in the water. If they sense that some trans-woman is not one of them, they can giggle, whisper, point, or inflict indignities and uncertainty that crumple the confidence of that trans-woman. It may be done with a simple glaring look, a snide remark, a laughing whisper to another nearby female, or just by exhibiting disgust at their recognition. Again, I would point out that their being female is a gift and they did nothing to earn that privilege. So, lighten up ladies! Case in point, how I was treated that night by the girls' soccer team ... and I looked darn good that night. I suppose that was more guilt by association.

This sort of treatment I have witnessed in public bathrooms and when out in public. Such behavior was not always directed at me, but rather it was at the novice trans-woman I was with, but I still felt the scorn and suffered along with her. When these sorts of things were done to a friend, it was like <u>throwing down a gauntlet</u> and <u>daring</u> her ... and <u>me</u> to enter their world. I took that challenge as a learning opportunity and rather than let their discrimination rule, I used it to overcome. A clever MTF trans-woman will learn the subtleties of how to dress, how to speak, and how to give off signals that she is female. Some people learn negatively, and I suppose I am no exception to that, for I learned a great deal from my pre-transition early forays into the scrutiny of the public. In many such cases, that scrutiny bred success. I finally realized that most of the time my fem presence wasn't the issue, but rather my height. In that case, most females likely thought me to just be a tall woman.

We must all face up to the realities of this world and separate ourselves from fantasy when we go 24 / 7 and think that everything will become suddenly rosy. Taxes, bills, child support, and making a living still happen after we transition. Few are immune to the economic challenges every adult human must face. **TANSTAAFL** is the name of a nightclub in Arlington, Texas. Its subtle name sends out a powerful message to all. Those letters in that name stand for: "There Ain't No Such Thing As A Free Lunch"!

"Show and Tell"

So, who do you tell and when? That is a very individual choice and one that the trans-woman regrets doing. I believe that the trans-woman should tell only those who need to know If she decides to "come clean" to family or friends, find around five people she'd like to tell first, confess her intentions, and then observe their reactions before telling anyone else. If the reactions are ones you can endure, then you might choose to reveal yourself to more family or friends.

The point is, don't rush in and tell those who might not be ready, or that don't need to know yet. I made that mistake with my siblings and some friends. I wasn't prepared to explain myself the way I should have and was clumsy in my methods, so I regret having told as many as I did … when I did. Having not sought to become Shannon until after my parents all passed on, I never had to deal with that scenario, so my heart goes out to those who do and must reveal to them about being transgender.

Of course, some of the biggest challenges that any trans-woman must face are those of a physical nature. I mentioned that my chromosomes are XXY and that afforded my body to adapt well to HRT and estrogens. Before I went in for breast implants, I had already developed into a C-cup, and that is rather near the top for hormonal growth for most secondary trans-women.

Pink Heart

The usual estrogenic hormonal effects occurred over time and I took on the overall body shape of a female.

Let me comment about <u>three</u> very important physical issues that <u>restrict</u> many trans-women I know:

A Hairy Situation

My true <u>cranial hair</u> is adequate and quite thick. I can style it to enhance my facial features. Still, some girls I knew were follicle challenged. Some had little to no cranial hair. Thus, they had to wear wigs all day, every day. I can tell you right now, for me it is no fun wearing a wig 24 / 7 when one is presenting oneself in public. Wigs are a wonderfully fun accessory and fine for a <u>temporary fix</u>, but they suck if they are required to become a staple of one's every day identity. Still, many of those girls I knew who were so challenged did wear them regularly. Ouch!

Is there an alternative? In some cases, hair transplants are an answer, but that is an expensive and painful option. Perhaps hair weaves and assistance from those skilled in hair extensions and appliances are the best solutions. Hormones help to restore some cranial hair loss, but even they have limits and can't re-establish growing hair to a bald palate. At my age, my hair has become sparser than when I was in my forties and fifties.

Also of note is the <u>facial hair</u> situation for MTF trans-women. Women do not have beards, and so removing unwanted facial hair is much preferred and required if one is to work and socialize in femme. I am lucky enough that what little facial hair I have left is fuzzy, light and even white or blond.

My skin did not bode well after ouch couch treatments, so I was cautious when I did a treatment and what part of my face I did it on. In time, the goal should be to remove all semblance of any male beard. In my and Nicole's case, we spent more time and almost as much money having our unwanted facial hair removed than the cost of GRS. Of all the things I did to become feminine, I deplored electrolysis the most. I tried laser treatments, but my hair follicles were so light the laser treatment didn't work properly.

One other encumbrance to a trans woman's passing might be her <u>voice</u>. For me, I was lucky enough to have a high tenor voice. I have trained myself to speak in feminine tones and to raise my voice accordingly. Thus, I am rarely read in public due to my voice. On the phone is another matter, for I have at times been taken for male on some calls. I would caution any girl that thinks her voice is too low that she should perhaps take voice lessons and train to <u>speak as a woman</u> before making surgery an option. Nicole has a low voice and she is very conscientious of that non-feminine quality.

She opted to have a <u>voice surgery</u> performed whereby her voice box was tilted and stretched. The theory behind this type of surgery is that the vocal cords are then stretched tighter and the voice pitch is raised to a higher decibel. To anyone considering this procedure, which by the way is costly, I would suggest you save your money and use it for voice lessons instead. Nicole was very disappointed in her voice surgery, and I've not been able to discern any difference in her voice tone now versus her voice previous to surgery. Both she and I feel it was a waste of time, pain, and money. There is apparently a medical procedure in Japan and Korea, plus other doctors in the U.S. that specialize in going through the mouth and using flex instruments to tighten the vocal cords to thereby raise the tone of the transwoman's voice. I've seen and heard the astounding results accomplished with such a surgery and it definitely seems to alter the male voice into the female range. I might have done it twenty years ago, but not now.

Nowadays, Nicole's made improvements in the sound of her voice and she has learned to lower the volume and to project her voice into higher, softer tones. This I find is more passable. Unless she or I slip, don't concentrate, and become too comfortable, then our voices are generally passable. Besides, <u>people are visual</u> and when one looks like a duck, walks like a duck, and acts like a duck ... they presume you to be a duck.

Unfortunately, even if everything else makes one appear to be female, the voice is still as big a factor at defining one, as are the other feminine signals one projects. If an MTF trans-woman expects to not be read as being male, she must attempt to <u>sound the part</u> of a female.

PART 6

Question 35: **When you did begin going out into the public as a woman, what were the reactions of those you encountered?**

Public Persona

At first, in my mind, I didn't dress as a decent woman should for someone my age. I loved low-cut blouses and dresses because they displayed the feminine me. I was in my forties when I did this, so I suppose it was to grasp at the femme youth I never got to encounter.

This was also true of my bedroom attire. In the life of almost every trans-woman I've known, we have all had a phase in which we had to learn what it is like to portray ourselves in the actual role of a female. For me, as well as many others that I've known, that process began in the <u>privacy of our boudoirs</u>.

Growing up, both my adoptive parents worked, so after I reached the age of eight in the summer months I was usually left at home until my mom got off work around 4:00 p.m. I used to take every private opportunity that came my way to rumble through my mom's closet where I'd withdraw a dress, blouse, or skirt that pleased me and try on a pair of heels … plus her panties and bras. This was an innocent attempt to makeover my boyish personae into that of a female. At best, I was clumsy and awkward at doing it. I'd apply far too much make-up and what usually resulted was the clownish-looking mockery of a female, one akin to what small little girls get when they play dress-up in mommy's clothes.

With no adult supervision or experience to call upon, I did the best I could to make myself appear feminine. I'd prance around, glaring at myself in a mirror, taking mental photographs of myself in this fashion and imagining myself being Vivian Leigh, Marilyn Monroe, or one of those typical beautiful women models I saw in magazines. I adored the smell of the compact powder back then, and even the taste of lipstick. Though I had no wig, I'd use a scarf, or one of mom's fancy hats to frame my childish face and make me look more girlish.

The key to making this all become a routine was to be extra stealthy and cautious. I had to keep the doors locked, the blinds closed, and I limited myself to portions of our small house where I knew nobody would see me. I tried being extra careful with what clothing of mom's that I tried. I knew her favorite dresses, and so I usually opted for the ones out of season or ones she rarely wore. The make-up I used was gaudy, old, flaky, and likely infested with bacteria, but back then I didn't care. It was all I had to work with then, so I used it.

Though I was always careful not to tear a seam or to get the dresses and blouses wrinkled or soiled in any way, one day I did get in a hurry and ripped one of her nicer winter dresses. In a panic, I also ripped the hem as I stepped out of it. I was horrified that I'd be found out, but she never mentioned the ripped seams or hem to me. We had two closets where mom kept her clothing, and on one occasion, I failed to hang a garment back in the right closet. She was confused over that and even confronted my dad, but she never questioned me as to why it was moved. I often wondered if she was actually wise to my goings-on and simply chose to ignore it, thinking it to be just a role-playing game or growing phase I was going through. God, how I wish I'd had the courage back then to allow her to catch me "dressed," and to have sat her down and explained to her my true femme desires.

My cross-dressing continued into adulthood and even after I was married. I'd manage to collect a few feminine garments and I'd use opportune times when the wife was away visiting at a friend's, at her mom's, or a social function and I was home alone. Being a sales rep during each of my marriages also afforded me out-of-town cross-dressing opportunities. I recall the very big rush I got when I bought my first wig and tried it on one evening when I was alone. It wasn't real hair, but it was an exciting moment all the same.

Over the years, I went through many stages of purge and denial, I'd gather up, and then discard garments in moments of frustration and overwhelming guilt about those feminine items I'd collected. This purging was expensive and always left me with a sense of disappointment, dread, and despair. Though I sometimes did become stimulated at the woman in my mirror, it was rare that I ever masturbated because of the incident. Instead, I most often got my satisfaction from seeing, if even for a brief, temporary moment in time, that which I aspired to become ... a female.

To answer the question about going out dressed in public, that came about first when I was around eleven years old. I was alone while my parents were visiting friends. I managed to muster enough courage to step out of my house one night and I walked up and down the sidewalk in our neighborhood. It was chilly and dark, and I was scantily dressed. To my knowledge, nobody saw me and I was relieved that they did not.

Years later, after I became a sales rep and traveled out of town to work accounts, I found new freedoms to dress up and did so as often as I could. Usually, after I was dressed, I'd find a moment, late at night, when few if anyone was around. As quickly as I could, I'd race out to my parked car drive around. It mattered not where I went, and sometimes these forays only lasted about fifteen minutes, but I was outside and if someone saw me, I wanted them to think me a female. Fortunately, I only once encountered a law enforcement officer during one of those nighttime forays. My heart almost sank into my girdle as I was pulled over and the officer came to my driver's side window and leaned his face inside. Except for the illumination from his headlights, it was dark and I was young and thin enough back then that I looked pretty convincing as a woman. He asked for my driver's license. In my best femme voice, I asked him what was wrong. He looked at my male name and photo on the license and then somberly replied, "You have a tail light out ... Shannon. Please see that you get it fixed as soon as possible." I calmly and politely replied, in my most feminine voice, "Thank you, officer, I shall have it looked at tomorrow morning."

Without further incident, he handed me back the license, turned, and walked back to his vehicle. My hands were so sweaty that I could barely hold onto the wheel. After I pulled away, I burst into tears, felt my wet panties, and knew that even though what I'd encountered was embarrassing, I'd somehow dodged a huge bullet. This incident was in deep redneck Texas. Why the guy was so lenient I cannot answer. Why he reacted as he did is to this day a mystery to me. Still, my sage advice to any novice trans-woman who drives is to get you a proper femme driver's license before doing so.

Over time, I became better at applying make-up, but I seemed to always overdo it. When I did that, I wound up looking more like a hooker than a housewife. I found my taste in the clothes I wore out was basic, but when I was alone, I was anything but conservative.

Boa Restrict-Her

I had my <u>Boa Stage</u> where I'd dress up in sexy lingerie. Obsessed with displaying my femme self, I took every opportunity to take photos of myself that provided the visual proof that the image I displayed was that of a female. Some of those photos were outrageous and hideous. Some phots herein are risqué, but not pornographic.

Later, after I began ingesting progesterone and estrogens secured via my trips into border towns in Mexico, I began to develop even a larger bust line than I'd had with my gynecomastia. Thus, in time I filled out those camisoles and the sexy laced garments I wore in private. I'm sad to say, this became an obsession, like nothing I put on returned to my mental vision a more feminine version of myself than when I was dressed in <u>sexy lingerie and low-cut blouses</u>. I essentially became a victim of the image portrayed in my masculine fantasies. Looking back, I was never prettier, but also not in touch with the decency I wanted to project to others. It took time to get over this obsession, but thank goodness ... I did.

Looking back on it, did this lingerie thing become a fetish to me? Honestly, I'd have to say it probably did somewhat, but although it seems trashy, I was not capable of seeing it like that. I know now that it simply was <u>one phase</u> of the process and one that I went through to arrive at and validate who I am today. Who was I endeavoring to tempt or to tease? <u>I was seducing myself</u> and attempting to create an image of a sexy female, and one that would be attractive to others. In retrospect, it was folly and I was too self-absorbed with imagination. Happily, as I pointed out, I did grow out of this stage

The realities of how good women dress and present themselves before others came to light when I began going out dressed on regular basis,

Pink Heart

especially in the light of day. I used the photos I'd taken from my lingerie and high heels days as a tool to correct and improve my image. When I did begin that and going out regularly, I managed to pass without drawing excessive attention to myself. My desire to wear low-cut blouses and dresses "did" obviously draw attention. I should mention one particular night, which happened to be my first month in Dallas when I moved away from X2. Mind you, I am not petite in any way, so it was foolish of the men involved in this episode to attempt what they did in the first place.

Anyway, I had been going out in Dallas with my trans-sister friends for about two years before coming to live there. I was comfortable being Shannon by then and had developed a lot of feminine traits. That evening after work, I got out of my work garb and got dressed to go out. After I'd gotten to the restaurant I'd gone to before with my friends, I realized that this time I was out … and completely alone.

The area of town was gay, lesbian, and transgender friendly, so I was not particularly worrisome. During dinner, I noticed two fairly large Caucasian men staring and watching me … with what appeared to be more than casual interest. I dismissed any notions that they might plan to do me harm. I figured it was just mere paranoia on my part. I had chosen to wear a nice pants suit and no high heels that chilly April evening, and it was fortunate that I did.

After dinner, as I went to find my parked car, I noticed that the parking lot behind the restaurant was not lit very well. I looked around for the two guys before leaving but didn't notice them, so I assumed they'd left.

As I hit the car key fob to unlock the door, the two large men stepped from the shadows. They made some crude, profane remarks, and then one of them tried to grab my arm, as they wielded a knife at me.

Without going into too much detail, I will tell you that later, one left in an ambulance, and the other was placed into a police car in handcuffs. Little did they know they had attacked someone trained in hand-to-hand combat that in the Army was trained to cripple or kill the prey or an enemy. I did not lose that technique or ability, despite my being weaker by hormones and loss of muscle. I was somewhat the "atomic blond."

Though I came out on top in that incident, I still had to explain myself to some confused and surprised cops, not to mention the feeling of vulnerability that I know women endure. Having to deal with some rough characters in sports, having once been raped, pushed around by school bullies, and also fondled by an adult male in a movie, I always had this overdose of adrenaline hit me when I was frightened or cornered. Sadly, I had to display that many times in the Army.

I was lucky that evening and yet foolish. As a result, I never put myself into that situation again. When I went out, I went with someone and I avoided dark parking lots. I try to always listen to my inner senses as a female and I am always aware of my surroundings and cognizant of strangers or if they might become a threat to me. I would recommend any MTF trans-woman follow that suggestion.

One thing I would like to tell every trans-woman. When you go out dressed as a female ... **BE** a female. If you feel threatened, or if you're uncomfortable or suspicious of how someone is acting, ask for assistance. Case in point: Once, Nicole and I went out and played billiards at a local pool hall (okay, so it's not the most feminine thing). We enjoyed it. A couple of inebriated Hispanic guys got a little belligerent and gave us some grief as we tried to attend to our game. We'd been coming to this place a lot in the past and the bouncers all knew and liked us. They treated us respectfully. They had not seen this particular incident, but Nicole and I were ready to leave and the Hispanics had gone out before us, with a glaring robust look of drunkenness and debauchery.

We explained the situation to the bouncers and asked them to accompany us to our car. Without hesitation, these adult males agreed to help protect their two female customers. They escorted us out and we left without further incident. There are gentlemen in this world and as women, we need to be aware that when we think we need help, we should not hesitate to ask them for it. Though being trained in self-defense is a plus for any woman, I prefer not to ever be tested again or have to use such techniques. It's best to use discretion and to leave one's macho past in the past. If one lives as a female, one must feel, act, and respond in the same manner as a woman ... at all times.

Question 36: What happens if an MTF trans-woman never gets her GRS surgery?

That's easy to answer. If she doesn't get GRS ... then she doesn't get GRS. The world will not end if the trans-woman fails to achieve their goal of having GRS. As I alluded to earlier, the MTF trans-woman was born female, only she considers that she has the wrong genitalia. Although a trans-woman does desperately desire to one day have a procedure to form the proper genitalia, it does not always preclude an overwhelming, all-consuming obsession.

I've heard the expression that a trans-woman not getting GRS as being compared to someone who is paralyzed being relegated to accepting their fate, as they must spend the remainder of their days of immobility in a wheelchair. Such a person would still be transportable and alive, she just wouldn't be able to walk or get around as easily as she'd hoped. A trans-woman may <u>not be as comfortable</u> with her handicap (remaining pre-op) as she'd prefer to be, but <u>she can survive</u> nonetheless.

To some trans-women, this may seem like a distressing situation, but the joys and challenges one receives from living as a woman usually outweigh the discomfort and inconvenience one receives from not yet having had her GRS. The sense of urgency is usually far more profound in younger trans-woman. Besides, for most, there is always hope, and folks as old as 70 can successfully endure the surgery if they are in reasonably good health. I think age plays a major factor in how one views the importance of having GRS. If one is under thirty, then it is more likely that the ability to have intercourse becomes a motivation than say someone in their sixties or upward of that. As I've pointed out previously, unless the transwoman is involved in a consensual sex relationship, having a functioning vagina may not be the ultimate goal. Also as I noted earlier, in non-sexual relationships or merely when viewed in public, a person's private parts are just that ... private ... and only the one with them knows exactly what's between their legs. Thus, unless engaged in a sexual union, it is nobody's business but her own.

Question 37: Are you concerned about the long-term effects of estrogens, and what it will have on you or other trans-women?

Shannon's Nutriments

So far as I know, there has been no definitive evidence that estrogens, in a vigilant physician-monitored regimen negatively affect a healthy MTF trans-woman. If one has pulmonary problems and high blood pressure, diabetes, or some other health issue, the doctor who is treating the trans-woman will likely be less aggressive with using as powerful an estrogenic substance as they might with those patients that exhibit no symptoms of circulation or heart problems. From a personal perspective, Nicole and I have had two trans-woman friends of ours have some bad incidents after they went on estrogens.

One of them developed a blot clot in her leg and was hospitalized. She has hypertension, but it was controlled by medicines. Still, the clot came about and because of it, last year that same person had to undergo a heart bypass surgery. This person's transition essentially came to a screeching halt. Since we both knew how much our friend wanted to transition, we were saddened by the incident. However, this friend survived and is fortunately still with us.

Our other dear trans-sister, Diane, was not so fortunate. For whatever reason, Diane suffered a complete coronary arrest and died almost instantly of SDS (sudden death syndrome). She too had hypertension, but it was supposedly under control .... or was it? She was a few weeks shy of her 50th birthday and her son and spouse were with her when she complained of shortness of breath. Before her spouse could summon help, our friend collapsed onto the floor. It's still difficult to believe she's gone from us. Attending Diane's funeral, one of Nicole's and my dearest friends, was one of the saddest and most sobering days of my life.

What role, if any, did estrogens have in the problems with these two trans-women? I have my suspicions, but no proof that estrogen contributed to their health problems. Nicole has hypertension as well, but she came through her GRS just fine and her blood pressure leveled off anyway after she lost weight. She still takes medicine to help control it though. At any rate, being healthy should have a lot to do with which estrogens one is prescribed, plus the dosage and effect are something that should be closely monitored.

My former gynecologist, now retired, used to tell all us girls that he had to be certain we all got what we needed and only what we needed when it came to prescribing our hormones. He said it was crucial to get a full blood workup and to be sure that we were physically capable of taking the prescribed regimen he tailored for each of us. He was very cautious and thorough. I recall him showing me how to examine my breasts for lumps, and he did a manual prostate check, (yes, I still have one, as do all who were genetically born males) which was not a lot of fun for me. His concern was that we not throw gasoline on a fire, as he put it. If there were the beginnings of a tumor or some benign lump, the estrogens would make that grow faster. Thus, he would carefully check us out to be sure we fit the physical profile before he'd prescribe.

So, to answer the question, I'd say that my choice is clear. I have no alternative but to take the estrogens. I am not some genetic female who had a hysterectomy, nor have I any ovaries to worry about being affected by the estrogen or progestin. So far as I know, most of the benefits I've received are beneficial. The only thing that has been a detriment to me with the use of estrogens has been that I was taken off them in 2009 and without them it caused my metabolism to come to a crawl. When on them I became hungrier, as estrogen increases one's appetite. Doing that, when I stopped them, I gained more weight than I wanted … even on a rigid diet and mild exercise program. I lost most of my rather nice girlish figure.

In regards to my worries about breast cancer, I can only hope that scourge will not affect Nicole, any of my friends, or me. (X1 and X2) have now both had a bout with breast cancer and each wound up taking chemo and radiation treatments, X1 had to have one of her breasts removed via surgery. We were not married at that time, but I saw her during that ordeal and my heart wept for her. X2 had a recent episode and chemo and radiation were done, but her breasts were spared, thank God.

Problems with breast cancer are a horrible experience for any woman and yet both my exes have endured it bravely. As I stated, my sister-in-law died from the complications of breast cancer. Except for giving birth to my kids, I think I admire them both more for how they've handled that than anything either has ever done. I'm not sure I would have had the same amount of courage that they displayed. Fortunately, cancer has not spread and both are fine today. So far as I know, none of my ancestral family has ever had any forms of breast cancer, so hopefully, I too will be spared the ravages of such a disease.

Question 38: Do you believe the Internet is a help or hindrance to those who are transgender?

Internet Hazards and Benefits

As an educational tool for anyone, be they transgender or not, the Internet is an invaluable entity. If there had been an Internet when I was a teen, I firmly believe I would have been able to avoid a lot of grief in my life and spared a lot of vexation from occurring in the lives of others. Why? The Internet provides proof, via chat rooms and the very informative websites and personal web pages of others who are transgender ... that I am not alone with this condition.

When I was growing up, the amount of written or visual information I received about gender dysphoria was sparse and was found either through adult bookstores or in outdated reference sections of a public or college library. The subject matter was by and large taboo, and though present in the world, a sex change, as it was referred to back then was something looked upon by the populace as being an aberration, an event poked fun at by comedians and not taken too seriously by society in general. Most people associated those effeminate men who sought such surgery as being homosexual drag queens, she-males, or female impersonators. As a teen, I knew no other trans-women, nor was I able to converse with any in real-time, as we can do today online in numerous chat rooms and Internet services.

The times changed and the subject matter of being transgender became less of an unmentionable, as societal restraints lessened somewhat. As much as anything, the Internet brought to view that there are numerous others out there, besides me that are transgender. One need only click onto one of the many Internet search engines and type in transgender to find dozens of sites that will offer up information. These searches can assist one in finding GRS surgeons, questions about the effects of estrogens and hormonal regimens, personal websites of other trans-women or transgender individuals, and all sorts of reference sites to explore and learn more about our condition.

My Advice is to Seek Advice from a Gender Counselor- '97

Indeed, if I'd known then what I know now, then I could have better enjoyed my young adulthood and become a woman years ago. I would have avoided two painful divorces. Perhaps my children would have been born into another family where their father was secure in his manhood. If the

Internet had been around then, I am certain that Gordon would not have existed near as long as he did. The Internet is in essence how Nicole and I met (at group meetings) and we located our gender counselor.

That said; let me throw in another caveat. Today it is easier to meet other trans-sisters, it is also easier for those who prey upon our community to locate us, to victimize us for some sexual purpose, or to target us for harm. Personally speaking, I have had some bad experiences with guys I met on the Internet. In many instances, they were not what they portrayed themselves to be online, and they only wanted to meet me out of some morbid sense of curiosity or to explore their sense of latent homosexuality.

I would caution anyone to keep up their guard if seeking a rendezvous with someone they chat with online. Use common sense and set rules for such meetings. DO NOT invite anyone you are meeting off the Internet for the first time into your home. Instead, I'd meet in an open and public place, preferably a popular restaurant or club for a drink … and not dinner. That way, if we didn't hit it off, we could say our graces and depart. There is no need to become paranoid, but use your radar, as my counselor stated, and keep up your guard.

Question 39: Nicole's mother belied the fact that her "son" did not exhibit any feminine behavior and mannerisms as a child. Did you? Don't all MTF transgender kids behave like sissies?

Oh, contraire! Like any young child, I learned early on from watching my parents, aunts, uncles, and so on what the different gender roles were for women and men. I was a responsible, obedient child, and I did my "chores" … be they washing dishes, making my bed, or as I grew older helping with yard work. From my perspective, I observed that my dad was the worker and considered to be the main provider. My mom was the nurturer, the one who kept us in clean clothes, ironed our pants, cooked our food, kept the house clean, bandaged my knee when I fell, wiped my runny nose, and brushed away my tears with her hugs.

Pink Heart

No doubt, in my sibling's household, they saw in my birth mother those traits, but also another role. She was the child-bearer as well as the child raiser. I knew from watching my grandmother on her old foot-treadle sewing machine that women mend, darn, and make dresses. From watching other girls, plus the little girl that lived next door that girls played with dolls and liked to play house, dress-up, played in make-up, and exhibited less aggressive behavior than the boys in the neighborhood did. Biological sex differences existed all right, but for me, I simply self-identified myself as a non-male, for I never truly felt masculine at any time of my life. Instead, I recognized myself anatomically by what I didn't have, rather than what I did. (Not having a vagina, rather than as someone with a penis)

I knew grown-up girls also had boobies, as other boys called them. As a child, I only knew that boobs made their shirts stick out in front and that there were two of them. I did not breastfeed as a child, so I had no direct point of reference, as I never saw either mother nude. Nor did I see so much as a photo of any nude woman until I was in high school. Thus, the true distinction between actual sexual anatomy, sex roles, and sex characteristics came long after I'd been mentally imprinted as being feminine. All I knew was I desired to become female. If that type of thinking was not pre-imprinted in my mind and instincts, then how else can it be explained?

Even though my primary caretaker was a woman, I did not have an oedipal complex, nor did I act or behave with any exaggerated effeminate mannerisms as a child. Most trans-sisters I've known did not exhibit such behavior either. In no way does that lessen our urge or desire to do so. We were refrained from feminine gesticulation because of our recognition that if we did, it would cause us to be questioned or looked upon with disdain and suspicion by others. That dread included disguising our desires from our parents, relatives, or peers.

To me, girls had an easier time learning their adult roles. For me, I was never able to ascertain or develop a stable masculine personality. I tried to model myself after my adoptive dad, but even he could not make me become like him. He tried to teach me to stalk, kill, and hunt animals or birds, but my heart was never in taking another life ... (As a hunter or in the military) ... even if it were a quail or dove. I never exhibited any of the macho mannerisms that he had, or the brisk, booming, authoritative voice he projected. He was a straightforward man, but a man nonetheless. I admired what he was, but I was not like him. The differentiation I had between myself and girls was that I felt unsightly compared to them. I desperately sought to join them and be able to grow my boobies and have my period. Instead, my body betrayed me and later poisoned me at puberty with a flood of testosterone.

I've learned that the attainment of a gender-role identity boils down to the fact that girls subsist, while boys must achieve. Feminine identity is then assigned and masculine identity is to be attained. A woman then must merely be a female, she does not have to do anything to become one. Comparatively, a boy must therefore be matured and converted into a man!

For me, I attempted to become a man by excelling at sports or macho endeavors in hopes that would bring me achievement. I tried doing what my dad wanted me to do to turn out to be a man. Despite it all, it did not! I also found it true that manliness is not a constant and has to be earned and continually re-earned. I recall when I was once at a funeral, an uncle reminded me that men do not cry openly, even though I did. He said it was a sign of weakness and was not masculine or the strong male thing to do.

I found that manner of thinking frustrating for I could never withhold my inner emotions when I was happy or sad. To me, crying was enabling and gave me a sense of relief that seemed natural, be it manly or not. I suspect my uncles saw early on that I was not the macho type of boy that my cousins were. In some ways, I think this embarrassed my dad, and I regret that, but the truth is ... I <u>was</u> different than them. I think dad knew I was unlike most boys, but in his heart, he could not accept that I was deficient in any way. He did his best to mold me into a man, but his chisel broke off at the handle! I will say, however, I was no sissy, nor did I act like one.

Now that I am free to be feminine, I can note the strong sense of relief it gives me when I need to express my emotions openly and without restraint. I can laugh when I feel like it, or cry when I am inclined to do so ... without the scrutiny or accusation that it's not appropriate.

Pink Heart

"If God Hadn't Meant Me to Fly"
By: Shannon O'Shea

She stands atop the precipice … her face up to the sky,
Her arms spread wide … imagining … what it's like to fly.
Birds fly among the clouds …she hears their joyful songs,
Calling her into the air … is that where she belongs?

Why could she not have been a bird … or butterfly … so fair?
One of God's special creatures … whose domain is in the air.
Why was "she" grounded … when her yearning is so strong?
She seeks to free her bonds … take flight … to right a wrong.

The tears she's shed could fill a lake … and spill into the sea,
Her heart bears deceitful scars … from dread of discovery.
She's tried to reach … beyond her fate … till now to no avail,
Are her wishes, hopes, and dreams … unjustly doomed to fail?

Behind her then comes the Sun … to light a brand-new day,
Its rays bring strength … that somehow … she will find a way.
She gives in to this blind faith … and the promise that it brings,
And noticing her shadow sees … behind her there … "wings."

In the poetry posted herein, I've used the reference about the trans-woman learning to fly. That's a metaphor describing what she needs to do to get her transition off the ground and into the freedom of the air … and from being male.

Clamp onto the good memories in life, and let go of those that cause you pain.

I did this in the Army! I learned that a parachute and LIFE each come with many strings attached.

Shannon's Favorite Place to Eat: In bed, or in my recliner.

Question 40: Did your adopted parents shape your attitudes toward the feminine gender role?

For most men, I think the threat of femininity is internal, which is the effect of being socialized as children by our mother, or a mother substitute. Although I doubt you'd get many to admit it, some men retain feminine qualities from their upbringing. Some, like me, even aspire to become women later on in life. Did this happen to me? Did my upbringing contribute to my becoming transgender? Gender or sexual difference is created through psychological, social, and cultural processes, as well as through relational experiences. However, except for my aforementioned adoption, no, I don't think anything my adopted parents did contribute to my being transgender.

They did not create the circumstances that lead to my being assigned to them to raise me as their own. They only reacted to a couple of their friends' situations and reached out to extend the offer to care for an infant. Other than that, they did all they could do to see that I had a comfortable and safe home life and upbringing.

Although I had internalization of feminine elements in my character, I am certain it was not due to anything that I derived from Hattie or Red. The internal pressures that I placed upon my psyche were mostly the result of the state of affairs of my adoption and that of my fixation that if I'd been a girl I'd not have been given away.

Did I want to play with dolls, clothe myself in dresses, and act frilly and feminine? Without a doubt, but in reality, I knew that mom and dad would expect me not to do so. I did anyway in private cross-dressing, as mentioned earlier. Thus, like almost every trans-person I've ever known, I too hid and repressed this unexplainable urge out of love for my parents. I dreaded facing the humiliation had I done so. As I noted earlier, I was able to do some and most of those things <u>in secret</u> playtime moments with the little girl next door and with my sister. I again make the point that I did not openly claim preference for feminine toys or anything feminine, and that brought me dismay, for I certainly did want to do so.

Ask almost any MTF trans-woman if they acted in a male manner, and I'd wager 90% or more of them will tell you they acted and reacted similarly. I found early on that the one thing fathers are apprehensive about is that their boy child will not exhibit non-masculine traits. God forbid that he would fail to develop … to become a man!

Thus, I would proclaim that the relationship, which my dad and I had, was one of <u>loving deception</u>. By that, I mean I had to present counterfeit manhood and attempt to not make him uncomfortable by thinking I was abnormal and wouldn't grow up to be the kind of man he wanted me to be. The same can be said of Nicole, who had a domineering, borderline abusive father.

Having lived in their gender, I would tell you that there is one secret that most men do not want you to know. Even as adults, men remain psychologically defensive and all have their insecurities! Men repress far too many things about themselves. Although the "man of steel and velvet" may be more in vogue today, most men are still paranoid about exhibiting any perceived feminine trait.

Mom-N-Ems

As a child, the relationship I envied most was that between my birth mother and my sister. The relation and the bonding connection that those two shared was something I coveted all the days of my childhood and on into adulthood. Mother-daughter relationships are almost always close anyway, but with my mother and sister, it was as if the two were but one. My sister never strayed far from my mother's shadow or vice versa. I reasoned that in a way, my mother needed my sister as much as she needed my mother. Perhaps my sister almost served as an endearing love object, a pacifier of sorts and means of gratification for mother's own tumultuous life and marriage.

It may have been that by clinging to my sister, my mother appeased her wounds and scars all the while strengthening the ties to her only daughter. To mother, my sister then became a living entity and a means to have someone to hold onto … someone that would always be there … for her. In point of fact, and to her credit…my sister always was there with and for her… to the end of life's road.

More often I was able to define what I was not far better than I could define what I was. I knew I was not like other boys. I knew I was not going to become the man my parents wished for. I knew I was not going to go through puberty as a girl or grow breasts and have a vagina. I knew I was not going to ever have a menstrual period, or be able to become a mother or give birth.

I reasoned that as Gordon, I was not going to be able to wear dresses, put on lipstick, play with dolls, grow my hair out, pierce my ears, wear high heels, silken panties, or paint my nails. I would not have the privilege of playing girl's games or looking back on my childhood and recalling the fun I would have had growing up in a PINK world. I was not going to have a supple feminine voice, or a soft, dainty, petite, curvy feminine body. I knew all that … and frankly … it pissed me off and disturbed me. Fortunately, some of those things "did" come to be in spite of my once male looking body being a challenge to alter

If you're going to become a female, it's a good idea to step into the light and cast your own shadow.

Esprit-De-Core

My recognition of gender differences no doubt emerged developmentally, but I also know that the feminine urge and relating to being female had to have been as I pointed out earlier. Those urges were ingrained into my psyche from birth or before. I perceived my lack of a vagina early on. Thus, for me ... my core gender identity was shaped before I was even three years old. Most boys and girls are fortunate enough that they do not suffer through this ambiguity and sense of wrongness about their gender. For example, my brothers both grew to establish their own identities and to emphasize their differences, not commonalities between themselves and females.

For me, the commonalities I felt toward females made me hunger even more to become one. The angst I had as a child did not wane and as for any true trans-woman, the desire only heightened over time. If women sometimes have penis envy, I am someone who always had femininity and vaginal envy. I greatly admire and covet everything of beauty and that which is feminine in a woman.

All trans-women start with a clean, empty canvass. The portrait that develops comes about by learning technique and how to paint with life's colors, shadows, and using the right brushstrokes to create the woman posing in her mind.

Fifth Year Fulltime

Question 41: Other than a tracheal shave, breast implants, and GRS, what other cosmetic surgeries or procedures might a trans-woman need or perhaps desire? What would such procedures entail?

Most MTF trans-women will rarely be completely satisfied with their facial appearance without having had some sort of cosmetic surgery to help feminize certain parts of it. When one looks at another's face, there are usually no problems identifying who is female and who is the male. The facial structures of a male versus that of a female are stark and easily noticed but rather subtle. The exact differences are not so easily identified by a layperson.

Things such as the upward angle of tilt of the nose, the absence of facial hair or sideburns, the more squared-off hairline, smoother rounded brow, fuller lips, thin eyebrows, a shorter distance between the upper lip and to where the nose begins, more alluring eyes, higher cheekbones, and a more pointed chin. All these are physical traits that help identify femininity in a face. It's what helps make a woman look like a woman.

There are several facial feminization procedures now available to an MTF trans-woman. Those trans-women I've seen on YouTube display astounding after transformations ending with gorgeous faces that look nothing like a male.

Those with a heavy male brow may wish to have it rounded and honed down. Skilled surgeons can indeed alter the cranial shape of a forehead, brow, and even give her a narrower, and more pointed feminine chin. Cheek implants, face-lifts, upper and lower eyelid surgery to remove bags or fat deposits, and of course the altering of the nose to give it a narrow and more feminine tilt creates an overall more aesthetic and pleasing look.

<u>I had the latter of that done and I love my nose now.</u>

The surgeon's goal is to alleviate and revise the male face to such an extent that when she is seen, even if she were in a nightgown and went to answer the doorbell, nobody would suspect or assign her to any gender other than female. I have known several of my trans-sisters that have had such extreme cosmetic surgery. I can attest that the results are nothing short of astonishing. The before person seldom resembles that feminine lady that emerges.

Immediately after the surgery, one's face looks as if she were hit by a train. Unless you have a lot of comp and vacation time built up, you may not want to do this radical surgery until you do have the time to recover. After the swelling subsides and scars are healed, these trans-women would never be thought of as anything but cis-women. I would note that such surgeries are expensive and can cost upwards of over $35,000 or more.

What is the Question?
Lovingly written by Shannon O'Shea

Many years have come and gone ... and now her time is near,
For Nicole to bloom as spring ... her day is almost here.
Each new day brings her closer ... to all her life's dreams,
In sweet anticipation ... having waited forever it seems.

Her question will always be ..." Why wasn't I born this way?"
She'll accept what she's given ... for comes her bright new day.
When she too can take her place ... beside her sisters' fair,
And feel at last that she belongs ... in this world all women share.

She'll proudly lift her head on high ... and face the joyful pain,
For her destiny awaits ... as sunshine comes ... no more rain.
Time will heal her body ... and it heals her heart and soul,
Anxiety becomes elation ... for she'll finally reach her goal!

As her day of dreams approaches ... Nicole then will find,
That at the rainbow's end ... is a tranquil peace of mind.
Inside her unbridled spirit ... womanhood does await,
And what once seemed remote ... will soon be blessed fate.

Weep not for dear Nicole ... her journey's nearly done,
By man's skill, blessed by God ... a woman...she'll become.
True happiness will come ... femme pleasures now shall treat her,
Having known the journey's toil ... will make it all the sweeter!

So make your wish upon a star ... for one day maybe you'll
Take your place upon the Earth ... and live out your dream too!

The previous poem I wrote and read to Nicole at our support group meeting two days before she left for her GRS in Montreal

Pink Heart

 To a trans-woman, <u>she who is within</u> is somewhat like using a bronchial dilator. One good blast of the feminine and she can more easily inhale and breathe.

 The Transwoman should carefully <u>weigh</u> <u>all</u> her options before deciding to transition.

Shannon's Special Talent:
Letting go of guilt / Breathing fresh air / Being reborn each new day

Nickname:
Nicole calls me her, "Luggette"

Favorite Place in Texas:
In the spring on a boat near a shoreline covered in bluebonnets; on a calm Texas Lake watching a golden sunset

Movies Most Interesting:

"Gone With the Wind" ... I am" Scarlet O'Hara ... I wish!
"Inherit the Wind" ... That's a lot of wind for one lifetime.
"Ben Hur" ... I've "Been Him," but now I'm "Hur ... er Her."
"Star Wars" ... It would've been much more interesting if Darth Vader had told Luke, "I am your father ... I used to be your mother."
"The Good, The Bad, and The Ugly" ... This Clint Eastwood spaghetti western pretty much sums up my existence, as I have felt like each of those adjectives at some point in my lifetime.
"Lawrence of Arabia" ... Peter O'Toole and Omar Shariff were incredible, as was the scenery and cinematography.

Favorite T.V. Shows:
"Jeopardy / Wheel of Fortune / "I Love Lucy" / "Whose Line Is It Anyway" / "NCIS" / Big Bang Theory / Young Sheldon / Yellowstone, The Voice, America's Got Talent, The Blacklist ... "Lonesome Dove"

Children:
Four out grazing the range and five grand-ones being corn fed in their corrals.

"Beyond life's Bend"
By: Shannon Leigh O'Shea

What lies beyond ... the river's bend?
Waits there a girl "child" ... at journey's end?
Will the world fall off ... and I fall down?
What wonders there ... will I have found?
Will there be a sea ... with a rising tide?
And cold, dark waters ... deep and wide?
Will my sails take me ... to a newfound land?
Will life become new ... when thereon I stand?
Will I be guided ... by a distant star?
Will my journey's end ... find I've traveled far?
Will my restless feet ... thereon be stilled?
Will dreams and hopes ... there be fulfilled?
Will I find peace ... when I reach the end?
Does happiness wait ... beyond the bend?

Conclusion

In our contemporary world, just how should a male act and react in today's society? What is he supposed to be like? What constitutes our ideal image of a bona fide <u>macho man</u>? Internal demands and impracticable ideals heaped upon males only end up depriving men of their individualism. From the get-go, I found that I couldn't <u>measure up</u> to being a man or that ideal of constant toughness and dominance. As a husband and father, I found that I could relate better to my children and women when I treated them as equals.

Men who no longer depend on false superiority complexes to define their masculinity will find that to be a relief from having to live up to impracticable standards for a stereotypical male. God forbid that a man with machismo is perceived as having vulnerabilities or being human!

A potted plant will only grow so big or tall if it is restrained inside a clay pot. Take it out, transplant it into an open flowerbed, and with fertile soil to expand in it can grow to its maximum genetic and inherent potential. Similarly, a plant that is cramped and constrained into a tight area may even reverse its growth and become a bizarre and distorted heap. Restraint from seeking one's true nature or dreams and a human too can and does often <u>suppress their growth potential</u>. This same sort of thing that happens to a refined potted plant can and does happen to exceptionally intelligent trans-people who sometimes end up suicidal or confined to mental institutions. As humans, be we trans-women or not, we flourish best by allowing ourselves the freedom to grow in unrestricted soil. Plow, plant, and cultivate your dreams in fertile ground and one day you might just reap a bountiful harvest.

Trans-women, in particular, seem to be born with an inbred need to win at life. By that, I don't mean it's a case where the trans-woman must beat down another person or make that person lose. She simply feels compelled to win over the odds and remake and remold herself into the woman she feels she is. A good example of this is the trans-woman **Amy Schneider**, the brilliant engineering manager / writer that won several times recently on television's "Jeopardy." I am very proud of her courage and integrity, plus admire her amazing knowledge and intellect.

Pink Heart

A trans-woman should avoid self-exile and should learn to overcome the oppression and injustices she will face in her lifetime. She should come to know her true self and realize that she is unique among humans and then learn to <u>accept and appreciate</u> that <u>uniqueness</u>. She will have her potential for growth, her abilities, and accomplishments as well as her limitations.

She should not let herself fall into the trap of being what others think she should be, but rather she should merely <u>be herself</u>! She should be autonomous and not see herself as being inferior or superior to a genetic woman but rather she is simply distinctive. A trans-woman should assume responsibility for her own life and respect the significance, dignity, and well-being of those with whom she is involved. I also believe that a trans-woman should adhere to <u>moral principles</u> and maintain her <u>dignity</u> and <u>integrity</u> if she's ever to be taken seriously by the world.

As trans-women, I believe we have an opportunity, <u>by example</u>, to exhibit to the world those things that make us worthy of the gift of femininity and life itself. Take pride in who you are, in what you are, and keep your mind open, your intellect sharpened, your eyes focused on the present as well as the future, your faith in God steadfast as is His love for you, and your heart set upon living the type of life you've always hoped for and dreamed about.

Through this story, I've had the privilege of writing the facts down, as I see them, and then hoping someone is willing and able to read all about it. So, if you did, <u>read it all</u>, what did you think? Did you learn anything? Do you have any questions that went unanswered, or did you perhaps disagree with some one or more of my viewpoints?

If you sought to find answers, then I hope you did. I would suppose what you found depends on what you were looking for. If you are one of my trans-sisters, then perhaps you discovered few new points of information herein. I provided you, the reader, with an open and honest assessment of my thoughts on the world, as I perceive it to be.

I've Concluded That We Took a Photo Every Time We Ate Out

Ever the optimist, I still see the world as being a glass-half-full ... and still overflowing with good and decent people. Although there are risks equated with being a trans-woman, I don't believe in being ruled by paranoia, fear, nor do I think anyone is deliberately out to get us. Rather, I think there is still a lot of work to be done so that legislators, leaders, employers, relatives, friends, and all others will become better informed and educated about who and what makes us transgender. There is yet more room to grow in unrestricted soil, cultivating understanding, and overcoming discrimination, thus attaining the life of peace most trans-women seek.

In our nation and world, we must work to create resolute revision in the way the general public perceives us. As a grouping of individuals, we must become "one voice and one body" to help instigate the positive changes that we'd all like to see happen.

Pink Heart

Skirt and Hose Days – Ms. Office Manager- 2003

If you are a family member, a parent, spouse, child, aunt, uncle, brother, sister, etc. of someone that is transgender, then I hope you kept an accessible, admissible open mind and came away with a better and clearer understanding of what a trans-woman is and isn't. None of us are perfect and likely as not, some of us will have stepped on your toes, tripped over your feet, pushed you aside, or even knocked you down and tread upon your heart in our efforts to discover who we are. In the end, there's no denying that being transgender is a self-seeking, self-centered condition, one that is overwhelming, and one that eventually consumes us like the spread of Covid-19 or cancer. In our efforts to reach out and ascertain that woman within us, you might believe we lose sight of the things most valuable and blur the big picture. I assure you that all of us who are trans-women come to realize the costs, risks, and consequences of revelation and of traveling roads that leave loved ones behind. Yet, we do it, for we can have no peace unless we do.

Shorter Wig - Older Me in 2020
Yes, I Own and Drive a Motorcycle

We do not reject, nor cast aside our love for you, but rather we must redirect our focus upon finding the truth about ourselves. That truth may hold before us a mirror that doesn't reflect the male you might know, respect, and admire; for most of us … that person reflected therein has been a sham and an illusion. We often lose the esteem and love that were once so strong a bond between those and us we most cared for and who cared for us.

Pink Heart

I can but apologize to those two women I facetiously referred to as X1 and X2, to my children, my siblings, and to friends I have known most of my life. They are all a reminder of the mistakes I made ... the lives I touched, and the love that I lost.

Despite my losses and theirs, I am still warm and breathing ... so I must be alive. My future looms before me in light made brighter each day by hope. I welcome the promise of tomorrow while clinging to the joys of today. If I look back over my shoulder, it's but to learn from previous mistakes and no longer repeat or linger upon them. I trust in my Lord and know the future holds two things ... either fer or faith. I have faith that He will guide me in my all my days, and throughout the remainder of this life's journey. I give Him praise, honor, and thank Him for forgiving my sins.

I have many new friends and a family of choice that supports me and loves me. I am blessed with Nicole, whose love and devotion mean the world to me. I am living joyously as Shannon. I've found a sense of peace within my heart and soul at long last.

In the television mini-series made from the great Larry McMurtry novel, "Lonesome Dove", an aspiring young reporter tells the retired Texas Ranger, Captain Woodrow Call, that he's heard the captain is a <u>man of vision</u>. Captain Call stops, his eyes moisten over, and in his mind, he envisions those lives that touched his own; his friends and those with whom he shared precious moments in his lifetime. He then alludes to that view of his past and those he knew being ... what he says is, "Yeah, a hell of a vision!"

I relate with Captain Call, for in my own life, I envision those lives that touched mine. I see my parents' smiling faces; hear their laughter, praise, and recall the warmth of their embrace. I see faces of old friends, cousins, aunts, uncles, brothers, my sister, and evoke the fond moments we had together. I see vividly the faces of my children and our loving times together. I see the faces of those two beautiful women who shared my love and life in such intimate and magnificent ways. I see the face of him I once was and I thank him for his sacrifices and this point in my life.

Yes, in so many ways ... I too am a person of vision. But, as I've said, there is no future in living in the past. So, as was said in the movie,

"Castaway", "I know what I have to do now ... I will keep on breathing; the sun will rise again ... and who knows what the tide will bring." As stated in the lyrics of Toto's song, "<u>Africa</u>:" "I bless the rains down in Africa. I'm going to take the time to do the things we never had."

So, I leave you with this one last "Garden of Eden" conundrum: If Adam was the perfect figure of a man, and Eve was so incredibly beautiful ... where have all the ugly people in the world come from? ;o)

Thanks for your time and attention. I hope you learned something.

MORE PHOTOS:

Pink Heart

Nicole and Me (I'm in a Wig)

Relaxing With an Orange Drink

Peek-a-Boo Shannon   **Quiet Moment Interupted**

A Studio Glamour Shot

I'm Female - It's Headline News! As If

Formal Function in Dallas

Celebrating a New Millennium

A Texas Gal Has to Have Boots

Posed Portrait – Wild Flowers for Trans-Women

Pink Heart

Shoe Shopping – Don't Ask What Size

At Home with My Poodles Before Going Fulltime

When I went out in this wig dressed as a cowgirl in Abilene, that was the start of me being Shannon and the end of my marriage.

Time Spent with a Dear Friend

Cool Off in The Pool

Spent a Christmas with My Older Brother, Vern

**Short Wig – Long Legs – Heels – I'm Too Tall
I Wore Them – But Didn't Like to Walk in Them**

Sharing a Toast Together

Pink Heart

Autumn in The Park

Dinner With a Friend

Do I Look Like I Belong in The Men's Restroom?

Posing by the Pond

Pink Heart

Nicole and Me at Bass Hall

Me Waving at You

Long Wig – On a Summer Day

Work Out Girl

Pink Heart

Hey, I Have to Buy it ... it's on Sale!

Glamour Shot- 2003

Jet Ski Weekend on The Lake

Even wet I Love a Parade   **My First Go at Heels – Ouch!- '97**

Pink Heart

At Home and at My Hairdresser's

Watching My Daughter Play in the Park

A Chili Dog Lunch in Texas

Pink Heart

With Three Good Friends- in '99

April Showers

To Thine Own Self be True

Nicole and Me at Razoos – 2010

Pink Heart

For … After All, Tomorrow is … Another Day!

Pink Heart

www.ingramcontent.com/pod-product-compliance
Lightning Source LLC
Chambersburg PA
CBHW032032150426
43194CB00006B/246